BUT IT'S SO SILLY

Other Titles by JonArno Lawson

Poetry
Enjoy It While It Hurts
Inklings
I Regret Everything
Love is an Observant Traveller
There, Devil, Eat That
This (and That was That)

Children's
Aloud in My Head
Black Stars in a White Night Sky
Down in the Bottom of the Bottom of the Box
The Hobo's Crowbar
Leap!
The Man in the Moon-fixer's Mask
Old MacDonald Had Her Farm
Sidewalk Flowers
Think Again
Uncle Holland
A Vole on a Roll (illustrator)
A Voweller's Bestiary

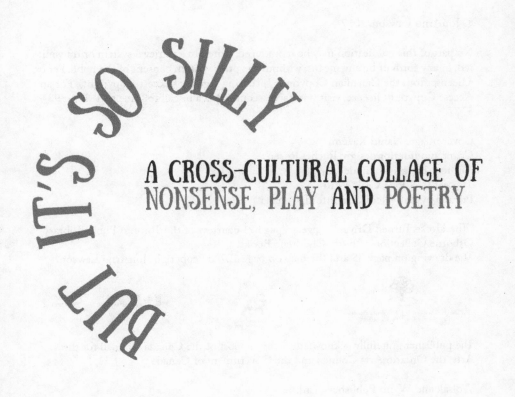

SO SILLY

BUT IT'S

A CROSS-CULTURAL COLLAGE OF
NONSENSE, PLAY AND POETRY

BY JONARNO LAWSON

WOLSAK
& WYNN

Cover image: Nahid Kazemi
Cover and interior design: Rachel Rosen
Author's image: Philip de Vos
Typeset in Adobe Caslon Pro
Printed by Ball Media, Brantford, Canada

"The Horse Turned Driver" image on page 91 courtesy of the Toronto Public Library Osborne Collection of Early Children's Books.
The drawing on page 35 and the map on page 127 are copyright JonArno Lawson.

The publisher gratefully acknowledges the support of the Canada Council for the Arts, the Ontario Arts Council and the Government of Canada.

Wolsak and Wynn Publishers, Ltd.
280 James Street North
Hamilton, ON
Canada L8R 2L3

Library and Archives Canada Cataloguing in Publication

Lawson, JonArno, author
     But it's so silly : a cross-cultural collage of nonsense, play and poetry / JonArno Lawson.

Includes bibliographical references and index.
ISBN 978-1-928088-45-5 (softcover)

    1. Play--Cross-cultural studies. 2. Finger play--Cross-cultural studies. 3. Games--Cross-cultural studies. 4. Rhyming games--Cross-cultural studies. 5. Children's poetry--Cross-cultural studies.
I. Title.

GR480.L38 2017   398.8   C2017-904860-0

This book is dedicated to those who, finding no way back, went forward.

Briefly and in passing: it is a sad thing that what is written has permanence, whereas what is said is often unnoticed.
  – Doris Lessing, *Walking in the Shade*

Logical, scientific, and verbal presentations are honored in our society. Less honored are spatial ability, grace in movement, and those aspects of a comprehensive awareness of relationships between objects or ideas which do not translate well into words.
  – Robert Ornstein, *The Mind Field*

The crucial driver of evolution, Darwin understood, was not nature's sense of purpose, but her sense of humor.
  – Siddhartha Mukherjee, *The Gene*

Korf invents some jokes of a new sort
That only many hours later work.
Everybody listens to them, bored.

Yet, like some still fuse glowing in the dark,
You wake up suddenly that night in bed
Beaming like a baby newly fed.
  – Christian Morgenstern, "Delayed Action"

We can all be explorers, and can all find wonderment wherever we are.
  – Tahir Shah

In art there is only one thing that counts: the thing you can't explain.
  – Georges Braque, *Illustrated Notebooks*

TABLE OF CONTENTS

PREFACE

The American anthropologist Edward T. Hall once wrote of the "absolute obligation that each of us has – in spite of the risks – to share our insights with others and the great loss when people lack the confidence, energy, or courage to describe systematically the conceptual worlds in which they live."

The thirteenth-century Scottish magician Michael Scot recorded the following story: "The tale is told of an ape or monkey with three young. When pursued, she takes the one she loves best by the hand, the second under her arm, and leaves the third, which she likes the least, to its fate. But it leaps onto its mother's back and alone escapes when she loses hold of the others."

This book could be read as a collection of shared insights from a fairly large number of people, but it could just as easily be described as a brief account of what's been achieved by that ape that escaped.

But what does the ape stand for? The bits of rhyme and play that live on in us after we lose hold of so much else? Or does it represent talkative, playful humanity – our own particular brand of primate that leapt free of its earlier hominid ancestors (who might have felt relieved to see the back of us when we departed) millions of years ago.

While I was writing my first books of poetry for children I made a sometimes careful, sometimes playful, study of English nursery verse and of English lap and finger rhyme games. I believed that extending this study to the rhythms, themes and dramatic movements of lap and finger rhyme games belonging to non-English languages and cultures could provide an important stimulus and grounding for further work I wanted to do as a children's poet, and that it might have a secondary importance, as well, as an archive of cultural artifacts that might otherwise disappear.

As I went along with my research, I started to take an interest in, and collect, other forms of brief poetry, games, entertaining traditions and other surprising (to me) approaches to play. In the end, this is a bit of a cultural collage . . . a chaotic compendium, even. And I've barely scratched the surface, if you look at this from a global point of view – most of what I gathered I gathered opportunistically from a handful of people representing a small number of nations and languages. There are hundreds more to be looked into.

You may want to (or even should?) check any (or all) of these on the Internet, or on YouTube, to see other versions (especially on the amazing Mama Lisa's World website – it's a treasure trove of information) and to get a "live" sense for how people use them. I can describe things here, but nothing beats actually watching these things being done. Not all of them are out there, though. A few of these, as of now, are gathered only here, including some I knew from my own childhood.

You ought to consider the fact that you, the reader, might be – probably are – the sole repository of a rhyme, game, joke or riddle – or at least of a unique, familial or regional variation of one, or of several.

While people who study education often look at how play is part of preparing a child for later stages of life, we sometimes forget that this goes both ways. Adults playing with children are also being reconnected to, or if there's no long break between generations, staying in touch with, something important that keeps their own minds and imaginations moving.

The physicist Richard Feynman (who cited his father's inquisitive nature and conversations with him when he was a child as a major influence) always taught first-year physics, at university, because he said it kept him in touch with the fundamental questions of physics all through his life.

The first-year students always asked the biggest, most difficult questions, and Feynman was reminded each time that most of those questions remained unanswered. He had to think about them again and explain what was known again in the simplest and most interesting terms he could think of, and he felt this kept his research fresh.

Writing for children has been similar for me – the work I'm happiest with almost always stems directly out of ideas or concerns my children expressed.

For instance:

My child Sophie (age seven): Imaginary aginary. Now that's a word, *imaginary*. What do you think of when you think of something imaginary? Aginary? I think of my poor self, with the very small, small elves.

My son Ashey (age four): We have to make all the elves and Cyclops stop because Noah said to God if those imaginary creatures build another ark I don't want them to build another because if they build another ark they'll squash our ark and our ark will go to pieces and all of us will die, and we'll see no people or animals we'll only see imaginary creatures.

Sophie: Said Noah to the imaginary animals
We're all packed up to go
God only sent for the other animals
So to you, we'll have to say, "No."

Shortly after this, I wrote a poem called "Our Imaginary Selves":

"I'm sorry," Noah said, "we've taken all that we can carry,
God never said I could save anyone imaginary . . ."
"Don't worry," said the gryphon, to the downcast dwarves
      and elves,
"We'll build another ark for our imaginary selves."

What interests me about this exchange is that I had no clear memory of this conversation with my kids when I wrote this poem. I knew Ashey had been worried about the other creatures and I remembered writing this to cheer him up. But I had no memory of jotting this conversation down on an envelope as they were talking. I had forgotten all about it when I was writing my own poem – I only came across the envelope again by chance, long after my poem was published.

Clearly my poem was based on their ideas and worries, and was scaffolded off of some subconscious memory of Sophie's brief poem – my poem comes at the idea a little differently, but the fundamental idea is entirely theirs.

Many of my poems are more consciously and clearly taken from things they've said or worried about – in response to them. My kids keep returning me to the fundamentals, and because they're still acquiring vocabulary and encountering old stories new, for the first time, they come out with great original expressions I'd never think of.

CHAPTER ONE
BABY PLAY, SCHOOL WORKSHOPS AND AN OJIBWE PERSPECTIVE

NOBODY PLAYS ENOUGH

Nobody plays enough – people get out of the habit.

Play, which can be part of almost everything you do, is often relegated to one room in the house, or to one part of the day, or even to one stage of life. Is this one of the reasons that so many new parents find their changed circumstances overwhelming? New parents sometimes feel isolated, lonely and bored. It can, and often does, take time, patience and a sense of humour to figure out your child's world, and to get to know yourself as an adult with children, if you're not used to being one. Play, in whatever form it takes, may be the best way to get you back on your feet and moving again.

TICK-TOCK

It was the sort of friendship that seemed destined to last forever. It didn't – it barely lasted a year – but I learned some important things from Jean-Marc before he and his family suddenly moved away and completely disappeared out of our lives.

The pursuit that became this book started as I watched Jean-Marc interact with his two-year-old son. I was sitting quietly on the floor with little baby Sophie, when Jean-Marc suddenly jumped up, put his son on his head and started spinning around.

I was shocked. Was that really safe? But his son squealed with delight – he loved it.

Next, Jean-Marc dropped his son down so that he was holding him upside down by his ankles. He opened his legs to brace himself, and started swinging his son back and forth like a pendulum. He chanted:

Tick-Tock
Tick-Tock
Sammy is a little clock

Boom Boom Boom!

When he said, "Boom Boom Boom!" he stopped swinging his son from side to side, and instead swung him back and forth through his open legs. His son couldn't get enough of this.

Watching Jean-Marc, I realized I had no idea how to physically play with a child, though to be fair, Sophie was still too small to play with in the vigorous way Jean-Marc was playing with his son. J.M. was originally from Brazil, though he'd lived in France, then in the United States and now was in Canada. I wondered in that moment – and still wonder – about the influence of culture on adult-child interactions. I had never seen an adult play with children like this when I was growing up. My father had bounced me on his lap while chanting a rhyme, but no one had tossed me about, or spun me – not that I could remember, anyway.

I was determined to learn how to do this. It was the sort of thing you could only learn by watching, and doing. But as time went on I also got up the courage to ask questions. I realized I didn't have to just passively wait to see this kind of play, here and there, randomly – I could go and actively seek what I was looking for, as well. Even though I wasn't exactly sure what it was I was looking for, I knew I would know when I found it.

I've assembled all of what's below in the hope that one or two pieces might be of fun, practical use, and that the rest might be at least entertaining.

As Alison Gopnik says in her book *The Gardener and the Carpenter*, "contemporary middle-class parents may allow themselves license to play only if they are convinced that it is part of the work of parenting. There is a famously puritan streak in America. We have a knack for taking what are simple pleasures in other cultures, from food to walks to sex, and turning them into strenuous work projects." Canada has a puritan streak, as well, though puritanical Protestant culture never gained as strong a foothold here, thanks largely to the counterbalancing influence of Roman Catholic French Canada. From the beginning of the colonial period the Protestants and Catholics were roughly equal, population-wise. The very large French-Canadian community in Canada has probably helped save Anglo-Protestant Canada from itself in more ways than I have time to go into here.

In any case, I'd hate for anything here to be taken in the Puritan way! I have no strenuous work projects to recommend. But as my child Sophie once said when she was very small, pretending to be Cinderella while she cleaned up her room (her idea, not ours!): "It's possible to do something real while you're pretending." In other words, while pretending to be Cinderella, cleaning up her evil stepmother's kitchen, she was actually just Sophie, cleaning up her own bedroom.

If you find something you can adapt in your own way, that's great. I used some of these for brief periods of time, and some not at all, because the time or stage I might have used it had passed, or the right opportunity hasn't yet presented itself.

I'll no doubt return to (and re-adapt) many of them, especially if a time comes again when I spend a lot of time with small children. It's never too late to put our insights to use, even if we only get to them later in life, or are among the last to make use of them.

YOU WILL EXPERIENCE LIFE AS A HUMAN

The grandfathers and the grandmothers are in the children; teach them well.
– Ojibwe proverb

Don't show them your mind. Show them your imagination.
– Thomas King [quoting his mother], *The Truth About Stories*

Over coffee at Pain Perdu on St. Clair Avenue, I told the storyteller Mariella Bertelli about the problems I was having finding sources and examples for First Nations versions of bouncing rhymes and finger games. I had found lullabies in First Nations languages, but always from secondary sources. Mariella, who had a personal and professional interest in bouncing and finger rhymes, as well, had found a similar dearth of this type of material from First Nations sources.

It was important to me to find First Nations examples of these rhymes and games, because I live on land that is part of the traditional territory of the Wendat, Anishinabek Nation, the Haudenosaunee Confederacy, the Mississaugas of the New Credit First Nations and the Métis Nation. I had grown up in a town (Dundas, ON) that had been Attawandaron territory for millenia. If I was gathering games and rhymes from global sources, I definitely wanted this book to contain examples from the part of the globe I call home.

Part of the problem, I realized, after a thoughtful email response from the Haida storyteller, Kung Jaadee, might have been my approach.

Though much of the material I gathered in this book came to me haphazardly, through people I met in everyday circumstances (through family and friends, on planes or while standing around on playgrounds), some of it I sought actively. If there was an area of the world that interested me, I would sometimes go looking for a source. Active looking was often less successful than casual collecting, but usually I got some kind of response.

I would write someone a brief letter, explaining what I was looking for,

16

or call a community centre and explain what I was after (or send a note on Facebook) and then follow up a little later if I didn't get a response right away.

Using this approach, I had written K̲ung Jaadee a quick, impersonal note about my research early in 2016 asking if she might know anything about Haida lap, finger and bouncing rhymes. I had never met her before, I had only read about her online, so I was writing as a complete stranger. By this point, I had already tried many other people from First Nations backgrounds without much success.

I'm including part of K̲ung Jaadee's response below, with her permission:

I'm wondering if you're interested in contacting other Aboriginal/ Metis/Inuit people, you might also let them know more about yourself; Indigenous people usually introduce themselves, telling us their English names, their traditional names, the Nation they come from.

Your message only let me know you're writing a book with rhymes, and actions with babies or toddlers. I'm only stating this because I'm sure other groups will feel more comfortable replying with their information if you say a bit more about yourself. Where do you come from? Have your written other books? Where were you raised?

These are things First Nations/Metis/Inuit are interested in knowing from others. It helps us to figure out more things about a person. And it helps build trust between people.

Thank you for asking me.

Haw'aa, thank you.
Good luck.
– K̲ung Jaadee

She could have just ignored me. Instead she trusted that my intentions were good, and took the time to reorient me. I really appreciated this. Her advice ended up being very useful as I went forward with the later stages of my research. It was good advice to put into practice when approaching anyone at all. She also said that – to the best of her knowledge, and from her own experience – Haida people didn't have or use these kinds of rhymes and games.

I took what Kung Jaadee said about her own experiences seriously, but I also wondered whether the residential school history might have had something to do with the lack of information. The relationships between Elders (primarily grandparents and parents) and their grandchildren and children had been under direct attack for generations, along with First Nations languages, cultural traditions and spiritual transmission. The First Nations have been undergoing (and, incredibly, persevering through) a genocide that's lasted for five hundred years.

How could things as fragile and ephemeral as games between adults and children *not* have been lost? At the same time, it's quite possible that, as Kung Jaadee said, they simply didn't exist in Haida culture, and maybe never had.

Still, I think it's worth considering something stated in the *Final Report of the Truth and Reconciliation Commission of Canada: "Cultural Genocide* is the destruction of those structures and practices that allow the group to continue as a group. . . . Most significantly to the issue at hand, families are disrupted to prevent the transmission of cultural values and identity from one generation to the next."

Sabrina Williams, an intergenerational Aboriginal survivor from British Colombia, is quoted in the same book: "I didn't realize until taking this language class how much we have lost – all the things that are attached to a language: it's family connections, it's oral history, it's traditions, it's ways of being, it's ways of knowing, it's medicine, it's song, it's dance, it's memory."

When I asked my friend Lylee Williams, a school librarian on the Kahnawà:ke reserve near Montreal, and the Mi'kmaw poet Rebecca Thomas the same question about rhymes, lap and finger games, I encountered the same answer. There were lullabies, but they didn't know any examples of lap bounces, or finger rhymes or games. Was it that that particular way of playing with infants was common in Europe, Asia and Africa, but wasn't something that was ever widely practised here, among the First Nations?

The fact that I didn't find what I was looking for didn't necessarily mean it had never existed, doesn't mean it doesn't exist now and doesn't mean it won't exist in the future. It might mean any or all of those things, though. I asked probably a dozen people from First Nations backgrounds or communities the same questions over a half-dozen years – still, however you look at it, that's a small sample over a brief period.

Luckily, though, Mariella knew Ojibwe storyteller Esther Osche through her work with the Toronto Storytelling Festival, and she suggested that I give her a call and tell her what I was looking for.

Esther Osche is an Ojibwe historian and storyteller of the Whitefish River First Nation. Anishinaabemowin is her first language. It's one of several languages of the Anishinaabe people, related to, among others, Fox, Cree and Potawatomi. There are close to three-quarters of a million Anishinaabe living in Canada and the United States. Osche has lived all her life on Birch Island, on the north shore of Lake Huron.

We had to speak on the phone, because I didn't have time to drive up to meet her. Even if I had, she was just about to take a leave from her regular job as a lands manager at the Atikameksheng Anishnawbek Band Office. I caught her at a lucky moment.

After we introduced ourselves, and talked a bit about who we were, and what we did, I went ahead and asked if she thought she might have any material along the lines I was asking about: Finger games, lap rhymes, interactive games between adults and children.

While Esther spoke I tried to jot everything down:

"We start talking to a child when it's in vitro – as if they weren't in vitro – as if they were already here. As soon as we find out we're pregnant, we start talking. They feel your energy. As the pregnancy progresses, the language used becomes more complex. We talk to it as a spirit. 'You are coming into human form.' 'You will experience life as a human.' We don't just let it float about in there alone, it isn't a passive relationship, it's direct.

"And when the child is born – 'See, now you're here – all is well – it's different here. . .' From the beginning we exercise them to build their strength, to motivate them, to engage them and capture their attention. It's important to draw their attention, to try to get them to listen, so that once they're mobile they'll really listen.

"When I was little my grandpa gave me a little wooden doll, little wooden toys he'd made. It's important to allow a small child to hold different things like this – flowers, feathers, leaves – to get them to look at them, to regard them. To really look, concentrate and examine. And then when they're done, when they've exhausted it, to go on to something else.

"We sing to the child in vitro, as well, with a drum. It's important to learn the parents' voices, and their energy. To make that bond, because that bond matters for everything. Everything at first will be experienced through that bond. We chant with the drum, not pronouncing words, but chanting. The chant goes up and down, which allows the child to deepen their understanding of themselves.

"The chants have patterns. Some, everyone knows. But some are invented by you alone – you go with the drum. The drum suggests, or underlies the patterns. You are teaching the child to go on a journey when it hears the drum.

"By the age of two and a half, the child is able to figure out a lot on their own. So it's important to take the child everywhere – not to let them run loose, but to take them everywhere to see everything. A cradleboard allows the child to stay in a fixed position, where they can see everything. They like to be standing, but they may not be strong enough. The cradleboard is for posture, and for strength – binding in a blanket may work that way, too.

"In a high chair, they won't be as happy – they can sit back, and squirm.

"By watching, they discover there is a purpose in everything. That there is a purpose also in themselves. You want them to engage with the world. You want them to have a good countenance, and posture – a good stance, which will give them confidence.

"I learned from my grandmother the ways of children. My mother was more modern – she liked Jack and Jill rhymes. But Jack and Jill is too flat. Nursery rhymes are flat. They quickly come to an end. I liked my grandmother's way better – it was more open.

"Out in nature with Elders, fishing, camping, having shore dinners, these are my early memories. Watching everyone working together – it all comes together – you learn by watching – and you know from observing. You know how to put yourself to a task. It teaches a purposeful way of living.

"Every day is purposeful. Every day has its menial tasks, and every day has its magic.

"Not just women sang, but men, too. Men and women did equally hard tasks. I never felt like I wasn't strong enough. The message was 'Try. See how strong you are.' And if you couldn't do it, you go away and practise, and come back again.

"We're boring babies to death with television and videos. I'm competing with devices, with my own grandchildren, but I still get them outside at every opportunity. I tap them on the shoulder, and say 'Imagine this . . .' I give them a few clues.

"I do a lot of storytelling with my grandchildren. They don't want a flat story about 'Do this, or that,' they like something richer. Not like Jack and Jill, where something happens, and then it ends. Something like 'How the North Star Came to Be.' They're listening, they may not understand the words, but they hear the tone of your voice. They can understand the energy. The voice that invites, or the voice that repels. They understand the difference.

"I became an expert at distracting a child. And I had fun with it! Make them forget what they're trying to control you with. You can shake something at them, something big, or shiny, something they haven't seen before. And they forget how important they are for a moment. Diffusing a child's sense of self-importance is important. The parent has to guide.

"If I was difficult with my parents, if I was being headstrong, my father would show me how creatures in nature interacted with their parents. He showed me to take cues from nature. We watched bears. The mother bear explored first. She found a bag, and explored it. She snarled at the cubs, at her babies, to give her room for safety. When they got too close she snarled, and they scrambled up a tree. Do they come down on their own, when they feel like it? No. The mother lets them know when it's time. And the cub who doesn't listen? Who comes down before she's ready? She bats it hard and it rolls away like a ball. So I also saw how much harsher the animal world was. My parents didn't treat me like that.

"Watching the bears spoke more loudly than my parents' words. This is why our people aren't big speakers. Have you noticed First Nations people aren't usually big speakers? It's all eyes and ears with us.

"But I'm different! I speak a lot. My grandmother said it was the French in me.

"And I want to add, that it's nice for a child to watch someone carve something. It's good for them to see the transformation, from a piece of wood, to transform it till it looks like someone they know."

I found myself wishing I'd met Esther Osche twenty years ago, before I'd had children. I loved particularly the idea of preparing the child for the world before it appears. By doing so, you are also developing intimacy, as well as preparing yourself for what lies ahead. And reminding yourself that no matter what, you, too, are experiencing life as a human.

WHEN IS CHILDHOOD OVER?

Childhood is never really over. We acquire thinner adult years that barely stretch, or in some cases, fit, over top of those initial dense layers of our early youth. For a while we grow physically bigger, but essentially most of us stay, internally, who we were as children. If we openly regress, it's often childhood behaviours that we regress to. At the same time, if we mature, it's often through the connection we've maintained to the sense of wonder and curiousity we had as children.

In any case, like many people who don't have younger siblings, once I reached adolescence, I thought childhood was over everywhere, for everyone. I didn't know children anymore, so I thought "That's it for childhood!"

I found it surprising when I started meeting children again later in life. Their existence seemed to offer surprising proof that childhood was still going on in the world without me. It had seemed like just a stage, just for me, and from my individual perspective, but childhood turned out to be a pervasive, widespread phenonemon, global in nature – a universal experience. Wherever you go, there are children, and even if you don't return to the place where you were a child for thirty or forty years, when you go back, you will, usually, still find children.

I realize that to many people, this isn't a strange thing, but to me, it really was a revelation. We become so familiar with ourselves that we forget that almost every self-discovery is an accident, at first. We forget that what we now take for granted we once had to learn.

AWAKENING YOUNG MINDS

I may not have thought much about children since I was a child, but in the late 1990s I came across a book called *Awakening Young Minds* that changed that completely. Denise Nessel, its editor, had selected a very wide-ranging set of essays on the nature of what education was and wasn't, while also exploring what it could and might be. Reading it made me feel like it was important to go out and explore life with children again. To see for myself.

My wife, Amy, and I had started talking about having a family, and I realized that I didn't know much about what I was doing. This was something I would re-realize again and again.

Re-realizing, by the way, is a word (and concept) that comes from my friend Geoffrey Corbet. He uses it to describe the process of realizing something important, then forgetting it, and then later, re-realizing it. Part of the sensation of re-realizing something is the sense of wonder you have that you could have ever forgotten it once you'd learned it.

In any case, I decided to volunteer at a local school. A friend of mine taught at Memorial Elementary School, in the east end of Hamilton, Ontario – coincidentally, it was the primary school that my grandmother had attended in the 1920s.

THE ICE PLANET

My friend who was a teacher there sent me students to work with one on one (and one by one), to do writing exercises.

There was a boy in grade four who brought his pencil case in which he had a single piece of paper folded up. He sat down at the table across from me. I asked him if he wanted to write a story. He nodded. He took out his piece of paper, and unfolded it. He wrote –

There was an ice planet.

Then he sat there looking at the paper. He didn't write anything more. After five or ten minutes, as I didn't want to rush him, I asked if he was done. He nodded. I sent him back to class.

The next week he returned. I asked him if he wanted to keep working on his story. He nodded, took out the paper and wrote under the first sentence:

The Ice King lived by himself in the ice.

Again he sat quietly, and again I asked if he was done. He nodded, and went back to class. He followed the same pattern the next week, adding:

On the other side of the ice planet, the Ice Queen lived by herself.

24

And the next week:

The King and the Queen of the ice planet never met.

That was it. A four-line story, or poem. He didn't come back again after that.

Many people would say he was not a good writer. He didn't add lots of detail and it was difficult for him to get even this much out, over the course of a month. But to me, this is a very powerful story, or poem. It underlined for me how important it is to let children do what they can do at their own pace.

There is a great push to categorize everything, to write by category, to publish by category, to react to – whether to reward, or punish – the work of certain people because of their reputations. All of that has its purpose, and works to a point, but most of that activity can become a hindrance, as well. Here we are twenty years later, and I can still recite this boy's poem from memory. His work became part of my personal anthology of important poems. It shouldn't surprise me, but it still surprises me, because I can't categorize him – I don't even remember his name.

His work works for me, and so I remember it. It's very probable that he himself, whomever he is (he'd be about thirty now), has no memory of it.

THERE WON'T BE ANY ROOM

I want to include one other brief, brilliant, anonymous example from another school workshop I did, because it's also a personal favourite. It emerged from a writing exercise I do with students from any age group, where I ask them to think of two seemingly incompatible types of animal, or thing (like the sun and the moon, or the shore and the sea) and imagine what would happen if they fell in love. Would it go well? Would it end in disaster? What would happen?

I tried this out with a grade seven (or eight?) class at Centennial

Regional High School in Longueuil, Quebec, a few years ago. A student in that class (I have no idea what her name was) came up with the following, which, like the Ice Planet poem above, ended up in my own private anthology:

The ceiling and the floor fell in love, but they realized they needed walls to keep them apart, if they wanted to be together. Without the walls they'd stop existing, because there wouldn't be any room.

WHY DO THEY MAKE THE CLOUDS BLUE?

"Why do they make the clouds blue?" an elementary school teacher once asked me. "How many times have they looked at the sky – I take them to the windows to look – but always – blue clouds. Jesus Christ! Clouds are white or grey! Maybe red – but never blue. And how many pictures they've made so beautiful, and in the middle of it they stick their own awful faces – huge, smiling – I could wring their necks . . ." She ended my session twenty minutes early so that she could "prepare the students for the end of the day." I was sure her students were prepared for the end of the day before it even started.

She was frightening, this teacher, but I found her question about the clouds so interesting. I would never have questioned blue clouds – something I myself have always drawn without thinking twice about it.

I don't mind blue clouds. But her observation seemed like one worth exploring even if her feelings about, and way of expressing, her observation were unfortunate.

If what we usually see is white or grey clouds floating in a blue sky, why do most children draw blue clouds in a white sky? My own feeling is that it's easier – to draw a blue cloud on white paper is quick, and most people looking at the picture would simply see white and blue – the right colours, and don't think about whether those colours are illustrating the right parts of what you'd normally see in the actual sky.

It wasn't the first or last time that I almost ignored a good question because I was frightened by (or disliked) the person who'd asked it.

SUNNY VIEW SCHOOL

Before I had published any children's books, I received a grant from the Artists in Education program of the Ontario Arts Council to run poetry workshops in six different schools. The trouble would be – though I didn't realize this at first – finding six schools that might want to work with me.

I thought it would be easy, but I was inexperienced, and principals and teachers I called out of the blue were, of course, leery about my lack of experience, and negligible credentials. After striking out over and over, I called my auntie Fran Kirsh, who's an elementary school teacher. She suggested that I call my cousin Ellen Little, who's also an elementary school teacher, who suggested that I call the principal of Sunny View Public School. She knew people there and said it was a remarkable place.

Sunny View is a school for special needs students in Toronto. It opened in 1953, and it's still going strong today in 2017. Close to a hundred students bused in from around the city receive intensive support to address multiple physical, communication, intellectual and health care needs. It sounded fascinating. This time when I called, I was invited over immediately by the principal, Annie Appleby. She wanted to get a sense of who I was and of what I was proposing. A meeting with Annie Appleby, I soon discovered, involves a great deal of walking – we walked around the entire school, around and around it, through every corridor and into every room as she introduced me to dozens of staff members and students. She wanted to know if I would be willing to work with all the different levels: primary, junior and intermediate.

I felt hesitant – I'd never worked with primary students before.

Really, I felt scared in general. What did I know about working with little people? Nothing. I had volunteered a little bit at Memorial Elementary School in Hamilton four years earlier, but I had worked with students there one on one: this was a school for students with special needs, and I would be working with entire classes.

Right from the beginning, before I had agreed to anything, Annie was introducing me as the poet who would be doing workshops at the school – she told people I would be starting right away!

Her energy and enthusiasm were captivating. It made me think of something I'd once read; that England's success at building an empire came about because it recognized two aristocracies – one of birth and one of ability. I'm not romanticizing the British Empire here – abilities, obviously, can be insidious, and/or used in insidious ways. Annie, I could see, came from the aristocracy of (non-insidious) ability. She was the undisputed captain of this ship, and her mission was to explore and make use of any opportunity for learning and self-expression that might be made available to her students.

She introduced me to the special projects art resource teacher, Gyongyi "Gingi" Venczel, and left me to talk with her. Gingi asked what my plans were. I didn't know what to say. I couldn't imagine how any of the workshops I'd thought of doing could fit with the needs or abilities of the students I'd just met. It didn't seem possible.

In fact – with a great deal of collaborative adaptation – it *was* possible, but at the beginning I wouldn't have believed it. I said I needed time to think, and then we chatted about our various teaching experiences. I described some of the things I'd done with students before. After a short while Annie came back and asked if I would come again later that week to see demonstrations of other creative classes that Gingi had worked on. They also gave me a copy of Tim Lefens' extraordinary book *Flying Colors*, to read in preparation.

Lefens describes an art class he conducted at the Matheny School in Peapack, New Jersey. His students were wheelchair-bound and had no use of their arms or hands. He had to devise ways to give them the freedom to express themselves through paint. The book is both practical and inspiring because it demonstrates the type of thinking that is necessary to adapt to what at first seems like an impossible situation. As the Spanish filmmaker Pedro Almodóvar once said, "When you believe that your situation doesn't have a solution, you become more spontaneous, you get involved in the lives of others, or if you like, the dangers of others."

Not knowing the students, but knowing that their abilities and levels varied widely, even within a single class, I felt as if I might be in a situation without a solution. Where should I start? Though I assured Annie on the first day we met that I'd love to do a workshop at the school, she later told me how reluctant I seemed, especially at the idea of working with students in the primary grades where I had very limited experience.

I was surprised she had sensed my reluctance – I thought I had hidden it well – but she was right. I had felt overwhelmed at first.

FRAME, MASK AND MIRROR

It took weeks of collaborative work to figure out how to do the writing workshops effectively – this one, my favourite of all of them – was dreamed up mostly by Gingi. I've included more about the other workshops in an appendix to the book.

I was going to have the students write a poem where every line started with the words *I am*. The idea was to have the students describe themselves in a variety of different ways, using strange images and trying out different moods. I was using "A Song of Amergin," a version of an ancient Irish calendar poem I found in an anthology called *Technicians of the Sacred*, as a model.

Each line in the poem begins with the words *I am*.

Gingi had a stroke of genius about how to model what we were after – she suggested doing a warm-up exercise using a picture frame, a lion mask and a large movable mirror.

The students sat in a semicircle in front of us as Gingi began her demonstration. She looked into the large mirror she'd set up in front of her. "Who am I?" she asked herself, and then she looked over at the class, and repeated, "Who am I?"

Students put up their hands – they answered: "Gingi," "An art teacher," "A good person."

"Okay," said Gingi, "but there are other ways I can look at myself." Now she held up the picture frame so it enclosed her face and she looked at herself in the mirror again, and then out at the class, looking from person to person. "Who am I now?" she asked. "A painting," "A picture," "The *Mona Lisa*." Now she put on the lion mask and repeated what she had just done with the frame. "And who am I now?" she asked.

"A lion," "A scary animal," "A monster" were some of the responses.

"Now I'm going to come around and I want you to ask yourself the same questions." She pulled up to the first student on her rolling chair and pushed the mirror in front of him. "Who are you?" she said. "Ask yourself who you are." The student stared deep into his own eyes for a long moment. He said his name.

Gingi said, "Now choose: the frame or the mask – which do you want?" The student chose the frame.

"Now who are you?" Gingi asked.

"A famous basketball player," said the student.

The students were incredibly quiet, fully concentrating as Gingi went to each one to repeat the exercise. There was a sense of heightened tension and expectation. Everyone was curious as, one after another, each was drawn into the mirror, and asked both to see themselves and to transform how they saw themselves.

Using this same exercise with a different class, a period later, Gingi said, "Now I'm going to be your mirror," and she held up the frame and whatever the student did she mirrored it back.

I felt anxious at the beginning of this – How would students feel who had limited control of their limbs, who couldn't help jerking their arms or splaying their fingers? But Gingi was in control of what she was doing, it was completely respectful and the students laughed and noticeably relaxed and the atmosphere lightened as Gingi acted the part of their reflections.

It struck me how liberating Gingi's exercises must be when I thought how much time many of these students spend trying to control their limbs and movements enough to communicate or to conform as much as possible to social norms. Part of what Gingi was communicating was "Just relax, this is you, have some fun with who you are. It's not all serious business."

During the question period, Gingi very politely reframed or re-answered questions I'd been asked, when she sensed that my answers might not to be meeting the needs of the children who asked them.

For instance, when I was asked by a student how old I was when I learned to read, I answered without thinking of what might be the intent behind the question: "I was young – three or four."

Gingi jumped in right away and said, "That *is* young! I was at least six before I started to read. I found it very difficult."

I knew as soon as Gingi said this what she was getting at. As she said to me after, "The student wanted to know if there was any hope for him as a writer – he was comparing himself to you, what age he was at when he started to read . . ."

Or when one student said she hoped to be a poet when she grew up.

I said, "I hope you will be, too." Gingi followed this up with "But you already are! Look at what you wrote today. You're already a poet."

This time I was a bit quicker and I said, "Gingi's right. You're already writing poetry. Just keep writing."

SELF-IMPERSONATION

The Victorian psychologist James Sully described the case of two sisters, aged five and seven, who spent the afternoon pretending to be sisters. Sully noted that the game had a strangely civilizing influence: the pretend sisters were much nicer to each other than the real sisters had been. Be yourself, for a change, the lesson seems to be. You might like what you find.
– Charles Fernyhough, *The Baby in the Mirror*

Wendy Doniger explores the phenomenon of self-impersonation in a wide range of stories from various mythologies and modern films in *The Woman Who Pretended to be Who She Was: Myths of Self-Imitation*. How do we discover ourselves through putting on masks, but also, by pretending to be who we already are, or feel we could be?

When my son Ashey was three, he was wearing a Batman costume one day. He said to me, "Your son is inside my costume! Look!" He then took off his mask, saying, "Here's your son's face!" It was a complicated bit of pretending – it was as if his own face had become the mask of Batman, who was speaking from within his body. And the Batman mask represented the true Batman, who had to wear the mask to conceal Ashey, who wasn't really him. He was Ashey, pretending to be Batman, pretending to be concealed within Ashey.

Dementia can put someone in this position, too. Someone can become quite good at pretending they are who you knew them to be, but who they no longer know *themselves* to be. We visited my aunt Jean a few years ago, when she was in her mid-nineties and had lost much of her memory. My wife, who frequently works with demented patients in her practice, pointed out to me afterwards how adept Aunt Jean had been at circling around questions she couldn't answer. She questioned back, and used humour, which helped mask the gaps in her memory.

There are times when actors play themselves in their own biopics. Aging rock stars often (more or less) impersonate their younger selves on stage. Plastic surgery is sometimes used by those who want to look like their younger selves, too.

I once had a good talk with the poet Robert Priest about self-presentation. We happened to be presenting together at Brock University, and while we were there, writer and professor Kari-Lynn Winters asked us about our school presentations for research she was doing.

It turned out both Robert and I had thought a lot about how we were perceived by students when we went into schools to present. Much depended on the age and size of the group, but also on the mood of the

group, the overall tone of the school itself, as well as the relationship between the students and the teacher (or teachers) in charge. There was often
the fear that your persona (and/or presentation) might get in the way of
how your work is received. Robert, though, is a natural onstage. He really
had nothing to worry about from my perspective.

But as the three of us talked, I realized that over time, the more I had
presented, the less I worried about how I was seen. It helped to realize
(through experience) that it was very, very rare to meet a hostile or indif-
ferent audience. As time went on, I also became more interested in learning from others who presented effectively, because I had become more
comfortable with my own awkwardness. I wasn't a showman. I recognized
my limits. But recognizing my limits meant better understanding how
I could refine my style of presenting within those limits. I couldn't go
beyond them, and become a song, dance and tricks man (however much I
wished, sometimes, that I had those talents!). But I could still find better
ways of engaging, by being more conscious of my body language and pacing, and of how and when I used humour. And I could then "impersonate"
the successes of those experiences the next time.

I talked about this issue with the poet Robert Heidbreder a few months
later in Vancouver, and he had his own fascinating account of how he'd
handled the difficult issue of presentation – he started to use puppets (as
a classroom teacher), and this was a huge success for him. The puppet
became his intermediary.

Mark Twain, apparently, kept careful note of how people reacted to his
public presentations, and revised his anecdotes, written work and future
public presentations according to what he'd learned from audience reac-
tions.

Erving Goffman wrote two fascinating books on the subject: *The
Presentation of Self in Everyday Life* and *Stigma: Notes on the Management
of Spoiled Identity*. In the first, Goffman analyzes the ways in which we
try (and often fail) to project a certain persona in social situations. He
analyzes the phenomenon as if it were acting on a stage. In the second, he

talks about the ways in which people try to reduce the discrimination they experience because of social stigmas imposed on them by society.

The Japanese psychologist Takeo Doi wrote one of the most helpful books I've ever read on the issue of the self among (and as defined by) others, *The Anatomy of Self: The Individual Versus Society*. He pointed out that we are all different with different people, and in different situations. He felt there was a greater understanding of this in Japanese culture than there is in the West. He said that in the West, we often worry too much about finding our true or authentic self, as if we had one true version, which gets hidden from view. We ask the question "who am I?" as if there was only one possible answer.

And that leads to enormous stress, because there is no single answer for any person.

BUMBOSITY

One of my maternal great-grandmothers, Nina Allen (nee Hindman), grew up in Syracuse, New York. I asked my great-aunt Eunice, who's ninety, if she remembered any rhymes her parents used with them when she and my grandfather were children. She produced this one, from her mother, straight away. She said she heard it many times as a child in the 1930s:

The very idosity
Of your curiosity
If I was your Mother
I would spank your bumbosity.

Beyond the fun of the wordplay, and the implicit threat, there's also the momentary mind-bending oddity of your mother saying, "If I was your mother." This dampens the threat a little – it's as if the speaker (the mother), by pretending not to be the mother, is saying, "Don't worry, since I'm not your mother, I'm not going to spank you." At the same time, the child might be thinking, "My mother might remember she's my mother at any moment, and then I'll be in big trouble!"

I searched the Internet for any exact matches or variants of this one, and found a single reference in comments to an online obituary for a man named Richard Sweeney, who was born in Salt Lake City, Utah, in 1935. As far as I can tell (from the family names) he wasn't a relative of mine. A family friend of Richard Sweeney notes that Richard's mother (back in the 1930s, or '40s?) would recite this verse:

Why the very idosity of your curiosity.
If I didn't have my white gloves on
I would spank your bumbosity.

I can't find a single other reference to this rhyme, and this version is quite different, since the mother pretending not to be the mother is replaced by a pair of white gloves.

KOO KOO! OPA!

In High Park one day I saw two parents, I think from Poland, playing with their child on a slide. The mother stood at the bottom and called up "Koo Koo!" to the child. When the child slid down and got to the bottom the father would shout an enthusiastic "Opa!" They did this over and over. I noticed because my two year old was watching and he wanted to do it, too. He continued repeating the two exclamations for a while afterwards. Koo Koo! and Opa! have a nice ring to them.

CHAPTER TWO

HAMILTON, TRINIDAD, JAMAICA AND CHECHNYA

THE VERY, VERY BEGINNING

We move about in a world of sound and rhythm in the womb. The heartbeats of our mothers, their digestion, their movements through space, their conversations – all of this surrounds us while we grow and move within our mother's bodies. We have our own heartbeats to keep us company in there, too. The rhythms of our own hearts and the motions (and sounds) of the bodies of the mothers who carry us may well be of interest to our fetal minds – minds that are made to detect, analyze and use patterns, and have no other source of stimulation while in the womb. There is much that's already familiar when we're born, much that we *don't* have to learn.

It's possible that our lifelong desire for, and hypnotized responsiveness to, rhythm comes about because birth deprives us of our close proximity to a constant heartbeat. While we're born into a new world of light and sound, no doubt there are things about our first world (the world of the womb) that we miss, and so we're attracted to things in the new world (the world outside the womb) that remind us of it.

Edward T. Hall talks extensively about the rhythms of human social interactions in his book *The Dance of Life*. Included in this book is a passage I've been rereading and thinking about for twenty-five years. It describes one of Hall's graduate students doing research on filmed interactions between children playing on a school playground. It influenced the depiction of the central character in a book I wrote called *Sidewalk Flowers*: "One very active little girl seemed to stand out from the rest. She was all over the place. Concentrating on that girl, my student noticed that whenever she was near a cluster of children the members of that group were in sync not only with each other, but with her . . . he realized that this girl, with her skipping and dancing and twirling, was actually orchestrating movements of the entire playground."

After reading this, I realized that there must be patterns (rhythmic arrangements) we were actively taking part in all the time without being aware of it. It also made me think about poetry.

Have rhythms become less varied, and of less interest, in modern poetry because our activities have become less varied than they once were? Kneading, chopping, weaving, laundering, knitting, hoeing, rowing, sewing, caring for animals in a variety of ways, carving – all sorts of physical rhythms that varied and demanded a chant or song aren't part of most Western lives anymore. This must have had (and is still having) an impact on verbal and rhythmic invention.

What sort of rhythm does a food processor have? Or buying a sweater? Or turning on the furnace?

Many, when they exercise, or drive, or do anything not requiring their full attention, listen passively to music with a drumbeat of some kind. Does this interfere in any way with cycles of boredom, excitement and invention in the quiet mind? What impact does it have? Is it, again, some kind of regression to life in the womb?

Dennis Lee wrote about how "Alligator Pie" emerged directly out of the physical effort he was making on a bicycle in the anthology *Aloud in My Head*: "My legs were going round and round as I pedaled, and there was a particular rhythm when my left foot, and then my right, pressed the pedal down. I began to hear snatches of words that echoed the rhythm: 'All-i-ga-tor pie . . . All-i-ga-tor pie' . . . Da dum-da, da dum-da . . . I think I'm gonna cry (sigh? die?)."

In her book of essays *What is Found There*, Adrienne Rich notes: "Fewer and fewer people in this country entertain each other with verbal games, recitations, charades, singing, playing on instruments, doing anything as amateurs – people who are good at something because they enjoy it. . . . To do moderately and pleasingly well, in short, a variety of things without solemn investment or disenabling awe – these were common talents till recently, crossing class and racial lines."

How many of us have stopped doing something because we were told we'd never be great at it? Never professional? Again, one of the discoveries for me, putting this book together, has been that it's okay to be my awkward self when I'm interacting with children. I may not have a natural gift for entertaining little people, but that doesn't mean I can't be a perfectly functional amateur.

And if I end up being a lifelong apprentice, that's fine. In any case, what choice do I have?

DAVID WRIGHT, HUMAN TRAFFIC LIGHT

I was at a potluck in Toronto one Saturday night, and there was a little boy there – not quite two, not saying anything. I'd never met him before. I happened to be sitting next to him at an outdoor table where he was drumming his feet rhythmically on his chair. I matched his drumming exactly with my feet on the ground. He looked happy that I was able to match what he was doing. So he did it again, then stopped and watched to see what I'd do. I did it again. Then he did something similar, but slightly different, with his hands on the table, and raised his eyebrows at me, as if to say, "And this? Can you match this?" I did the same. Then he smiled and raised a palm, and reached it toward me. I didn't understand this at first, but then (I'm so slow sometimes . . .) I got it, and pressed my palm against his. He laughed. That was the whole interaction. We never exchanged a word.

A few months later I was at a bicycle rental shop in Mont Tremblant, Quebec. While Amy filled out a rental form, I drummed on the counter –

an unusual rhythm a friend had taught me once. We were the only people in the shop, aside from a man sitting behind a desk on the other side of the shop, looking at something on a computer screen. He wasn't looking our way. A moment after I finished drumming out the rhythm, he drummed exactly the same rhythm on the edge of his desk. I could tell looking over at him that it was unconscious. He was imitating what he'd heard without seeming to be aware of it.

It reminded me of something from my childhood. My brother and I squabbled a lot, but I remember that if I was singing somewhere in the house – say I was sitting in the living room, and my brother was passing by in the hall – he would often whistle or hum a little in harmony with my song. It seemed completely unconscious – I never asked him about it, but it made me happy when he did that.

But there are other kinds of imitation that people don't like at all.

Before the time of computerized traffic signals, which have existed in Ontario for about fifty years, most major intersections in large cities had to have people who stood high up on poles, who were in charge of traffic control.

My great-great-grandfather David Wright was a human traffic light at the corner of Barton and James, in Hamilton, back in the 1920s. I only know this because my grandmother, his granddaughter, didn't like him. He had insulted her father once, and she never forgave him. To antagonize him, she would go stand at the corner of the intersection and imitate his arm and body movements, which infuriated him. He couldn't gesture back at her without putting cars and horses at risk, he could only shout at her. He was trapped in a series of set movements, indicating which lane could go, which could turn, which had to stop.

Before a child innovates, linguistically, or in their movements, they usually have to learn to repeat a sound or movement. It's quite exciting when they first learn to mimic us, and then exciting when the next part happens – when they start to move free of repetition, and to innovate. Schools are so hard on children for plagiarizing the words of others, but in other areas

– when it comes to how they dress, or how they move their bodies – when it comes to *actions* (especially the actions of being a consumer!), our culture encourages us to value copying above all else.

LAP, FINGER AND BOUNCING RHYMES

In the lap and finger rhyme games of infancy we discover the most fundamental forms of human entertainment. Most lap, finger and bouncing rhymes are an addictive mix of euphonic, rhythmic language matched with simple melodies, often accompanied by the slapstick drama of tickles, joltings and sudden drops.

And so we are introduced all at once, and very economically, to poetry, music, drama and much else besides. One could argue we are experiencing, at the most basic level, the rhythms of our culture, or cultures, and there's some evidence that we're also helping to hard wire a child's sense of balance, and of risk taking.

While lap and finger rhyme games are universal, appearing in every language and culture on earth, very little cross-cultural research has been done on them. Even though a lot of good children's poetry is rooted in a definite knowledge and understanding of nursery verse and the overlapping genre of lap and finger rhymes, there has been relatively little transfer between cultures, especially between cultures that, until recently, were geographically and/or historically distant.

This is understandable; they are considered ephemeral entertainments by most. This is part of their charm, and many people forget them before they reach adolescence.

But maybe it's important to actively take part in the maintenance of and transfer of these ephemeral entertainments. Especially now, with the proliferation of electronic devices, and the pressures on parents to divert their children with toys and gadgets that encourage passive and isolated *play*. It's also a problem – from the point of view of passing on these games – that families in the West have fewer children and longer time gaps between generations, during which much of this material may be getting lost.

In regular speech, we avoid repeating the same sounds and similar sounding words close together over and over again. We also usually avoid ambiguity or duplicity of meaning, as well as flights of fancy and nonsense words. Rarely, if ever, do we match our actions to the words we're saying – except, perhaps, when we're angry, being loving or giving directions. Lap and finger rhyme games for children, it seems, take advantage of these taboos, by reversing our usual tendencies and making something novel and entertaining out of them.

WHAT THEY DON'T DO

It's quite interesting that lap, finger and bouncing rhymes are rarely used as vehicles of indoctrination. Perhaps because they'd be useless. They are mostly sound and action based – they have to do, usually, with animals, or people in the present moment. They are nearly always free of religious dogma and gender norms.

In this sense, they've been able to live and evolve in a way that poetry for older readers and listeners hasn't always. Jacob Burckhardt pointed out in his lovely book *The Age of Constantine the Great*, that Christianity, in the form it was imposed on the West, had a stifling affect on poetry and the imagination. There were always fears about dogma being undermined.

He contrasted this with the great energy and richness of imagination that existed in the Greek system of belief (referring to the stories of the ancient Greek gods). By this, I believe Burckhardt meant there were dozens, even hundreds, of variants of the stories and myths told about the Greek gods – the stories were treated as departure points, things to be retold, but also stripped down and then re-embellished again by whomever happened to be telling the tales. They weren't meant to be taken as fixed and unalterable, they were treated as a dynamic shape-shifting force of their own, to be engaged with imaginatively. The stories certainly weren't understood to be the word of God. Monotheist scriptures were (and often still are) treated quite differently.

In the Greek stories, tales of heroes or heroines are the medium through which the gods make themselves known on earth, while in Judaism, Christianity and Islam, the prophets are God's exemplars, and their words are meant be passed on with exactitude. There isn't much room for play there.

I don't feel it's possible to promote a cause or grind an axe with a children's rhyme. If you try, the rhyme dies on the spot. On the other hand, they can also become the source for more successful parodies, as Isaac Watts and Robert Southey's didactic poems were parodied by Lewis Carroll.

Having said that, I'll give you an example that seems to be contradictory to this idea at first glance. This is a bouncing rhyme taught to me by Elaina Ryan, director of Children's Books Ireland, when I was in Dublin for a conference she was running. She first heard it in Waterford, Ireland, at the age of ten.

You bounce the child on your lap, saying:

There was a little lass
Who didn't go to mass
And she fell into a
Deep
Dark
Hole!

When you say "Deep dark hole!" you drop the child through your knees, which you suddenly open.

At first, it does sound like a bit of indoctrination. You're telling the little lass you're bouncing that if she doesn't go to mass, something bad is going to happen to her. Is this sudden opening between your knees supposed to be *hell* that you're dropping her into?

If so, the fun of the rhyme, and the thrill of the drop, almost guarantee that the child will beg to be dropped into the "deep dark hole" again and again. Is the rhyme actually subverting the idea of punishment for skipping mass? The outcome, at least in the action accompanying the rhyme, is, I'd say, more reward than punishment.

SOME CONJECTURES ABOUT THE ROLE OF NURSERY RHYMES IN LANGUAGE ACQUISITION

I suspect that with nursery rhymes, and related nonsense, the repetition of sounds and rhythms has something to do with preparing the mind, and the mouth, for spoken language. They expand a child's ability to string words together in a meaningful way. Sort of like laying the track before the train. By the time you start trying to speak, you've been spending a lot of time and expending a lot of effort preparing. Nonsense and nursery rhymes give the child's tongue something to hold onto. It's as if you're saying to them, "Yes, you're making nonsensical noises, and I'm giving you something slightly less nonsensical in return. It's a bridge between the way I talk and the way you talk. I'm going to start with something you'd say, KooKoo KoKo Tsip Tsap, and then I'm going to link it to something closer to what I'd say." You give the language a muscle memory, too, in the rest of the body – you're rooting the language in what the child has already learned, and is currently learning, often to walk.

Yet nursery rhymes aren't just designed for language acquisition. They have other functions, as well – they're entertaining. You're painting pictures in the child's mind – odd ones – but as an adult, you're repainting those same odd pictures in your own mind at the same time. It's a two-way street. The pleasure is mutual. I wonder if this sort of thing rejuvenates the adult mind in subtle ways while simultaneously stimulating the mind of the child.

As I worked on the second draft of this book, my publisher, Noelle Allen, sent me a link to an online BBC article by Pallab Ghosh she thought I'd find interesting. It discusses research that Dr. Victoria Leong of Cambridge University has been doing on learning, the infant brain and the importance of parent-child interactions, which seems to confirm some of my conjectures:

> Dr. Victoria Leong, who is leading the research, has discovered that babies learn well when their mums speak to them in a soothing sing-song voice which she calls "motherese."
>
> Dr. Leong's research shows that nursery rhymes are a particularly good way for the mums in her study to get in sync with their babies.
>
> "Although it sounds odd to us, babies really love listening to motherese even more than adult speech. It holds their attention better and the speech sounds clearer to them. So we know the more motherese the baby hears, the better the language development," she said.

The idea that there are *ways* of speaking more suited to certain times of life might be something worth exploring in relation to other age groups, as well. The more knowledgeable we are about the subtleties of communication, the better able we'll be to communicate with each other.

DOE DOE PETIT POE POE

In the mid 1970s I had the great fortune to have Lee Davies (later Qarib) as my babysitter. Lee was my father's student at McMaster University. She had come to study foreign languages, along with several of her friends from Trinidad and Tobago. Lee was one of the sweetest adults I knew as a child – loving, funny, good-natured. I was very sad when she graduated and went away. But we stayed in touch. I wrote her letters, and she always wrote back. As a child, I hadn't realized that Lee wasn't that much older than I was.

While doing graduate work in Spain, she met and married Adnan Qarib, a young Palestinian also studying far from home, and they ended up moving to Louisiana, where Lee works to this day as a schoolteacher.

I told Lee about my research, and she sent this back:

Doe Doe Petit Poe Poe
Petit Poe Poe pas v'lez Doe Doe
Doe Doe Petit Poe Poe
Petit Poe Poe pas v'lez Doe Doe

The language is Antillean (French-based) Creole, which is spoken by about a million people among the Caribbean nations. Lee understood it to mean, "Go to sleep, little baby."

"I think my granny sang her version of it because she had difficulties learning English. It was something she sang while rubbing or patting our backs.

"I grew up mostly in San Fernando and my grandmother, Antonia Cavada, was from Santander in Spain. She was very poor, growing up. She won a lottery as a young woman and bought a ticket to Cuba where she married my Trinidadian grandfather, Stedman Cory Davies. She was a firecracker for her time – very no nonsense, and she adored her grandchildren. All 'white' families in Trinidad had local women care for and raise their children. We grew up closer to these women than to our parents. My grandmother was often shunned for being darker skinned. She was a very hands-on granny and not into society at all."

Later, Lee said her grandfather became so difficult that her grandmother divorced him.

He returned to Cuba, and – for those interested in twentieth-century American novelists – sometimes took Ernest Hemingway for fishing and drinking expeditions.

MANUEL ROAD

The poet and novelist Pamela Mordecai was born in Kingston, Jamaica, in the early 1940s and she's lived in Canada since the early 1990s, though she studied in several other countries along the way. Her *de book of Mary* is my all-time favourite retelling of the Gospels – to me it's the perfect example of how powerful, striking stories will always, in every place and era, find exactly the right person to retell them.

When I met Pamela and her husband, Martin, at a common friend's in 2014 and told her about the work I was doing she promised to help out. A short while later, Pam sent me several emails filled with interesting information, including songs as she remembered them from her own childhood, and references to scholarly work others had done on Jamaican children's games and rhymes.

"Here's the version I know of 'Manuel Road.' You can go as high up with the numbers as you wish, as I recall, but not after they got to two-syllable digits."

Manuel Road [probably originally "Emmanuel Road"]

Go dung a Manuel Road, *gal an bwoy,*
Fe go bruk rock stone, *gal an bwoy.*
Go dung a Manuel Road, *gal an bwoy,*
Fe go bruk rock stone, *gal an bwoy.*
Bruk dem one by one, *gal an bwoy,*
Bruk dem two by two, *gal an bwoy,*
Finga mash, no cry, *gal an bwoy,*
Memba a play we a play, *gal an bwoy.*
Go dung a Manuel Road, *gal an bwoy,*
Fe go bruk rock stone, *gal an bwoy.*
Go dung a Manuel Road, *gal an bwoy,*
Fe go bruk rock stone, *gal an bwoy.*
Bruk dem two by two, *gal an bwoy,*
Bruk dem three by three, *gal an bwoy,*
Finga mash, no cry, *gal an bwoy,*
Memba a play we a play, *gal an bwoy.*

The form of English (and spelling) Pamela is using here is Jamaican Patois, called Jamaican Creole by some linguists.

"I can't remember playing the game myself, but I'm pretty sure there was no element of 'winning' involved.

"Olive Lewin, an ethnomusicologist that we knew well, is a reliable source. There's some debate as to whether 'Manuel Road' is a worksong, and I associate it (perhaps arbitrarily) with women breaking stones in the quarry near our family house when I was growing up. See the second quote from Olive Lewin.

"'In 'Manuel Road,' the most popular [Jamaican] stone game, six or more players kneel in a circle, each tapping a fairly large stone on the ground in time to the song. The speed thus established, the game begins in earnest. Players pass the stones to the right. If the movement coincides with the accents of the song (indicating the passing of the stones) all is well. If not, a finger can be crushed as a stone lands on it heavily,' (Lewin, 80)."

"Olive says: 'Manual labour was such an all-pervading feature in the life of black Jamaicans that music from other areas of activity was borrowed to accompany it. . . . Work movements and rhythms also inspired play activities, such as stone passing games. I remember women in my childhood, sitting facing piles of stones, breaking them for covering dusty or water-pocked roads. They worked rhythmically, whether singly or in groups, to let the "music carry the work" and make it easier for them. The same rhythm was transferred to games such as "Manuel Road"' (Lewin, 101)."

Below is another song Pam recommended. I watched many different YouTube clips of people, often at community or family gatherings, dancing to this song, along with my kids, and pretty soon we were all singing it. It's very catchy. In some danced versions, the dancers touch their heads and spin when they sing, "Peel head John Crow sit pan the treetop." In all the versions I watched, people – mostly women – reached out and took each other's hands while singing, "Come let mi hole yuh hand."

Long Time Gal Mi Neva See You

Dis long time gal mi neva see you
Come let mi hole yuh han
Dis long time gal mi neva see you
Come let mi hole yuh hand.
Peel head John Crow sit pan the treetop
Pick out the blossom
Let mi hole yuh han gal
Let mi hole yuh han.

Dis long time gal mi neva see you
Come let mi wheel an' tun
Dis long time gal mi neva see you
Come let mi wheel an' tun.
Peel head John Crow sit pan the treetop
Pick out the blossom
Let mi wheel an' tun gal
Let mi wheel an' tun.

Dis long time gal mi neva see you
Come let mi walk and talk
Dis long time gal mi neva see you
Come let mi walk and talk.
Peel head John Crow sit pan the treetop
Pick out the blossom
Let mi walk and talk gal
Let mi walk and talk.

Dis long time gal mi neva see you
Come let me wheel an' jig
Dis long time gal mi neva see you

Come let me wheel an' jig.
Peel head John Crow sit pan the treetop
Pick out the blossom
Let me wheel an' jig gal
Let me wheel an' jig.

Let mi hole yuh han gal
Let mi hole yuh han.

There's a lovely sense of homecoming, intimacy and happy restlessness in the song and the way it's danced. And it's as accessible, as a dance, to the elderly as it is to children.

IF YOU DON'T KNOW HOW TO DANCE, HOW DO YOU KNOW WHO YOU ARE?

It took months to arrange a meeting with the Taramovs – a Chechen refugee family living in one of the St. James Town apartment complexes in downtown Toronto. It's incredibly difficult to meet with people who don't have time – the poor and the rich have this in common. Only the middle class has time and money, and they complain most about the lack of both. (I can attest to this, being a complaining member of this class myself.)

In any case, I arrived early, which was lucky: the entrance to the building was craftily hidden far from the street behind crumbling cement walls. As with so much of 1960s architecture, you couldn't help feeling that whoever had dreamed the building up had been inspired by a mouse maze – the entrance had been put in the place where you'd least expect to find it.

When I finally found their door, I was greeted by a young man with dark spiky hair.

"I'm Aslan," he said, "and this is my mother." He told me her name, but I didn't catch it, and later I was too embarrassed to ask for it again.

I was tempted to ask Aslan if he'd read the Narnia books – and made a note to find out where C.S. Lewis found the name for his famous lion. Chechnya, after all, is between the Caspian and Black Seas, and Caspian was another name Lewis was clearly fond of. I later found out that Aslan means *lion* in Turkish.

I took off my shoes. Aslan at once offered me some large white slippers.

I declined the slippers Aslan was offering, which I thought was the polite thing to do. Aslan insisted. I could tell from his expression that it would be a mistake not to put them on. Later, when I told my son Ashey about this, he asked how Aslan had known my shoe size.

I told him that he must be very good at guessing, just like a shoe sales- man. "If it's their custom, no doubt they learn well and early how to guess which slippers will fit."

I was served an enormous meal. I should have guessed, from what I'd read about social customs in the mountainous Caucasus region (sand- wiched between Turkey, Iran and Russia, as well as the Black and Caspian Seas) that I'd be shown this kind of hospitality, but I hadn't considered it from any sort of practical angle when I'd eaten a large lunch an hour or so before.

One large plate was heaped with chicken, another with deep-fried meat patties that I later found out were called belishi. A third plate held a loaf of freshly baked bread. There was also a chopped vegetable salad, and, in front of my plate, a litre-sized glass filled with apricot juice.

I ate, and ate, and ate. They were so generous, and the food was deli- cious – but I was full when I arrived. And I'm a vegetarian. I hadn't eaten meat in years. I couldn't possibly eat as much as they were expecting me to eat – though I knew I was being a terrible (but hopefully not typical Canadian) guest.

"My mother wants to know why you aren't eating more," said Aslan, after his mother muttered something to him out of the kitchen. "You don't like our food?" The "our" made it more personal, and general, and embar- rassing.

"It's just delicious, so good, but I'm not a big eater. . ." I said, which was true. Occasionally I forget about lunch altogether, and I had just eaten two unexpected and entire plates of meat and deep-fried fritters.

Trying to move away from the subject of lunch, I started to ask some general questions – we talked a little bit about politics, about the problems of the Chechens getting endless bad press in the West – how the Russian government successfully feeds Western newspapers and Internet news sites all sorts of nonsense that they simply print without independent investigation. This was a problem for Western news in general – it wasn't just reporting on Chechnya that had become weak – but Chechnya and the Chechens got a disproportionate amount of bad press, and it hurt their chances for survival, for just plain physical survival, let alone the survival of their language, their customs and culture.

The Taramovs had lived through both Russian invasions of Chechnya: the first being 1994–1996; the second in 1999, followed by a guerrilla war that lasted almost a decade. A conservative estimate puts civilian deaths in these wars at between fifty and eighty thousand people. Chechens in Russian custody are routinely tortured, and many of those who are abducted by Russian security forces are never seen again.

Today (in 2017) Chechnya is technically ruled by a Chechen named Kadyrov, but he was installed as the country's dictator because he swore absolute loyalty to Vladimir Putin. At the behest of Putin, Kadyrov tortures and murders his own people, most recently conducting a homicidal campaign against gay men, in keeping with Putin's recent legislative campaign to empower those who seek to persecute Russia's LGBTQ community.

Aslan talked a bit about being in exile. "We have no tradition of being a diaspora community," he said. "We've been in the same place for a few thousand years, maybe longer." He gave me some statistics – in Toronto there are roughly two hundred Chechens, many living in the St. James Town apartment towers. "By staying together, we make it possible to open up to the outside. If we're separated, we close up, because there's nowhere to be ourselves, to speak our language, eat our food, listen to our music. We die. But as long as we have our community, then we can open to the larger community, as well."

All of this made perfect sense.

Aslan talked also about how his grandmother used to make the entire family come to her farm at the same time to help with chores. Back then, he said, he couldn't understand it – there were so many of them, and it wasn't a big farm – she could have had just a few of them come and it would have been enough. But later he realized she wanted to create a sense of community in the family. She wanted them to talk to each other, and work together, and while they worked, she told them stories. She was educating them on the sly – she said they were there to help her, and they *were* helping her, but she was helping *them* at the same time, preparing them individually, but also as a group, for life.

Aslan put on a videotape of a party the community had had in the winter. It was dominated by dancing – all different people. The men danced with very fast complicated steps, legs and feet working so quickly it was hard to see where they were going or where they'd come from – fancy footwork would be less than an understatement. The women concentrated more on hand and arm movements – fluid wavelike gestures. Both men and women showed enormous pride in the way they held themselves, a definite uprightness, but without a hint of arrogance.

I thought of my mother, who'd been rediscovering her Scottish heritage as she got older, and how much of this rediscovery had happened for her through the groups she'd joined to learn Scottish dancing. I told Aslan about this. He asked me, incredulous, "You mean you didn't learn to dance when you were growing up?" I told him no – in high school I'd danced at school dances, thrashing about to pop music, but otherwise, I'd never danced.

"But if you don't dance, how do you know who you are? And how can anyone else know you?"

That how a person dances might provide you with important information about that person was a revelation to me. It would make sense that how a community dances would tell you a great deal about that community, as well. Wouldn't it be fascinating to slowly travel the globe, keeping track of the subtle changes in dance from one town to the next? The changes in body language would probably be as gradual as those in spoken language. At least it would be in parts of the world where people haven't managed to, or been forced to, quickly jettison the greater part of their cultural inheritance – and no doubt you would find relationships between both language and movement.

* * *

Aslan thought he'd be able to find some Chechen children's games to show me by the next time we met, but I was never able to locate him again. His questions stayed with me, though – and it fascinated me how often the subject of dance came up as I continued doing this research.

IF THE NUT FALLS, WHAT WILL HAPPEN?

Victoria Poupko (originally from Moscow) is the most tireless supporter of human rights I've ever met. In fact, we've never met. We almost met once in Boston – unfortunately I had to cancel my trip because of a ruptured appendix.

For years, though, we've been exchanging emails about the plight of Chechen refugees, and when I was unable to locate the Taramov family again, I asked Victoria if she could connect me with someone else from Chechnya.

She immediately connected me with the Chechen novelist Mustafa Edilbiev.

The pieces below became a three-way collaboration. Mustafa provided the Chechen versions, with rough translations into Russian, which he then gave to Victoria. Victoria made rough translations into English. Then Victoria and I refined those English translations together – all three of us sending questions back and forth about the meanings of words as we went along. We have tried to be accurate – in doing so, it's possible we've created something completely new, or at least somewhat different, instead – there's no way of knowing.

Edilbiev's work hasn't been translated into English, but he's well known in Russia as the government-persecuted author of a book called *Solomon, the Magician* (*Solomon-volshebnik*), which takes a stand against anti-Semitism in Russia. Edilbiev was born in 1951 in Kyrgyzstan. In February 1944 the entire Chechen nation had been deported to Kyrgyzstan on Stalin's orders as the first step in a government-sponsored genocide

Between a third and a half of the population of five hundred thousand died during the deportation. Half of the deportees were children. Like all children of deportees, Edilbiev had rickets. He didn't start walking until he was three and a half years old. He remembers most of all the terrible hunger. Among them were deportees of many different nationalities and all were struggling against famine.

In 1958, during the time of Khrushchev, the Chechens were returned to Chechnya. Mustafa said, "I was not yet eight years old when I was brought home, in the same cold, unheated carriages used for transporting livestock, the same that were used during the deportation. The return was terrible."

Chechnya had been settled by Russians, who were brought in after the eviction of the Chechens. Some vacated the Chechen homes, but most didn't want to. Chechens lived in barns and hastily built shacks. There was fighting, and Russians conducted pogroms against the returning Chechens.

Mustafa's earliest memories were the local authorities arming the Russians who then broke into Chechen shacks, caught Chechens and Ingush in the streets, and killed them.

"They killed everyone. Each day and every night for me – an eight-year-old child – was filled with the horror of waiting for brutal Russian mobs. Petrified with fear, we fell asleep in the arms of our parents and grandparents. They did not sleep at night, ready to die for us." Edilbiev and his children live at risk to this day. Games like this one, below, have survived against incredible odds.

Chechen Children's Game

The children make a circle around a teacher, or whomever leads the game. The game is intended for children who are six or seven years old.

Adult: What is flying way over there? [Gesture to somewhere far away.]

If there are no answers, or the answers aren't what's needed, the adult answers: A black, black crow!

Adult: What does it have in its beak? [There may be many answers. If a kid says something meaningful everybody applauds them. Whatever is said, the adult continues.]

Adult: Could it be a nut in a green mossy shell? And what will happen if the nut drops? [You may get many answers. Praise whatever answers you get.]

Adult: We put out a big carpet to catch the nut. And if the carpet is torn what should we do? [Many usually scream the right answer.]

Adult: Yes! We take a needle and thread and fix it! And what if the needle breaks? [You may get almost no answers. If somebody says something, suggesting anything at all, the teacher responds, pointing to that child.]

Adult: "You will become the master and fix it." [And they might be given a needle as a reward.]

This could be done in any number of ways. The point is to give the children an opportunity to think, to imagine and to answer. You can be leading the story in a certain direction, but at the same time be positive about and encourage answers that go in different directions. As the adult, you can also think creatively about how to use the answers to head toward the end you have in mind, or toward a new end, suggested by the children.

This next game, again, can be done in a number of ways. Essentially, you ask children what the meaning of a number is, and then listen to what kinds of ideas or images they produce. The answers below are examples Mustafa provided – these could be used as examples for a child, as well.

"One": What does it mean?
What could be more desirable than a single soul?

"Two": What does this mean?
What could shine brighter than two eyes?

"Three": What does this mean?
A three-legged stool stays where you put it.

"Four": What's the meaning of four?
The house with four walls remains where it's built.

"Five": What does this mean?
If five tie a man, it will be hard for one to free him.

This final rhyme is, I believe, meant for the fingers. Victoria thought it might be a classroom game. Unfortunately we couldn't reach Mustafa after we did a first version of the translation, and so we had to guess. The imagery we agreed on, but the question we were left with was – what is it for?

I imagine it as a tickle game – each finger gets a bun, but the hungry hand (the wolf) is left with a crust, and runs up the arm to tickle.

Give this bun to the turkey
And this one to the duck
This one's for the rooster
And this one for the bunny
The last is for the wolf cub . . .

And we give the wolf the crust –
He's angry – and we all quickly flee!

KHIN-NAAN AND THE SHRINKING WATERS

Through Facebook, I connected with one other Chechen source. His name is Adam Tsopa – I don't know much else about him. I connected with him while he was back home, travelling in Chechnya. I believe he lives somewhere else now – possibly in the UK. I asked him if he had any information about playing with children, or stories for children.

He responded: "I did find one tale that was used to keep children out of big lakes and rivers. It is called khin-naan, the mother of the waters. This is a fictional creature created by our culture, always described as a mystical and big mother-monster living inside the deepest waters.

"The tale was told mainly to keep children out of dangerous places."

By chance, I had just come across a reference to the Ojibwe sea leopard, Mishibijiw (also called Mishipeshu), a kind of underwater composite-creature sea monster that lived in Gitchi-Gami (Lake Superior). It was feared, and considered dangerous. There is also the Iroquoian legend of the horned serpent Oniare, a dangerous underwater monster of the Great Lakes. It makes good sense, placing storied creatures in places of real danger. The possibility of seeing (or having to face) the unseen creature would keep a young person alert.

There is also the corollary, of the mystical invisible figure that we look for (or sense) in places or times of real magic (Santa Claus, Elijah, Khidr, et cetera). It's the opposite of feeling like there's something unseen waiting under the bed, under the bridge or in the closet – something invisible that you hope *won't* become visible. Instead, there's this invisible wonderful force, or figure, which you hope you *will* get a glimpse of. It's the hopeful belief in the invisible figure, as opposed to the fearful belief in the invisible figure – but in both cases we personify the unseen.

But myths, stories and surprising beliefs about water are, understandably, quite universal. The Loch Ness monster and the kraken are well known. There is the leviathan in the book of Job, and it's interesting to consider the range of water stories in the Torah, the Gospels and the Quran.

In the story of Noah (or Nuh), Noah has an ark to float above the water that covers the entire earth for forty days and forty nights. In the story of Moses (Moshe, Musa), God parts the Red Sea and the Israelites walk across the sea floor. In the story of Jonah (Dhul-Nun – which in Arabic means *the one in the whale*), Jonah is under the water, inside the whale, where he survives, this time for three days and three nights. In the story of Jesus (Isa) walking on water, the walk seems to be very brief. And interestingly, the storm ceases once Jesus gets into the boat, implying that Jesus wasn't just walking on a quiet surface, but on waves.

And so we go from floating on it in a boat, to walking through it after it splits into two walls, to moving through it, as if in a submarine, under the surface, to walking across the surface of it.

It's also interesting that the bodies of water shrink as the stories go on – Noah's flood covers the world, Moses crosses the Red Sea, which is an inlet of the Indian ocean, Jonah's ordeal take place in the Mediterranean and Jesus walks on the Sea of Galilee, which is really an inland freshwater lake. Finally, Jesus turns water into wine – a cup of water is a very small body of water! The final water miracle in the monotheist tradition is told in one of the traditions of Muhammad, when Muhammad takes a small amount of water and makes more of it, for those who are thirsty. Considered from all sorts of perspectives, aside from the visual possibilities, there's a lot to think about here.

Why, as times goes on, does the amount of water in the stories keep shrinking?

CHAPTER THREE
DUTCH AMERICA, THE NETHERLANDS AND SOUTH AFRICA

WHEN I WAS WALKING DOWN THE ROAD

I was feeling a kind of quiet ancestral awe as I walked down Lawson Road in the tiny hamlet of New Hamburg, New York, on the east bank of the Hudson River. I knew that as a small boy in the 1890s, in one of the little houses we were walking past, my grandfather had learned the lap-drop game I would learn eighty years later when I was a small boy in the town of Dundas, Ontario.

It gave me a funny feeling, because it's the only living piece of my grandfather's childhood left, as far as I know. I know very little about Palmer Lawson's life before the 1930s, when my father was a boy in Albany, New York. Even then, my grandfather was a quiet and private man, from all accounts. Family members remember him chasing butterflies at picnics – looking for specimens to pin under glass in his collection, or watching the fish in his fish tank while puffing on his pipe.

No one seems to remember a single thing he said. But my father remembered being bounced on his lap as he chanted, "When I was walking down the road – Look out!"

How many of us *can* quote a single line said by our great-grandparents? And how many of us know even the general outlines of the lives our ancestors lived two generations back?

I haven't been able to find any exact matches for this rhyme that I learned as a boy, and it's possible it was simply invented by one of my great- or great-great-grandparents. But below is a verse variant from the folk song "Old Dan Tucker," as recorded by John and Alan Lomax in *American Ballads and Folk Songs*. This is the verse:

As I come down de new cut road,
I spied de peckerwood and de toad,
And every time de toad would jump
De peckerwood hopped upon de stump.

Here's the Lawson version:

As I was [went, came] walking down the road – Look out!
I spied a toad upon the road – Look out!

I ran this by my uncle Ivan, who lives in Voorheesville, New York, outside Albany. I asked him if he did it with his own children. Ivan made a characteristic Lawson look of surprise: he opened his eyes wide, raised his eyebrows as high as they'd go and maintained – for a moment – the dramatic pause of a professional mime.

"Now you mention it, I never did do this with my own children . . . I wonder how I forgot? And it's too late now. But I remember my father doing it with me. And by the way, you've forgotten the last line. It's: 'Plop!' (or . . . maybe it was '*Pop*'?) 'Goes the toad in the hole.'"

Uncle Ivan was right. I'd forgotten that. My father hadn't remembered it either. He sometimes inserted his own extra line toward the end – "Diddle diddle dumpling my son John" – where he'd escalate the beat, before suddenly dropping us through his knees.

I checked the rhyme with my father's older sister, Jean, too. She was ninety-nine years old in 2016, and living in a nursing home in Guilderland, near Albany. She remembered it immediately when I recited it and acted it out, but had nothing to add. She also remembered doing this with her own children, but when I checked with my cousins, none I spoke with remembered it, and so hadn't done it with their children or grandchildren.

Part of me had hoped to find a Dutch prototype for the rhyme, but my grandfather's mother was descended from English settlers that traced themselves to Yorkshire. It really isn't possible to know its origins – only to guess a little from contemporary records of rhymes that look similar.

Part of what makes me wonder about "Old Dan Tucker" as the source is my memory of *came* being used interchangeably with *was* or *went* in the first line, and also the use of *spied* instead of *saw*, which was common in songs from that time. Though whether *spied* was also used interchangeably with *saw* in American English in the nineteenth century is something I'm not sure of.

The "Old Dan Tucker" verse also has those compelling jumping and hopping images. A creative adult listening to that song – and it was popular in its time – might easily have chosen to adapt it for a lap bounce.

According to Martha McCulloch-Williams, quoted by the Lomaxes, the song was often used as a lullaby, and new verses of the song were often improvised, many of them nonsensical. This might also have caught the ear and imagination of an adult aiming to entertain a small child. I used to extend the verses of "Hush, Little Baby, Don't Say a Word" in a similar way. This sort of song is a gift to parents soothing babies because it can go on for as long as you need it to – the only limit being your ability to rhyme and the nature of your imagination.

"Extend the verses" is often a euphemism for "I couldn't remember, so I improvised." I usually get lost after the diamond ring. Over the course of singing to three babies I improvised many versions of the song – I was so pleased with one improvisation session that I jotted it down:

Daddy's gonna buy you a room that's dark,
and if that room that's dark gets light,
Daddy's gonna buy you an endless night,
but if that endless night won't end,
Daddy's gonna buy you a cloud to mend,

61

and if that cloud won't take a stitch,
Daddy's gonna buy you a mud-filled ditch,
and if that mud-filled ditch goes dry,
Daddy's gonna buy you a big blue sky . . .

And so on, it got worse again after that . . .

I'm including this because it shows how taking liberties can be liberating, or, at the very least, how a bad memory can be liberating.

But back to "Old Dan Tucker" – *peckerwood* was Southern slang meaning either woodpecker or a poor white person. It's unlikely the word would have meant anything to people in the Hudson Valley, which might explain why the word was dropped. If, in fact, this song was adapted by one of my relatives.

I made up an extended play version of the song I grew up with for my own kids, which they all seemed to like. They asked me to do it over and over, so something about it was working:

When I was walking down the road – Look out!
I spied a toad upon the road – Look out!
The road was slipp'ry, it had snowed
I slipped and slid toward the toad
When suddenly I spun
And turned about!

Hippety hippety hop hop hop
Nobody knows where the toad will stop
A toadstool, a rock or a bump on a log
Don't mistake him for a frog
Ribbet!

FRAGMENTS AND THEIR USES

I remember many little fragments of poems, songs and even bits of TV theme songs that fired my imagination – especially my verbal imagination. Some part of me must have already been planning what I'd be doing in the future, and these were among the verbal exemplars I encountered in my early childhood.

I can't reproduce them in full, but here is a line or two from some of my childhood favourites. In fact, these little bits were most of what I remembered, anyway – I was never good at retaining more than a line or two:

The turtle lives 'twixt plated decks,
Which practically conceal his sex.
– Ogden Nash, *The Turtle*

Is he strong? – Listen bud, he's got radioactive blood!
– Paul Francis Webster, "Spider-Man"

Completely round is the perfect pearl the oyster manufactures,
Completely round is the steering wheel that leads to compound fractures.
– Sheldon Harnick, "The Shape of Things"

I could while away the hours, conferrin' with the flowers, consultin' with the rain.
– Yip Harburg, "If I Only Had a Brain"

One day when she had nothing to do, rickety-tickety-tin, One day when she had nothing to do, She cut her baby brother in two.
– Tom Lehrer, "The Irish Ballad"

Several fragments were from songs my father sang to us accompanied by his guitar. This is how I knew the Harnick and Lehrer songs, though my father always thought the Harnick song, "The Shape of Things," was by Ogden Nash. The song follows a brilliant conceit – a different shape inspires each verse. When I found out the song was actually by Sheldon Harnick, who is probably best known for *Fiddler on the Roof*, I decided to write to him to ask him about the genesis of the song. I wanted to know if he'd tried out even more shapes, and if he'd had to work on it for a long time. It all flows so naturally, but to me it looked like a very tricky piece of work.

Harnick generously responded to my questions in his response to my letter:

"'The Shape of Things' was a once-in-a-lifetime experience. At North-western University I had a classmate named Charlotte Rae. After graduation she went to New York to pursue her career. When I relocated to New York (from Chicago), Charlotte was trying to put together a cabaret act. She asked me to write her a piece of special material. I said yes – but couldn't think of anything to write for her.

"Then one night, about four a.m., I woke up with a song running through my head. I wrote it down and went back to sleep.

"The next morning I was curious to see what I had written. To my astonishment, I had written three stanzas, both words and music, of what seemed to be a first-rate song! I have no idea where 'The Shape of Things' came from! The fourth stanza was inherent in the first three and came very easily. Charlotte loved the song and has used it throughout her career. I've never had that experience again. I have no drafts of the song."

It came to him in a dream, nearly finished! That certainly doesn't sit well, or fit well with most conceptions of how people ought to do their work. Harnick himself admits that it only happened to him this one time.

My favourite of all the songs, though, was "The Fox Went Out on the Town One Night" (more commonly known as "The Fox Went Out on a Chilly Night").

My father played this one in a strange way. Instead of strumming, he'd drum his fingers on the guitar strings while holding down the chords, or sometimes he'd just drum his fingers on the wooden sound box of the guitar.

These are a few of the verses as I heard them, in the early 1970s in
Dundas, Ontario:

He grabbed the grey goose by the neck,
throwed a duck across his back;
he didn't mind their quack, quack, quack,
and their legs all a-dangling
down-o, down-o, down-o,
he didn't mind their quack, quack, quack,
and their legs all a-dangling down-o.

Well little Johnny ran to the top of the hill
And he blew his horn both loud and shrill
The fox he said "I better flee with my kill
Cause they'll soon be on my trail-o, trail-o, trail-o,"
The fox he said.

The fox he ran right back to his den
And he counted his children eight, nine, ten
They said, "Daddy, you better go back again
Cause it must be a mighty fine town-o."

Now the fox and his wife without any strife
They cut up the goose with a spoon and a knife
They never had such a supper in their life
And the little ones chewed on the bones-o.

And now, these are similar verses for the same song, as sung around
1500, in England:

He hente a goose all by the heye,
Faste the goose began to creye!

Oowte yede men as they might heye,
And seyde "fals fox, ley it doowne!"

"Nay" he saide, "soo mot I the –
sche shall go unto the wode with me;
sche and I unther a tre,
e-mange the beryis browne.

"I haue a wyf, and sche lyeth seke;
Many smale whelppis sche haue to eke –
Many bonys they muste pike
Will they ley a-downe."

Interesting to see how little the story has changed, though the vocabulary is very different five hundred years later. And it's a funny reminder of a time when English sounded more like Swedish. Unfortunately, no intermediate versions of the song have been discovered. We can only guess at the gradual changes that had to be made to the song. And this brings up an interesting issue – the issue of transformation.

Changing something to keep it the same: in this case a song, clearly much loved over the past five hundred years or it wouldn't have survived. The language has been continually modernized as time went on so that it could be enjoyed just as it was when it was first written. We can assume the foremost desire of those who changed it over time was to keep the song accessible – the song remains the same by changing. Would the person who first wrote it have approved of the changes?

It really doesn't matter. All that matters is that the song is a living thing that needs to be cared for and kept alive. People recognized this as a song that needed to be taken care of.

On the other hand, things are sometimes kept the same to make them, or to allow them, to be different, as everything else around them changes. The clothing of nuns, for instance, was not remarkable when it was first adopted hundreds of years ago, but the clothing of nuns didn't change as clothing fashions changed – and so what was at first not exceptional, became exceptional.

A SEVENTEENTH-CENTURY SUITCASE

A colleague of my father's was looking at a folklore newsletter sometime in the early 1990s, and twigged on the last name of one of the contributors – the unusual last name Burhans – recognizing it as my grandmother's maiden name. The article, by Barbara Burhans of Richmond, Virginia, was about how she had learned a rhyme made up of nonsense words from her father in the 1930s when she was a child. When she grew up, she realized that the nonsense was actually, for the most part, Dutch.

I tracked down the address of Barbara Burhans – it turned out we were cousins several times removed. Our last common ancestor had lived in the early 1800s. The rhyme she remembered started "Trip a trop a troon-je." There are several words that migrated from Dutch to English in the United States – some widely used words like *cookie* and *coleslaw*, and some which are more regional, like *stoop*. Concepts like thirteen being a baker's dozen actually came from a Hudson Valley Dutch bakery. An article by Tom Bijvoet in *DUTCH the Magazine* states that the eighth president of the United States, Martin Van Buren (who was born near Albany in 1782), had a "marked Dutch accent" though he grew up in the Hudson Valley.

The Dutch have largely been assimilated into Anglo-American culture, but looking at farm maps of the Hudson Valley, as recently as the later nineteenth century, you can see how the Dutch family names continued clustering together, right down to the time of my grandmother's childhood. The families continued to intermarry, and aspects of their culture survived.

In a book called *The Dutch-American Farm*, David Steven Cohen included some of the Dutch rhymes that had been collected among Hudson Valley families as late as 1907. By this time my own grandparents were already adults. This is one of them:

> Slaap, kindje, slaap!
> Daar buiten loopt een schapt!
> Een schapt met witte voetjes;
> Dat drink zijn melk zoo zoetjes;
> Slaap, kindje, slaap! toe;
> Slaap, kindje, slaap!

I wrote to Wilma Seijbel, the Dutch historian and canny contemporary owner of the publishing company Uitgeverij Karmijn (in the Netherlands), to ask if this was still known in modern-day Holland. She confirmed that it was something people still used – she herself knew it. "We still sing it!" she wrote, but she pointed out that there were differences in the spelling to make note of:

Slaap kindje slaap,	Sleep baby sleep,
daar buiten loopt een schaap.	out there is a sheep.
Een schaap met witte voetjes,	A sheep with white feet,
die drinkt zijn melk zo zoetjes.	drinking his milk so sweetly.
Slaap kindje slaap,	Sleep baby sleep –
daar buiten loopt een schaap.	out there is a sheep.

After that, I wrote to my friend Philip de Vos, a South African children's poet. Philip writes in both Afrikaans and English. When he came to visit us a few years ago, it struck me right away how much he physically resembled my father's family. His Dutch ancestors had arrived in South Africa at almost exactly the same time that my Dutch ancestors arrived in the Hudson Valley, over three hundred years ago.

I asked him about "Slaap," and it turned out the same rhyme was still used in the Afrikaans community today, as well. Again, with some interesting differences:

Slaap, kindjie, slaap.	Sleep, little child, sleep.
Daar buite loop 'n skaap.	A sheep is walking outside.
'N Skaap met witte voetjies,	A sheep with white feet,
hy drink sy melk so soetjies,	who quietly drinks his milk,
skapie met sy witte wol,	a sheep with white wool,
kindjie drink sy magie vol.	little child is also filling his belly
Slaap, kindjie, slaap.	[with milk].
	Sleep, little child, sleep.

According to Hedwig Knötig, an Austrian university student who happened to be sitting next to me on a flight to Cuba while I was editing this book, there is also a German version of this, which must have a common source with the Dutch version, though there are interesting differences:

Schlaf, kindlein, schlaf,	Sleep, little one, sleep,
Der vater hüt die schaf,	The father herds the sheep,
Die mutter schüttelts	The mother shakes the little
bäumelein,	branches,
Da fällt herab ein träumelein.	Falling into a dream.
Schlaf, kindlein, schlaf!	Sleep, little one, sleep!

I ran this rhyme by two other Austrians (of different generations), and they both had clear memories of what the rhyme had conjured up in their minds when they were children. Ingo Ermanovics, who was born in Gmünd, but grew up in Klagenfurt though he immigrated to Canada when he was still a boy, said, "This is a famous lullaby to which I still remember the tune. The mother shakes the little tree from which sandman dust (Gefusel dust), containing a sweet dream, falls."

Veronika Mayer-Miedl, born a generation later in Linz, said in response to Ingo's memory, "In my imagination it is not dust or 'Gefusel' that comes down materially as from a sandman, although this is one possible interpretation. In my eyes they are the dreams themselves coming from the spirit world. The tree's branches reach high up to the spirit spheres, where our ancestors are and other spirits sending us messages to help us on our way ... the roots of the tree are rooted in our material world – the earth, and the branches are rooted in the spirit world, from where the dreams fall down. Mother has the skill to contact the ancestors by shaking the tree. As I child I imagined it this way."

Wilma Seijbel didn't know the next rhyme, which is also from David Cohen's book, but Philip did. This is the one that my distant cousin knew a version of in the 1930s:

> Trip a trop a troontjes,
> De varkens in de boontjes
> De koetjes in de klaver,
> De paarden in de haver.
> De eendes in de water-plas,
> De kalf in de lange grass;
> So grott mijn kleine poppetje was.

Another version recorded near Albany in the Van Alstyne family in the 1750s sounded more like this:

> Trip a trop a troenje;
> De varken en de boenjan,
> De koejen en de klaver,
> De paardje en de haver,
> De kalfie en de langen gras,
> De eenjen en de vater-plas;
> So groet myn klyne pappatje vas.

According to a translation I found online, which unfortunately isn't sourced and doesn't have contact information, the implication of the first line is "Up and down the throne," where the throne is represented by the parents' knees. I understood this to mean that the child is being bounced:

Up and down the little throne
the pigs are in the beans,
the cows are in the clover,
the colts are in the stable,
the calf is in the long grass,
the ducks are in the pond,
so big my little baby [literally, "little papa"] was.

Philip had an Afrikaans version of this one, too:

Trippe trappe trone,	Trippe trappe trone [nonsense
varkies in die bone,	words],
koeitjies in die klawer,	the pigs are among the beans,
perdjies in die hawer,	the cows among the clover,
eendjies op die waterplas,	the horses among the hay,
gansies in die groene gras.	the ducklings in the pond,
Ek wens dat kindjie groter was	the geese in the green grass.
om al die diertjies op te pas.	I wish my child was older
	to be able to look after all the animals.

That all of these different versions have survived in different communities that came from a common source is fascinating. The small changes are interesting, and the overall sameness, as well. For me, it creates a sense of cousinship, and continuity, with my friends in the Netherlands and in South Africa.

* * *

In my bedroom, full of old clothes and teddy bears, I have what looks like a pirate's trunk. I've had it in my room since I was little. My father told me that his mother, Ella Vesta Burhans, said it had been passed down in the Burhans family since the 1600s. The Burhans family had brought it with them when they left Deventer, in the Netherlands, and came to Wil-twyck (now Kingston, New York) in the Hudson Valley during the time of the Dutch plantations.

When the family arrived in what's now New York State, the Hudson River was called the Muhheakantuck and the land they were "settling" was already settled – it belonged to the Munsee-speaking Lenape Nation. Wil-twyck was then called Esopus, after the community of Lenape who lived there originally. My family, sadly, came as part of an invasion force.

To have acknowledged and understood the humanity of the people they were robbing, my ancestors would have had to acknowledge and understand their own humanity. It's impossible to dehumanize others without at the same time dehumanizing yourself. By this, I mean if you decide that another human being isn't actually human in the way you are because they look different, or act differently than you, you are destroying a bit of your own human identity. By seeing someone else as less than they actually are, you are seeing yourself as more than you actually are. The resulting dehumanization goes both ways.

The enormity of this missed opportunity is tragic. The linguistic, cultural and spiritual exchange that could have taken place in the Americas if the Europeans had arrived with different motives, and greater self-understanding, is almost beyond imagining. There is no such thing as "bringing civilization" from one place to another, but there are always new opportunities to increase your knowledge, wherever you come from, and the Europeans generally chose not to increase their knowledge when they arrived in new (to them) lands.

They arrived as they arrived, with their guns and trunks, looking for free land and gold.

When I was little, I believed that the trunk, which was now in my childhood bedroom, was as old as my father said. But as I got older, and thought about it more, it seemed pretty unlikely to me. What were the chances that a trunk could be passed down through a family for twelve or thirteen generations? It did look very old – it didn't resemble a regular blanket chest. It definitely looked like a pirate sea-chest from a Disney cartoon, but could it really have been in the family for three hundred fifty years?

A few years ago my cousin Mark Lawson, of Mark Lawson Antiques, was visiting. He happens to be an expert in ascertaining the age and value of old and unusual objects, so I asked him to take a look at the trunk. He ran his hands over it, opening it up and looking closely at the underside of the domed lid and the forged ironwork. He shut it again, turned to me and said, "How the hell did *you* get this?"

Mark said there was no question that it was a seventeenth-century trunk. The design was Dutch, as well. And so, in all likelihood, the trunk had indeed been passed down through the family since the sixteen hundreds.

It was, essentially, a well-made wood-and-iron seventeenth-century suitcase, which had been holding a varied and ever-changing assortment of family belongings for centuries. I could list you the names of all of its owners from the 1600s down to today, but I couldn't tell you a single other thing about most of them.

This suitcase had seen the transition of my family from Calvinist Dutch-speaking soldier land-robbers, to Dutch-speaking colonial farmers conquered by English land-robbers, to culturally Dutch but English-speaking American farmers, to Anglo-American city dwellers, to Anglo-Jewish Canadian city folk . . . it had seen a lot. If only it could talk!

Or maybe it's better that it can't.

Most of us, of course, know more about the celebrities who appear in supermarket-aisle magazines than we do about our own ancestors, two generations back. I don't know much about the previous owners of my seventeenth-century suitcase. But I do, luckily, have a couple of hand games passed down by its ninth or tenth owner, my grandmother.

PITTY-DE-PAT

I never met my grandmother (the one through whom I inherited the trunk) because she died before I was born. But I do have this rhyme from her – my father remembered her doing this with him, and with her older grandchildren. She had learned it from her older sisters in Arlington (now a suburb of Poughkeepsie), New York, in the 1890s.

She would sit behind the person she was playing this with, and drum it out on their upper back:

> Pitty-de-pat
> Upon the back
> Pretty good fella to hold the luck
> How many fingers do I hold up?

The "patter" holds up between one and ten fingers at this point. The "patee" can't see the patter's fingers, of course. They call out their guess. If the patee was wrong, then the patter would say, "One s/he says, but five there are!"

And then start over, with the top four lines.

If the patee was right, then the patter would say, "One s/he says, and one it was!"

And then the two people would change places.

CREEP MOUSEY

Creep mousey isn't really a rhyme. My father would walk his fingers up your arm saying – "Creep mousey creep mousey creep mousey – kitty kitty kitty kitty!" – building the tempo until the sudden tickle (kitty) in the neck. This one also came from his mother.

LANI-FLANNY-TEE-ALLA-GO-WHANNY

This one my father learned in Albany in the 1930s. He couldn't remember the source, but he did it all the time when we were growing up, trying it out with any name he came across.

It alters according to the name. For instance, if your name was Lani, it would be:

Lani, Flanny-tee-alla-go-whanny
Tee-legged toe-legged bowlegged Lani.

If your name was Paul, it could be:

Paul, fall, tee-alla-go-wall
Tee-legged toe-legged bowlegged Paul.

Or if your name was Galina, it might be:

Galina, Falina, tee-alla-go-Mina,
Tee-legged toe-legged bowlegged Galina.

Note that with multisyllabic names, you can only rhyme on the last syllable of the name at the end of the first line, and you have to alter the rhythm of the second line a bit, shifting the emphasis of the "Tee-legged" phrases from the first syllable to the second.

IF I WERE YOU AND YOU WERE ME

When I told my cousin Noelle Nanci that I was gathering old rhymes together, she brought out a few pages of rhymes her mother, my aunt Jean, had made up for her and her siblings in the 1940s and '50s when they were little. I have them all in a folder somewhere, but this was my favourite, which I have right here in my head:

> If I were you and you were me
> And we all set out to go to sea
> How many of us would there be?

My aunt Jean was great with children. I used to spend hours talking with her when I was thirteen or fourteen. She once told me a funny story about something she did with my cousin Kathy Clegg, when Kathy was a little girl. She couldn't remember if this was her own idea, or if she'd read about it somewhere, but she had Kathy close her eyes, and using makeup, she painted eyes onto her eyelids.

Then they went out and walked hand in hand down a busy street in Schenectady, where they lived. Kathy had her eyes closed, and Jean said she wished she could have photographed people's expressions as they looked at Kathy. Sometimes Kathy would blink her eyes open and shut, which added to the passing pedestrians' shock factor.

CHAPTER FOUR

MALTA

IS MORRIS MICKLEWHITE MALTESE?

Gawdi ghax mid-dinja m'ghandna xejn.
Enjoy yourself, for there is nothing in the world we can call our own.
– Maltese proverb

I met Christine Baldacchino shortly after her book *Morris Micklewhite and the Tangerine Dress* came out. Morris had quickly become one of my favourite picture books, a sentiment shared by all three of my children. While open homophobia has become increasingly unacceptable in Canadian culture over the past ten years, transphobia has remained a pervasive problem, though there are hopeful signs that this is finally starting to change, too. *Morris Micklewhite*, illustrated by Isabelle Malenfent, is a carefully structured, whimsical and highly entertaining book that opens possibilities, at home and in the classroom, for conversations about gender nonconforming experience. It's a brave book by a brave writer.

I was eager to meet with Christine because I was a big fan, and by luck she lives in the same neighbourhood. We met at the (now defunct) King Falafel at Bathurst and Eglinton. While we spoke, I mentioned I was working on this book, and right away she brought up the Maltese Għana, which she remembered from Maltese community picnics when she was little.

Malta, for those who haven't heard of it before, is a small island country of half a million people in the middle of the Mediterranean, between Sicily and North Africa, conquered dozens of times over several thousand years by a very large number of invaders from three different continents. Maltese has the distinction of being the only Semitic national language in Europe (it's related to Arabic, Hebrew and Tigrinya), though the vocabulary of the language has been heavily influenced by Latinate borrowings over the centuries.

Christine suggested that we meet again with her father, Victor Balda-cchino, who was more knowledgable about the history of the Għana. A few months later, the three of us met up at the food court at Yorkdale to talk. Beforehand, Mr. Baldacchino sent me a Għana that he himself had written, and translated for me.

In this song, two friends engage in a duel of words, but the words are sung – there's an improvisational vaudevillian humour to it. With his per-mission, I'm including it below:

1. Ahna gejna hawn il lejla
Sabiex nghaddu naqra zmien
L-ewwel nghidu x-ghandna nghidu
Imbaghad niehdu drink flimkien.

1. We came here this evening
Just to pass the time
First we say what we want to say
Then we'll have a drink together.

2. Nispera li giebt flus mieghek,
Kulhadd jaf li interessat,
Dejjem tieha m-ghand haddiehor
Imma int ma thallas qatt.

2. I hope you brought some money
Everybody knows you're a miser
Always bumming from the others
But you never buy yourself.

3. Forsi jiena nibqa lura,
Mux ghax jien interessat
Meta jiena hrigt ma ohtok
Hriegt ta ragel, Sibt jew Hadd.

3. Maybe there are times when I
skip some
But not because I'm tight
Cause when I took your sister out,
I paid, be it Saturday or Sunday.

4. Jiena hriegt ma l-mara tieghek,
Steak u lobster hallastila,
Kienet ila sena gewwa
Ghaliex inti kont taqfila.

4. I took your wife out
Bought her steak and lobster
She hadn't gone out for a year,
Cause you keep her locked up.

5. Ghandek rasek bhal kabocca
U saqajk mghawwgin bhal granc
Zaqqek bhal ta mara tqila
U bilkemm izzom bilanc.

5. Your head looks like a cabbage,
And you're bowlegged
You look like a pregnant woman,
And you can hardly balance yourself.

This form of singing is unique to Malta. The Għana (the *Għ* is silent – it's pronounced more like *A-na*) can refer to two different types of song. The Għana tal-Fatt is more of a traditional ballad, while the Spirtu Pront is the type Christine remembered from her childhood. It's also the type that influenced what her father wrote, above.

I asked Mr. Baldacchino if he knew anything about the history of the form.

"Spirtu Pront is a kind of improvised insult song two people sing back and forth at each other. A guy walks into a bar, and he sees his friend. And he starts singing – he makes fun of the friend, and the friend picks up the thread – he sings an insult back – but there's a set way of doing it. It has to rhyme, there has to be some wit in the way it's done."

I asked if there was any risk of making the other person mad. Did fights ever start over the songs?

"Never. If you're sensitive, you don't get into it. You don't take part. But everyone knows it's in good fun. And at the end, you shake hands, you have a drink. That's it. If you said the same thing instead of singing it, of course, you'd get punched in the nose. It's the form, and the singing – that's what makes it okay. Everyone understands."

I asked if he knew how or where the form started.

"It was based on insult songs washer women sang at each other from rooftops, or at wells. There's a well tap back in Malta they're going to put a plaque on, to commemorate where they say it all started. Because it was based on the singing of women, men sing these songs in a high-pitched voice – it's actually a requirement – if you try to sing it in a regular low voice you won't be taken seriously."

This made me think of research I read about a few years ago where two scientists in England, musicologist Dr. Alison Pawley and psychologist Dr. Daniel Mullensiefen, had discovered that the most successful pop songs usually have a male singer singing in a high-pitched voice, making a noticeable effort to achieve the affect, for at least part of the song. An example would be Queen's "We are the Champions," but there are many, many others, when you start looking for them: The Beatles' "Hey Jude," Aerosmith's "Dream On," U2's "One." Those are all older examples, but modern releases have just as many men aiming for the high notes.

I wonder if this is related, in some way, to the benefits of the motherese way of talking? Does a (male?) voice singing in a higher range elicit some kind of sympathetic response? What's being communicated? Is it appealing because women's voices tend to be in a higher range, and it sounds like the man is attempting to cross into that realm – that there's something a bit gender nonconformist about it?

I asked Christine and her father if they thought the songs had a cultural or social benefit? What impact did they have on children? Christine had enjoyed them as a child – what had she liked about them?

"It's a point of pride. It's something specific to Malta. You hear a Għana and you feel like it's something you can be proud of, that it helps give you your identity as a Maltese, no matter how old you are, no matter where in the world you happen to live," said Mr. Baldacchino.

"It also teaches you good sportsmanship," Christine added. "As a child listening to these, maybe you learn not to take yourself too seriously. You're listening to adults sing their insults creatively, in a set form, with wit and humour. There's wordplay involved. And you discover how other people see you doesn't really matter. It's just a song. In the end, they shake hands. There aren't any hard feelings."

"Exactly," said Mr. Baldacchino. "I'm just a little guy, from a little village, in a little country, but I've done all right – we've done all right. And part of that comes from knowing who I am, and where I'm from. I love Canada; it's the best country in the world. But I'm a Maltese who's a resident of Canada."

Victor Baldacchino actually isn't a little guy – he's at least six feet tall.

And as we spoke, I noticed that Mr. Baldacchino and Christine both spoke in this kind of evocative picture-book quality language. I kept wanting to jot down things they were saying for future use.

"Once there was a little man, from a little village, in a little country far away . . ." Right away, a clear picture formed in your mind.

They used the same kind of language to tell anecdotes and describe eccentric relatives – they illustrated these relatives (and also themselves) with quick verbal sketches, compelling mini-portraits built out of brief, humorous details.

Mr. Baldacchino once applied for a job, but he was turned down because he was told he was too short, even though he was taller than everyone else in the line. A relative had a lifelong job where all he got to do was sit at the bottom of a set of stairs and, with a wave of his hand, direct people left or right. Another relative only answered his door at a certain predetermined moment or not at all. For instance, if you said you'd come by at seven, he would only answer the door if you knocked at precisely seven o'clock. If you knocked a minute early or late, he wouldn't answer. Another ate bananas with a knife and fork, and wouldn't eat at all unless he had a serviette cushioning his elbows.

I asked Mr. Baldacchino what (or who) had influenced him in his ability to write songs and tell stories. He attributed this to both of his parents. "My mother couldn't read, but she could make a rhyme or a song out of anything. For instance, we might be sitting with her at the end of the day – she'd be sitting there, and suddenly she'd start singing:

I'm sitting here by myself
Waiting for my husband to return
And now I'm going to go fold laundry

"But in Maltese. All the rhymes would work, she was just making some fun out of what was happening to her at that moment. We learned from that."

"And what about your father?" I asked.

"He was a great storyteller. He was in the Royal Navy for twenty-two years, and another thirty years in the merchant navy. But he also liked to rhyme. He'd leave my mother a note, written in verses. We'd have to read it to her, of course … but it was clever, and funny, and all the rhymes worked."

I asked Christine if she thought this family tradition of playing with words, and of storytelling, had influenced her own writing. Christine's sister, Charlene Challenger, is also an author – and the many positive reviews of her novel *The Voices in Between* make special note of the musicality of her language.

Christine pointed out the euphonic multisyllabic title *Morris Micklewhite and the Tangerine Dress* as an example of where she saw the influence of her family, and of how they used language.

Later, responding to other questions I sent her regarding the influence of her family, she wrote:

"Char and I were very lucky in that we had not only our parents and their love of music as an influence on our writing (and on our views on life in general), but we also had our older siblings and their love of music. So Char and I would get to listen to Roy Orbison, Talking Heads, Patsy Cline, the Bee Gees, the Ramones, and Echo and the Bunnymen in a single day. In *Morris Micklewhite*, Morris loves the colour of the dress, but he also loves the symphony of sounds he and the dress are able to create together. Char has a background in musical theatre, and it's all there in her writing. In a scene that first introduces us to a 'piper' named Ritter, she describes his singing voice and you can hear it quite strikingly in your head as you're reading – how his voice becomes three voices harmonizing with each other, how it somehow manages to breach logic and become something the main character can see and touch. Despite the fact that the man is singing in a language the main character has never heard before, the main character is still able to understand the song's message – something I think everyone can relate to. My tongue would turn to sand in my mouth if someone were to ask me to describe music the way Char is able to."

Christine's response made me think about a theory I have about the influence of the German language on modern English poetry. It had suddenly occurred to me one day that a very large number of English and American poets and lyricists had heard German or Yiddish spoken in their homes when they were growing up. A partial list would include Robert Graves, Gertrude Stein, Sylvia Plath, Theodore Roethke, Theodor Geisel (Dr. Seuss), Shel Silverstein, Yip Harburg, Sheldon Harnick, Muriel Rukeyser, Laura Riding, Allen Ginsberg, Irving Layton and Leonard Cohen. It might also be worth noting, here, that the Israeli poet Yehuda Amichai was born in Würzburg, Germany, and lived there till he was eleven years old. So German lay just underneath his Hebrew – just as many Russian poets, such as Osip Mandelstam, would have heard, and in some cases used, Yiddish and/or German growing up, as well.

Is it possible that the rhythms and even the vocabulary of German and Yiddish had an important influence on how these poets heard (and wrote) their various languages? I once wrote to Sheldon Harnick to tell him my theory, and he wrote back that though he couldn't speak Yiddish, he understood it, and he thought his work had definitely been influenced by the inflections of the language.

I wrote to Christine to ask her the names of her grandparents to include in the book. Here's what she said:

"Believe it or not, I have to ask my dad how he wants his parents' names written. In Malta, that generation mostly used nicknames, then there are the Maltese versions of their names and the English versions. In English my grandparents are Joseph and Josephine, but in Maltese my grandfather's name was Giuseppe (or Guzeppi) and I believe my grandmother's was Giuseppina. It's weird how such a simple question yields so many different answers. Only in Malta."

But reading this, I thought that there are benefits to this kind of complexity. It's like a constant reminder that everything can be more than one thing, and we can be known by more than one name, as well.

The multi- and cross-generational creative playfulness of the Baldacchinos survived its passage from one language into another, and across cultures, and time. Formal education hasn't had anything to do with it – it's a family and home-based inheritance – this lively, living approach to language in everyday life.

Finally, Mr. Baldacchino entrusted me with a small group of his favourite nursery rhymes and poems from his childhood. "These were extremely popular. We learned them at school. But our parents knew them, too. My mother, without being able to read, was able to help me learn them because she knew them by heart."

Sajjied ta' Xewqtu	**A Cuschieri**
Kemm nixtieq kelli	I wish I had
Ġewlaq sabiħ	A nice basket,
U xlief u qasba	A rod and fishing line
Għall-ħut tal-qiegħ.	To catch the fish.
Fuq blata, waħdi,	By myself on a rock,
Bil-ġewlaq ħdejja,	With the basket near me,
Qalziet imxammar	Rolled up pants
Fuq irkobbtejja,	Up to my knees,

x-xemx fuq wiċċi,
Bil-qasba f'idi,
Hemm trid tarani,
Ja ħija sidi!

Hemm trid tarani
Nillixka d-dud,
Inlikkem, niġbed,
Naqbad il-ħut!

Issa nwaħħallek
Burqax sabiħ,
Issa xi sparlu,
Jew xi buxiħ;

U meta l-ġewlaq
Bil-ħut nimlieh,
Immur għand ommi
Ngħidilha: aqlih!

With the sun in my face,
The rod in my hand,
You should see me,
My brother and master!

You should see me,
Putting worms on the hook,
Trawling and pulling,
And hooking fish!

I'll hook
A nice [type of fish],
Or a [type of fish],
Or a [type of fish];

And when the basket
is filled with fish
I'll go to mother's
and tell her to fry them.

Il-Pupa

Għandi pupa wisq sabiħa,
aħmar, wiċċha bħall-peprin.
B'par għajnejn minn lewn is-se ma,
bħalha żgur ma ssibx ħelwin.

Il-mama bħali tlibbisha,
mid-drapp stess tal-libsa tiegħi.
Oħti ż-żgħira nisthajjilha,
meta jien noħroġha miegħi.

Fejn immur dejjem noħodha
għax mingħajrha ma jien xejn.
minn fejn ngħaddi nisma' jgħidu:
"Dawna donnhom pupi t-tnejn!"

Grandma's Big Big Kiss

Waqt li Toninu kien qiegħed jaqra,
b'qattus magenbu u kelb daqs naqra,
daħlet in-nanna inkiss inkiss
u tatu bewsa kif kien imiss.

The Doll

I have a very nice doll,
Her face is as red as a poppy,
Eyes the colour of the sky,
You won't find any dolls as
                beautiful.

My mother dresses her like me,
From the same material,
I imagine her as my younger sister,
When I take her out with me.

Wherever I go I always take her,
Cause without her I'm nothing,
Wherever we go I hear them say,
They both look like dolls.

Grandma's Big Big Kiss

While Toninu was reading
with a cat by his side, and a small dog
in came his grandmother, silently
and gave him a big big kiss!

CHAPTER FIVE

ISRAEL, BRAZIL, VENEZUELA, MEXICO, CUBA, NURSERY RHYMES AND MY FATHER'S STROKE

PINKIE MAKES PEACE

We met Hadas Leviner and her husband, Uri Kochavi, shortly after they moved to Toronto from Tel Aviv, sometime in 2004 when their son Daniel became friends with our child Sophie at the Helene Comay Nursery School. We spent a lot of happy times with them, including many of the Jewish holidays, before they returned to Israel a few years later.

Hadas learned this little play rhyme from her friend when her friend had a child. Apparently it's very well known in Tel Aviv. She only learned the first two verses, and thought that was the entire song. Hadas also assumed it was just an anonymous finger rhyme, so – with her first son – she taught him just this part. But when the family moved back to Israel, and they had another son, Michael, Hadas discovered that in fact there were more verses, and also that the song had a known author, Rivka Davidit.

Davidit was born in Bendery, Bessarabia (now Bender, Moldova, also part of the breakaway region of Transnistria), in 1908, and died in Tel Aviv, Israel, in 1970. She was a pioneer of Israeli children's literature. Any infant rhymes and games that existed in Hebrew would have disappeared almost two thousand years earlier. Davidit was one of the first to start experimenting with how to bring Hebrew to life again for infants and toddlers. Today, Hebrew is spoken by about nine million people, over half of them living in Israel.

Her success at doing this is demonstrated by the fact that Hadas had no idea where this came from at first. It's similar to the way most people who sing "Twinkle, Twinkle, Little Star" have no idea who wrote the words, or that it's only the first part of a longer poem. That Davidit was on the right track is also shown in the way that parents adapted this poem by adding actions to it – which is part of how Hadas learned it.

I think it's interesting that the verse Hadas showed me (and remembered) when she was still in Canada had a mix of lines from different verses – and that those were exactly the lines that worked best with actions.

Original Version Hadas Showed Me:

Ten fingers I have, they can do everything. [Hold your ten fingers up and shake them.]

To paint and to scribble, to beat a drum. [Pretend to do all of these actions.] Such a tiny house I have, with a chair and a table. [Make your fingers like the roof of the house, then a chair – one hand flat against the middle of the other, then do the table.]

Circular glasses I have on the tip of my nose. [Spectacles – make fingers into spectacles, then touch the child's nose.]

יש לי אצבעות עשר	Eser etzbaot li yesh
הן בונות דבר כל	Kol davar osot hen
שש בו ויונים שובך	Shovah veyonim Bo shesh
הן הומות גור גור גור.	Gur gur gur homot he
קטן לי בית הנה	Hineh bayit li katan
שולחן וגם כסא בו	Bo kisee vegam shulhan
עגולים משקפיים	Mishkafayim agulim
החוטם בקצה לי.	Li biktze hahotem

יש לי אצבעות עשר

הן יודעות והכל

ולקשקש לצייר

הן מכות בתוף גם.

רע לילד אוי אבל

עושה נו נו נו אצבע

אצבעות ברוגז בוהן

מתפייסות הן. זרת

Eser etzbaot li yesh

Vehakol yodot hen

Letzayer ulekashkesh

Gam batof makot hen

Aval oy leyeled ra

Etzba nu nu nu osah

Bohen brogez etzbaot

Zeret mitpaysot hen

As Hadas Learned It After Returning to Israel:

Ten fingers I have
They can build everything
Dovecote with six doves
Gur gur gur they sing

Here's my little house
It has a chair and a table
Round glasses
I have at the tip of my nose

Ten fingers I have
Everything they know
To draw and to scribble
Even to play the drum

But oy for the bad boy
Finger does nununu
Toes are quarrelling
Pinkie makes peace

JONARNO LAWSON

The hardest work, you'll notice, is left to the smallest!

And now, a brief diversion about "Twinkle, Twinkle, Little Star": Jane Taylor published it as the first verse of the poem "The Star" in the book she wrote with her sister Ann, *Rhymes for the Nursery* published in 1806. The Taylor family moved about quite a bit in southern England, but it seems they were living in Colchester, Essex, when Jane wrote the rhyme. Later it was sung to a melody popularized by Mozart, along with the English alphabet song, "The ABCs," and "Baa, Baa, Black Sheep":

Twinkle, twinkle, little star,
How I wonder what you are!
Up above the world so high,
Like a diamond in the sky.

The Taylors also wrote a first-rate book of children's poetry that's been almost entirely forgotten, though I think it would be popular still if it had been kept in print.

It's called *Signor Topsy-Turvy's Wonderful Magic Lantern.* The book was recommended to me by my friend Lissa Paul, one of the editors of the *Norton Anthology of Children's Literature.* She told me there was a copy of it in the Toronto Public Library's Osborne Collection of Early Children's Books, so I went to see it, and read through it. It's small – the size of an average-sized adult hand – and it's a work of art.

It was considered too political when it came out in 1810, shortly after the French Revolution, because it presents a topsy-turvy social order, where animals overthrow their human masters, and inflict the same terrible lives on them.

This seems to be why it disappeared almost right away. Here's a sample poem from the book:

90

The Horse Turned Driver

A poor looking hack,
Had long borne on his back
A groom, who did nothing but chide her,
Till at length unto her
Came a thought, "My good Sir,"
Quoth she, "I've a mind to turn rider."

So stirrup and bit,
She had alter'd to fit,
Nor of bridle and spur was she sparing;
And the groom she displays
In a saddle or chaise,
Whenever she goes for an airing.

If he dare to complain,
She but tightens the rein,
And whips him for going no faster;
But some people say,
She had trudg'd to this day,
If he'd been a merciful master.

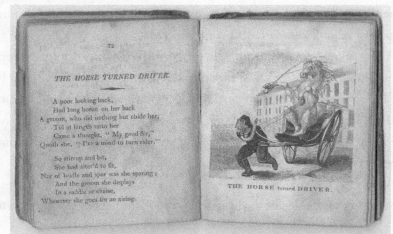

MY FATHER'S STROKE AND "THE ABCs"

I think all of us tend to either use internal speech or internal music to organize ourselves to some extent. One has things like nursery rhymes – "One two, buckle my shoe" – or marching songs, or work songs, but the *song* as a unit of organization became tremendously important and crucial for this man who was so totally lost visually.
– Oliver Sacks, *The Last Interview and Other Conversations*

As I mentioned above, the tune that was popularized by Mozart and used as the melody for "Twinkle, Twinkle, Little Star" was also used for "Baa, Baa, Black Sheep," as well as "The ABCs."

I can remember the moment I realized, as a child, that all three songs had the same melody. I wondered if anyone else had ever realized this! I couldn't believe it – each song was so important and completely distinct in my mind – how was it possible they all shared a tune, and that it took me so long to notice this?

I thought more about the importance of the connection in 2002, when my father had a stroke.

My sister called to tell me what had happened from the hospital. Luckily she was visiting my father at the time, so she was able to call an ambulance while he was still having the stroke. I live an hour away – I rushed over, and when I got to the hospital my father was alert, but unable to speak. He looked terrified, of course.

A few hours later, my brother, Stephen, arrived from Montreal. Stephen is a multidisciplinary artist – I mention this because I think it's possible that his occupation is at least partially relevant to what follows. I think my brother's intensive training and practise as a stage performer might have given him a more integrated and cohesive sense of how the mind, memory, voice and body work together.

As soon as he came in and took in the fact that our father couldn't speak, he went over to the side of the hospital bed, took his hand and started to sing to him "A-B-C-D-E-F-G." He said later that he had no idea why he did this. It could be he just had an instinct to try soothing him with a childhood melody. But maybe it also had to do with his years of stage work, where memory, movement and voice all had to work seamlessly together. On the stage, of course, it's very important not to forget your lines. Quick, accurate recall is part of the job.

My father said it was as if he was at the bottom of a dark well, and someone threw down a ladder. Just like that, out of the silence the stroke had imposed on him hours before, he started singing along with my brother.

He looked startled. We all laughed with relief. And then they kept singing together – the rest of "The ABCs," then "Baa, Baa, Black Sheep," then "Twinkle, Twinkle" – the same melody scaffolding all three sets of lyrics. My father's speech was back. He crawled back to language on the alphabet song, as provided, providentially, by my brother at exactly the right moment.

It's possible he might have regained his speech anyway. On the other hand, who knows? This seemed to be the trigger, and it might be that he really needed that ladder to get out. Is it possible that one of the functions of nursery rhymes and songs is that they act as an early (maybe brief, but important) bridge between sound, rhythm and language?

In Charles Fernyhough's remarkable book *The Baby in the Mirror*, he talked about his daughter lifting word patterns from nursery rhymes like "all fall down," and how this was exciting to hear when a child first starts speaking. But he thought the next stage was even more exciting, when they start coming up with their own phrases, like "no gone" – something they haven't heard an adult say, but through which they can make themselves understood.

I wrote to Fernyhough to ask him whether he thought nursery rhymes might play an important role in early language acquisition. I was delighted when he responded: "I'm sure they do. A very important bridge, I'm sure. Not really aware of any specific research on this, though."

If that was the case, then maybe it was possible they could spark a damaged mind and help with its repair if the language centres in the mind were affected?

Charles Darwin, in his "A Biographical Sketch of an Infant," noted not just the types of sounds his son made, but also the quality of the sounds:

> I was particularly struck with the fact that when asking for food by the word *mum* he gave to it (I will copy the words written down at the time) "a most strongly marked interrogatory sound at the end." He also gave to "Ah," which he chiefly used at first when recognising any person or his own image in a mirror, an exclamatory sound, such as we employ when surprised. I remark in my notes that the use of these intonations seemed to have arisen instinctively, and I regret that more observations were not made on this subject. I record, however, in my notes that at a rather later period, when between 18 and 21 months old, he modulated his voice in refusing peremptorily to do anything by a defiant whine, so as to express "That I won't"; and again his humph of assent expressed "Yes, to be sure." M. Taine also insists strongly on the highly expressive tones of the sounds made by his infant before she had learnt to speak. The interrogatory sound which my child gave to the word *mum* when asking for food is especially curious; for if anyone will use a single word or a short sentence in this manner, he will find that the musical pitch of his voice rises considerably at the close. I did not then see that this fact bears on the view which I have elsewhere maintained that before man used articulate language, he uttered notes in a true musical scale as does the anthropoid ape Hylobates.

That infants understand from the beginning the subtle but definite importance of tone (how both they and others use it) can be shown from more modern research, too. And so we touch again on the subject of motherese, and hitting high notes: According to Brian Boyd's *Origin of Stories*, "Infants prefer recordings of lullabies sung by mothers while a child was present to those recorded without children present, and adults also judge these versions more loving."

Is it possible that my father responded as he did not just because of the mechanics of "The ABCs," but because my brother had taken my father's hand and sung the song in a soothing way? Did part of the healing come from his loving approach?

ZAPA, ZAPA, ZAPATERO

I was introduced to Lietzka Graterol by my old friend Lourdes Zelaya. Lourdes used to work at an organization called Skills for Change – a resource centre for newcomers to Canada – which is a ten-minute walk from my house. Lietzka came from Caracas, Venezuela. We only spoke for twenty minutes or so, but she had a whole slew of games and rhymes to teach me – I could barely keep up with her.

The first one she said is mostly played in kindergarten, or grade one, when you're six or seven.

Zapa, Zapa, Zapatero;	Shoeshiner, shoeshiner
Tiene Tinta en el Tintero;	Do you have polish in the tin?
Tienes alguien que to quiera;	Do you have somebody who loves
Como se llama?	you?
Si [any name] te quiere	What's his/her name?
Tienes que mover este piecito!	If [any name] loves you
	You have to move your little foot!

Several children sit in a circle, putting their feet in. This game of elimination is played one syllable per foot (similar to "Eeny, Meeny, Miny, Moe") and if your foot is hit on the last syllable, that foot is out.

SEA SNAKE

The interesting thing about this rhyme, and game, is that in Spanish it's called "A la bibora de la mar" (viper of the sea, or sea snake). The Spanish word for snake (or viper) is *víbora*. Lietzka thought the word might mean snake, but she said she wasn't sure. It was a nonsense word to her, as it stood. Given the many centuries of connection between the widespread Spanish colonies, it doesn't seem impossible to me that the name of the game (even if no other part of it) might have had its origins in the Philippines, or at least as a nod to Filipino pronunciation.

The Tagalog (Filipino) word for snake is *bibora*, which I'm assuming comes from the Spanish word. Filipinos started arriving in South America in the sixteenth century, during the Spanish colonial period, which took place at exactly the same time in both Venezuela and the Philippines. Filipinos are the oldest, and one of the largest, Asian communities in South and Central America.

A la bibora de la mar	Snake of the sea
por aqui podra pasan	Here you pass!
el de adelante	Those in front run quickly
corre mucho y el de amao se	And those behind
quedará	He will catch, he will catch, he
se quedará, se quedará, se que-	will catch!
dará	
se quedo.	

In this game, two children create a bridge with their arms. The other children have to run under the arm-bridge. If those making the bridge can lower their arms and catch the one running through, that one has to stand behind one of the catchers. Once everyone has been caught, there's a tug-of-war between the two groups.

CHICLET MAS CHICLET, AMERICANO

This game takes three kids to play. Two children hold a rope (or long elastic) around their legs, while the third child stands to the side of the rope. Those holding the rope chant:

Chiclet Mas Chiclet, Americano! Tie tieto, tie abro, tie cierro, y tie salgo!	Chiclet plus Chiclet, American! Go in, go open, go closed, go out!

Each time the children chant an instruction, the other child has to jump in and out of the "trough" made by the rope or elastic. You can't touch, or you're out. And after each round of the chant, the rope is raised a few inches, to make the jumping more difficult.

FOR YOUR DAD, WHO GIVES YOU NOTHING!

And finally, this is a clapping game played with babies:

Arepita de Manteca, Para mama que da teta Manteca Arepita de cebada Para papa que no da nada!	Pancake of lard For mama, who fed you from her breast Pancake of barley, For your dad, who gives you nothing!

That final scorching line! It's hard not to love the blunt, bitter humour of this one. (Unless you happen to be a dad who gives your child nothing? In which case you probably wouldn't be around to hear this clapping game anyway . . .)

Lietzka demonstrated how you alter the direction of your hands with each clap – fingers of one hand forward, then fingers of the other hand forward.

97

FIVE LITTLE WOLVES HID BEHIND A BROOM

In 2008, on a shuttle bus between Calgary and Banff, I happened to sit next to the Mexican poet Coral Bracho. A selection of Bracho's work (*Firefly Under the Tongue*) had just been translated into English, and she had been invited up to Calgary's Wordfest to read from it.

As the foothills outside the bus turned into mountains, we chatted about our work, and I told her that I wrote mostly poetry for children. She said that children's poetry had always been of great interest to her. Her family had moved to England for a year when she was a child, and during her time there she discovered English nursery rhymes. "This was my first experience of poetry," she told me, "and it was a revelation. I loved them."

I told her what Robert Graves had said about English nursery rhymes. I paraphrased what I remembered, but this is the exact quote: "very few of them are moralistic, historical, scientific, devotional, or merely literary; and that is why the best of the older ones are nearer to poetry than the greater part of the 'Oxford Book of English Verse.'"

Bracho agreed wholeheartedly.

I asked her about Mexican nursery rhymes, and right away she showed me this one:

Cinco lobitos tiene la loba	Five little wolves has the mother wolf
Cinco lobitos detras de la escoba	Five little wolves behind the broom

She then showed me how to do it. "Wiggle the fingers of one hand behind the fingers of the other, opening the fingers of the first hand to show the fingers behind." It was so simple, and compelling. I had never thought of my fingers as little wolves before. I liked it so much I couldn't stop thinking about it and expanded it into something longer for my own kids. I'm including it below because it went over well with my children.

Adaptation:

Five little wolves
Hid behind the broom
One jumped out because there wasn't any room.

[Have first hand hide behind the second hand, then have one finger of the first hand jump over the top of the second hand.]

Four little wolves
Hid behind the broom
One tripped and fell, down a well, boom boom boom

[Have the next finger of the first hand appear between each set of fingers from the second hand as it falls, boom boom boom.]

Three little wolves
Hid behind the broom
One hopped out, and howled at the moon

[The next finger of the first hand should jump over the second hand and wiggle as it howls.]

Two little wolves
Hid behind the broom
One came to play this morning
But stayed all afternoon!

[The offending finger of the first hand should poke "aggressively" out from over the second hand.]

One little wolf
Hid behind the broom
He raced to chase the tail of a raggedy raccoon

[The last finger of the first hand goes running off over the second hand.]

Five little wolves back behind the broom to play
But their mother came and found them
And she swept them all away.

[First hand completely behind the second hand now, second hand becomes surprised mother, which makes sweeping motion at first hand, and both hands can now go tickling child.]

I never saw Coral Bracho again, but this little rhyme always stuck with me, becoming part of my own active repertoire.

MARINERO QUE SE FUE A LA MAR

I met Kali Nino when she was singing with the artist/writer/illustrator/performer Alec Dempster (my co-collaborator on two books) in Toronto. She's a Nahuatl speaker, with her roots in Tuxtla, in southern Mexico. Nahuatl is spoken by about one and a half million people.

She said this was one of her favourite active rhymes from her early childhood. Though she grew up speaking Nahuatl, she didn't know of any children or infant rhymes in the language – but she also grew up speaking Spanish, and in Spanish Kali knew this rhyme, which she shared below.

Marinero que se fue a la mar	The sailor has gone to sea
Para ver lo que podia ver	To see what he can see
Y lo unico que pudo ver	But all that he can see
Fue el fondo de la mar.	Is the bottom of the sea.

Kali said, "The first time you do the rhyme, you cross your hands back and forth with your partner, clapping your hands together, and touching your forehead on the word *sea*. The second time you go through the rhyme, you cross your arms. The third time, you slap your thighs. And then you just keep going, but each time you increase the speed."

Kali talked, too, about the importance of toys in her town. She said this has changed, because of electronics, but when she was little, children played a skilled game with a pretty wooden toy called a balero (cup and ball), and another with a toy called a Cayuco Trompo (a top, also known as El Trompo).

THREE SAD TIGERS EATING WHEAT

Seven years after meeting Coral Bracho, I met Salvador Alanis and Ximena Berecochea on the school playground at Forest Hill – they always made eye contact and said hello – not a given on any Toronto school playground I've been on! In fact, Salvador and Ximena said this was one way they could often spot people in Toronto who came from Latin America – they made friendly, easy eye contact with strangers in public places.

When I told them about my long ago meeting with Coral Bracho, they told me that, coming from Mexico City as they did, they could expand the Mexican section for me, so we arranged to meet a few days later at the Aroma Espresso Bar on Spadina Avenue. With notebooks and nursery rhyme books spread out on the table, we started talking.

Ximena said, "These are the ones my parents used to do with me – or at least the ones that I remember – and that I did with own children, Matias and Pablo. This first one is a variation of the one Coral Bracho taught you:

Cinco lobitos	Five little wolves
tuvo la loba	had mother wolf
blancos y negros	white and black
tras de la escoba.	behind the broom.
Cinco crió	Five she raised
cinco cuidó	five she took care of
y a todos ellos	and all of them
solita enseñó.	she taught by herself.

"For this next one, you sit the baby/child on your lap and with your fingers you pretend to 'walk' from the wrist of the kid to his/her upper arm and end up tickling him/her:

Andaba la hormiguita	The little ant was walking
juntando su comidita	grabbing its tiny food
vino un aguacerito	a tiny downpour[1]
¡corrió hacia su casita!	it ran to its tiny house!
¡y entró a su covachita!	and entered its tiny room![2]

"For the following one, you say the words while you move the kid from sitting position to leaning back and so on. We just used one hand to hold and with the other hand tickled our kids' necks at the end – our sons, Matias and Pablo, loved this one.

"The words that I used:

---

1. It's a bit nonsense but that's the way it is: *aguacero* is *downpour* but as you can see *hormiga*, *comida* and *aguacero* are used with diminutives *ito*. *Aguacerito* would be something like a tiny/huge rain.

2. *Covacha* is a storage room; I'm not sure how you would translate this in the context of the rhyme.

Riquirran	**Riquirran** [this word means
Riquirran	nothing]
Los maderos de San Juan	Riquirran
Piden pan	The timbers of San Juan
Y no les dan	They ask for bread
Piden queso	That they don't get
Y le dan un hueso	They ask for cheese
Que se les atora	And they get a bone
En el meritito[3] pesquezo.	That gets stuck
	In the throat."

After Ximena shared these, Salvador showed me this one, which he learned from his grandmother Graciela, who came from San Luis Potosí, Mexico. His mother also did this with him.

El niño chiquito	The little boy
El señor de los anillos	The lord of the rings
El tonto y loco	The dumb and crazy
El lame cazuelas ...	The bowl licker
y el mata piojos!	And the lice killer!

The adult holds the child facing outward on his/her lap. Holding the child's hand, you start with the pinky (the little boy), and then work your way over to the thumb. At the end, you tickle the child.

Salvador said that he didn't really think about what the words meant until he was ten or so – he took it for granted just as it was, and later on, he thought about why each finger was given that specific title.

---

3. At the word *meritito* you tickle a very specific spot: the throat.

This was another of Salvador's:

Este era un gato	Once there was a cat
Con los pies de trapo	With paws made of cloth
Y los ojos al reves	And its eyes were twisted
Quieres que te lo cuente	Do you want me to tell you again?
Otra vez?	

Salvador said this was said over and over to a child, while tickling them. Whether the child answered yes or no, the adult continued to do it. It was pure nonsense. The child would beg the adult to stop, and this was part of the game.

Salvador, Ximena and I talked about this oddity of tickling. There is something terrible about it, but also compelling. You could be laughing, while seriously asking the other person to stop. It was a fine line with children. On the one hand, it was often okay. If all went well, there was something enjoyable about the hysteria involved in being tickled. But tickling could also go wrong. Many adults have memories of unwanted tickling when they were children. It seems to be something adults are more conscious of, now.

Salvador wanted to know if I was interested in tongue twisters. I said I was. He recommended this one:

Tres tristes tigres tragaban trigo en un trigal.	Three sad tigers were eating wheat in a wheat field.

He said the Cuban writer Guillermo Cabrera Infante used the beginning of this tongue twister as the title for his novel *Three Trapped Tigers*, noted for its wordplay. He was surprised I'd never heard of it. I promised him I'd track it down.

Ximena then jumped in with this one, taught to her by her grandmother Carola Fernandez, who also came from Mexico City.

Al paso, al paso, al paso	In step, in step, in step
van las señoras;	go the ladies;
al trote, al trote, al trote	trot, trot, trot
van los señores;	go the lords;
al galope, al galope, al galope	galloping, galloping, galloping
van los caballerangos!	go the horsemen!

This was done as a lap game, and the adult bouncing the child would go faster and faster and faster as the rhyme went along.

And then from Salvador again:

Tengo manita	I have a little hand
No tengo manita	I don't have a hand
Parquet la tengo	Because it is
Desconchabadita.	Broken down.

Salvador said you did this with a very small child, or infant, to get the child to imitate the hand movement. *Desconchabadita* is Mexican Spanish for *twisted, sprained, broken down.* Your hand moves with a motion similar to what you'd use to screw in a light bulb.

As he thought through these, Salvador realized he often had to do the movements to remember the words – as if he was thinking with his body. The body-memory brought back the word-memories.

The last one they taught me was a rhyme to gently shake a child's leg to:

Cuando me voy	When I go
Casa Tio Juan	To Uncle Juan's house
Con la patita	With the leg
Toco el zaguán.	I knock on the door.

Salvador said that the first line is a contraction, which sounds good, though the grammar is bad. He said it was the grammar of someone not fluent in regular Spanish. If you used the proper grammar it would be: "Cuando voy a la casa del tio Juan." But it's a rhyme for children, so sound trumps meaning!

RR CON RR CON RR BARRIL

We met Yanelis Lopez Forcade at a resort in Cayo Coco, Cuba, in the winter of 2013. Yanelis worked in the dining room where we ate all of our meals, so we saw her several times a day. Gradually we got to know her a little – her children were close in age to ours. You could tell she adored her children from the way she talked about them, and she was curious about our children, as well.

She was working, so we couldn't talk for long, but we exchanged email addresses so that we could talk more later. I told Yanelis about my research, and she offered these two rhymes from Morón in the province of Ciego de Ávila in central Cuba, where she grew up and still lives. The first is:

Arruru mi niño	Arruru my child
Arruru mi amor	Arruru my love
Arruru pedazo de mi corazon	Arruru piece of my heart
Ese niño lindo q nacio de dia	That cute boy who was born
quieren q lo lleven a la dulceria	in the daytime
ese niño lindo q nacio de noche	wants to be taken to the candy
quieren q lo lleven a pasear en	shop
coche.	that cute boy who is born at
	night
	wants to be taken on a ride.

Ximena Berecochea regularized the Spanish below:

Arruru mi niño
Arruru mi amor

Arruru pedazo de mi corazón
Ese niño lindo que nació de día quiere que lo lleven a la dulcería
Ese niño lindo que nació de noche quiere que lo lleven a pasear en
   coche.

The second rhyme from Yanelis is:

Duermete niño duermete	Sleep, child, go to sleep
ya que viene el cucu y te	or the bogeyman will come
comera	and eat you
Rr con rr con rr barril	Rr with rr with rr barrelling
Rapido pasan los carro por la	Rapidly the cars pass on the
linea del Ferro-Carril.	Ferrocarril line.

Again, Ximena regularized the Spanish:

Duérmete niño duérmete ya, que viene el cucu y te comerá
Rr con rr con rr barril
Rápido pasan los carros por la línea del ferrocarril.

Apparently this song is well known (with variations) all over the Span-
ish-speaking world. But the Ferrocarril line is the Cuban national railroad,
making this very much a local version.

THE COCKROACH SAYS THERE ARE SEVEN RAINBOW SHIRTS

We hired Maria Artuso to clean for us shortly after we bought our
house in 2002. She and her husband had moved to Toronto from Brazil in
the early 1990s. Maria had been a high school science teacher in São Pau-
lo, though she came from São Domingos do Prata, Minas Gerais, in Belo
Horizonte, and she'd hoped to teach again in Canada, but it hadn't been

possible. She had to make money and look after her daughter, and re-qual-ification was costly and time consuming. Becoming proficient enough in written English to teach would also have been a big challenge. But Maria said she thought the sacrifices were worth it, because she felt her daughter would have more options in Canada.

When I told Maria about the project I was doing, she started writing things down for me on the spot.

1. A Barata diz que tem!
Sete saia de felo
E' mentira da Barata,
Que ela tem uma so!
Ha, Ha, Ho, Ho, Ho.

1. The cockroach says
There are seven rainbow shirts
The cockroach is lying –
There's only one!
Ha, Ha, Ho, Ho, Ho.

A Barata diz que tem
Um ariel du formatura!
E' montira da barata
Que ela tem e' easca dura.

The cockroach says she has
A graduation ring
It's a lie, all she has
Is an old nutshell.

2. Boi, boi, boi da cara preta –
Vem pegar crianca que
Tem medo de careta!

2. Bull, bull, black-hearted bull
Come take the kids
Who have frightened faces!

3. Dorme nenem
Nenem do coração
Dorme sem medo
Do bidro papais
Mamãe foi a fonte
Papai foi trabalhar

3. Sleep baby,
Baby of my heart
Sleep without being afraid
Of the monster
Mommy went to the well
And Daddy to work

Dorme nenem	Sleep baby,
O bicho vai pegar	The monster's going to get you …
Mamãe va dormir	Mom's going to sleep,
E papai trabalhar.	Dad's going to work.

Maria, looking these over after, commented on the frightening nature of the last two. She said it was common in Brazilian rhymes and lullabies to have a monster figure. She thought it probably made the rhymes more compelling to small children, but she wondered, too, about what the point was, if the lullabies were supposed to be soothing? She speculated that it might have to do with taking away the power of something that's feared by naming it.

CHAPTER SIX
COLOMBIA, HALLOWE'EN AND MEXICO

RHYMES FOR SPECIAL DAYS

The American anthropologist Donald Brown had some interesting things to say about children's culture in his book *Human Universals*. This book deals with what aspects of human culture are common to all known human groups:

> The Universal People know how to dance and have music. At least some of their dance (and at least some of their religious activity) is accompanied by music. They include melody, rhythm, repetition, re-dundancy, and variation in their music, which is always seen as an art, a creation. Their music includes vocals, and the vocals include words – i.e. a conjunction of music and poetry. *The UP have children's music.*
>
> The UP, particularly their youngsters, play and playfight. Their play, besides being fun, provides training in skills that will be useful in adult-hood. (italics mine)

The phrase *trick or treat* was, apparently, the invention of children in Blackie, Alberta, not far from Calgary. This was where the phrase first appeared in print in 1927, in a newspaper article describing the raucous behaviour of young people on Hallowe'en Eve, which included their use of this chant to get treats in exchange for not committing mischievous acts.

Later additions to the rhyme varied through time and by location –

"Trick or treat, trick or treat, give me something good to eat"; "Trick or treat, smell my feet"; and so on – but on the whole *trick or treat* was the phrase that stuck.

In Mexico, there is a similar phrase used during the Mexican Día de los Muertos (Day of the Dead), which is associated with English North America's Hallowe'en, though this phrase is not as widespread: "*¿Me da mi calaverita?*" "Can you give me my little skull?" This refers to a small skull made of sugar or chocolate, given to children by adults.

There are many phrases, songs and rhymes that are only used at certain times. "Auld Lang Syne" on New Year's Eve. Christmas carols, which are only sung in the month or so leading up to Christmas. The songs that are used in Passover Seders, and Diwali devotional songs. Almost all cultures have songs that conjure up a great deal of nostalgia for those who grew up with those traditions.

It seems that we need, or in some cases feel the need to impose, a certain amount of repetition in the things we say and certainly in the things we sing. Some of it happens daily, such as the singing of the national anthem, lullabies, prayers before bed, grace before meals, certain formulaic greetings. Some of it is weekly, especially for the religious, in services. But some of it only happens yearly, again, more commonly during religious holidays, but also during secular holidays like Hallowe'en or New Year's. And then there are phrases like "the Queen is dead, God save the King," which might only happen once or twice a century.

A lullaby also has its usual time and place – usually by a child's bed, just before the child falls asleep. It may be that it's evolved as it has because it conjures up the quieter rhythms in the mind required for sleep. We often make the mistake of ascribing a single purpose to something – an event, action or desire; ours or someone else's – but that's rarely the case. I have no doubt that there might be more to a lullaby than just its sound, rhythm or imagery. It may be doing more to, and with, our minds than just putting us to sleep.

It's an odd paradox of the remarkably complicated human mind that it often ignores the complexity of its reasons for doing anything, and reduces, categorizes, summarizes and judges until finally settling on a single explanation, to its own relief! Variety is lost, though our minds themselves are various, as are our relationships and motivations.

While we live in an increasingly secular world, the need for repetitive phrasing and singing hasn't changed much – many of us can easily sing advertising jingles, memorable bits of pop songs and theme songs for television shows or movies. These can often conjure up powerful childhood memories, as well as memories from later in life. They remind you of where you were, what you were doing, how you were feeling and who you were with. It may be worth thinking about the emotional power of these melody-based memories – how they may both form our identities, and, at the same time, fragment us.

AGUINALDOS

Le cuento el milagro pero no el santo.
I'll tell you the miracle, but not the saint.
– Colombian saying

I first asked Monica Sarmiento about Colombian children's games when she was my son Ashey's kindergarten teacher, back in 2009. Monica, in those days we knew her as Ms. Sarmiento, told me about a game played near Christmastime, involving feet. But we didn't sit down to really talk about the subject until six years later, by which time our families had become close friends.

Monica; her husband, Andres Lopez; their son, Mateo; and Monica's mother, Gloria, came for lunch one spring day. We had decided ahead of time that the conversation would be dedicated exclusively to aguinaldos. I had tried to talk about this many times in the past, but a conversation with the Sarmiento-Lopez family inevitably went in any and every direction, and into this easy, organic flow of talk, research questions felt bureaucratic and out of place. But my book now had a deadline. It happened to be a piece of great luck that Monica's mother, Gloria, was visiting from Miami.

"What *is* an aguinaldo?" I asked. "What does it mean? And when does it happen?"

The adults conferred in a mix of English and Spanish. How to translate the word? The term could be used to describe a small birthday gift, but in Colombia, it referred to a series of Christmas games played between December 16 and December 25, corresponding with the novena. A novena, in certain branches of the Christian church, is the term for nine days of prayers that lead up to a special occasion of some kind, often in anticipation of a church feast.

The aguinaldos were usually played with the same group of people – family and friends – over the course of the nine days and evenings. Each evening someone else takes a turn at hosting.

Below are the five most commonly played games. For each one you might have a different competitive partner; all different ages participate and partner with each other. Over the nine days, you tally up your points.

1. Pajita en boca (grass in mouth) – In this game, you have to keep a piece of grass in your mouth at all times. Doing your chores, reading, cooking, everything – the piece of grass has to be there. If you're confronted by whomever you're in competition with to show the piece of grass, and it's not there, you lose a point (or they gain a point!).

2. Beso robado (stolen kiss) – You must not allow yourself to be kissed by the one you're competing with! You have to dodge away, crawl under a table – whatever you need to do. Andres said that this was often a way to kiss (or be kissed by) someone you liked. Because it was all very public, it was considered a non-threatening and safe form of courtship. In some cases, this might be your big chance to reveal your interest in someone. Or of discovering that the one you like doesn't like you back.

3. Sí et no (yes and no) – Monica and Andres said this one was super-fun, one of their favourites. In your pair, you decide that one of you has to say "yes" all the time, and the other one has to say "no," no matter what the question is. And so you can make the other person admit to, or deny, ridiculous or embarrassing things (or they risk losing a point). Do you have a boyfriend? Are you in love with so-and-so? Are you ugly? Et cetera.

4. Hablar e no contester (Talk, but don't answer) – You are not supposed to answer any question in this game. Andres said this one was particularly tricky, because, supposing he was playing against Monica, she could say, "Andres, did you pay the phone bill?" and Andres might automatically say, "Of course," and lose a point.

5. Tres pies (three feet) – This one requires stealth. You have to sneak up behind your opponent, and put your foot between their feet so it appears, from the front, as if they have three feet.

We moved on to to other topics. Andres, Monica and Mateo had come for New Year's Eve that year, and they'd brought grapes for all of us to eat at midnight. "How do the grapes and the wishes work again?" I asked them. They made it clear there was no religious connection.

"Where did the custom come from?" I asked.

"It must have been some witch," said Gloria, laughing. "You go to church, but you also visit a sorcerer for good luck, for health, to help with problems. Not everything is ruled by reason."

Monica told us about a complicated ritual with a dove, performed by a sorcerer on the beach in Miami. It had been done to help her find a good husband, and indeed, she and Andres did seem very happy.

In any case, the grapes: You had to eat twelve grapes in the course of a single minute at midnight, making a wish on each grape. And if you don't manage to eat the grape within that minute, the reverse of your wish happens, so the stakes are high.

There are several other ways to ensure good luck on New Year's Eve in

Colombia. You can wear yellow underwear for good luck on New Year's Eve. It's also considered good luck to run around the block with a suitcase in hand. Monica said in Colombia this isn't a big deal, but in Canada, in high heels on an icy night, it required extra effort.

You are also supposed to put a glass of water under your bed with an egg in it, and in the morning an expert could then prognosticate the year ahead for you by interpreting the meanings in the egg.

WHO'S DEAD?

Colombia is different from many of its national neighbours because of the significant African and First Nations influence. The Afro-Colombians live mostly in rural areas along the Pacific coast, the First Nations of Colombia are mostly in the mountains and the interior, and Euro-Colombians tend to be mostly in the cities. The river brings everyone together, and the different cultures have mixed in many ways. But each region has its own distinctive music.

According to Andres, everything involves dancing in Colombia – but this isn't the case in nearby Chile. Chileans listen to music, but they don't dance. Music is very, very important to Colombians, no matter where they are in the country. If there isn't music, the first question is "Who's dead?" The first thing you buy, when you have money, is a source of music – a CD player, a guitar, anything to make music with.

Toward the end of our conversation, Monica and Gloria recounted a finger (or toe) rhyme (done while pulling a child's fingers, or toes, one at a time):

Éste compró un huevito	This one bought an egg [pinky]
Éste lo cocinó	This one cooked it [ring]
Éste le echo la sal	This one added salt [middle]
Éste lo rebullo	This one mixed it [pointer]
Éste picaro ladrón se le robo!	This mischievous one stole it! [thumb]

And this song, which Andres had never heard, was sung by Gloria to her children as a lullaby:

Somos cinco negritos
y todos cinco primos hermanos
compramos una guitarra
y todos cinco en ella tocamos
Rumeque que maca
Rumeque que fue
Donde navega mi corazón
Ya sale el sol loco brillar
los pajaritos contando estan?
y los negrotis amos alla
y de nosotros tened piedad.

Mateo had a soccer game, so before anyone had a chance to translate this one, the Sarmiento-Lopez clan had to depart. Summer holidays intervened shortly after.

But six weeks later, Monica sent this email about the song, with her translation:

"I started working on the translation yesterday and only then I realized how sad this song is. I contacted various friends and inquired about your questions and my perceptions. It sparked really interesting and thought-provoking conversations. My translation of this song takes into account what I know about the black communities in the northern part of Colombia, and my basic knowledge of Colombian history.

"According to my sources and myself, though none of us are scholars, we think this song arrived in Bogotá through domestic help coming from the coast. So here it goes.

"Rumeque is a name and they (the children) are asking Rumeque what's going on by using the word *maca*. It's a game of words. It totally makes sense as this song is sung to shift the attention of children when they are about to cry, or get upset.

"I wish I had a better command of the language to express the feelings the song conveys, but unfortunately that's not the case so I apologize for my translation:

We are five black children and cousins all of us
Together we bought a guitar that we all get to play
Rumeque what is going on?
Rumeque what happened?
Where does my heart sail?
I see the sun
I see it pass
I hear the birds and the songs they sing
And without knowing, we all drift there
Have pity on us!"

OFRENDAS

Back to Ximena once more! I asked Ximena Berecochea about Hallowe'en/Day of the Dead traditions in Mexico, particularly about how: "¿Me da mi calaverita?" ["Can you give me my little skull?"] might be connected with "trick or treat." I wanted to know if it was widespread, going to door to door to ask for this.

Ximena responded: "About the calaverita, I think it was more a random thing. Some people did and some didn't. It was far from the way trick-or-treat is done here in Canada and also in the US.

"I never went trick-or-treating or asking for my calaverita . . . I don't have any memories to share about that. Salvador didn't do it either, and neither did my friends (that I remember). What was, and still is very common though, even today, is to do the 'ofrendas' at home for the family members that already died."

I asked Ximena if she could explain this more: what did it mean to her as a child? How did she remember it? Did it help her to remember the person who had died, or, if she hadn't met them, did it help her to imagine them?

An ofrenda is set up like a small altar in the home, and it's dedicated to a particular person who's died. Their picture is often at the top, and things that were important to that person – things they liked, or enjoyed – are included on the altar.

"Regarding the ofrendas. It was a very exciting thing, to prepare them, to buy little things, the person's favourites things, etc. As a kid it was something like an arts activity but with a deep meaning and with the delicious element, the 'pan de muertos' which you got to eat while doing this. Of course, this tradition, somehow, brought the dead person back in a very colourful, celebratory and warm way. If it was someone that I hadn't met, as for example my mom's grandma, this practice made me feel I had met her, it's hard to describe, it was something like having her there. Does this make sense?"

It made complete sense. I remember listening to stories about my grandmother – the one I never met – and feeling like I'd met her. As if she was watching over me, even. The same when we made Christmas cookies she had made, particularly pecan balls, or when I held things I knew she'd also held and loved.

But the tradition of ofrendas makes it more of an open and conscious experience – something consciously and lovingly shared within a family.

This is a tradition I feel very drawn to trying out myself.

CHAPTER SEVEN

RUSSIA, BELORUSSIA, THE UKRAINE AND POLAND

LULLABIES ARE ESSENTIAL

Everyone has gone to sleep, the children have cried themselves out and they have been asleep for a long time, but the woman does not sleep. She thinks and listens to the roaring of the sea.
– Anton Chekhov, *The Island: A Journey to Sakhalin*

Much of my research ended up being done through talking to adults on school playgrounds. My wife teased me about the importance of these playground conversations to my social life, since I spend most of my time working in the basement by myself.

She was joking, but of course she was right – my brief chats with other parents dropping off or picking up their kids at school sometimes comprised the whole of my social activity for the day. Because Toronto is so cosmopolitan, it's an opportunity to hear pieces of stories, to guess about families, to learn about other cultures and to fill in the picture of a person in small pieces, sometimes over years.

It was in exactly this way that I met Natalia Grayfer, during pickups and drop-offs at school – our sons were in the same split grade one/two class.

She and her husband, Igor, had emigrated from Russia, and they were both interested in children's culture, especially books and films. Natalia was originally from Retchitza, in the Gomel region of Belorussia (now Belarus). She said, "There was a vast Jewish population at the time. My mom was living in Leningrad – what St. Petersburg was called then – and I lived with my grandparents." Igor, she said, came from a Tartar background. Natalia said she understood exactly what I was looking for. When she got home she emailed me this:

"The challenge for me was to choose between the numerous variations that, as I discovered, exist. The text below is the simplest version, and, again, it is often changed and modified depending on parents' creative abilities.

"I remember seeing adults do this with children, it's really very popular. But there is no one accepted version. In my personal recollections, the text that adults in my family used was even shorter, and follows this one.

1. Longer version

Поехали с орехами	Poehali s orehami	Here we go with nuts
На бочке, на бочке	Na bochke, na bochke	On a barrel, on a barrel
По ровной дорожке,	Po rovnoy dorozgke	Down a smooth road
По кочкам, по кочкам,	Po kochkam, po kochka	Through bumps, through bumps,
По оврагам, по оврагам,	Po ovragam, po ovragam	Through ravines, through ravines
По ухабам, по ухабам,	Po uhabam, po uhabam	Through humps, through humps,
На высокую горку,	Na visokuyu gorku,	Up to the high hill
В ямку бух!	V yamku – booh!	Down into the pit – Whoop!

My family version:

По кочкам, по кочкам. По ровненьким дорожкам, По ухабам, по ухабам, В яму – бух!	Po kochkam, po kochkam Po rovnenkim dorozgkam Po uhabam, po uhabam V yamu – booh!	Through bumps, through bumps, Down smooth roads, Through humps, through humps, Down into the pit – whoop!

"I used your word *whoop* as it is closer to the meaning of *booh*.

"I'm not sure about the word *bulges* in this context, maybe you can help me find a synonym to *bumps on the road*. The third line is really close to the first one.

"Igor wasn't around small children a lot, so even though he remembers seeing adults do this, he doesn't know the words of the rhyme. He is not sure if he saw it in his family or somewhere else. I asked him to ask his mother when he gets a chance. His parents are in Russia. I thought having a Tartar version, if it exists, would be beneficial for your research!

"I'm also attaching the most popular finger game. Again, there are numerous variations but this is the most common in my opinion. There is one word in it that I need your help with. I'm not sure how to translate it. It is a general term used for oatmeal, buckwheat, etc., as a type of food. Do you have something similar in English? [I was able to figure this out immediately, because my wife is a big fan of kasha].

Text	Action	Transliteration	Translation
Сорока-ворона кашу варила, деток кормила	Mom moves her finger on the kid's palm	Soroka-vorona kashu varila, detok kormila	Magpie was cooking kasha, feeding her children
Этому дала	Mom bends kid's little finger	Etomu dala	She gave some to this one
Этому дала	Mom bends next finger	Etomu dala	She gave some to this one
Этому дала	Mom bends next finger	Etomu dala	She gave some to this one
А этому не дала	She doesn't bend this finger and, instead, wags this finger	A etomu ne dala	But to this one she gave none!
«Ты – дров не рубил, кашу не варил, мне не помогал: ты каши не получишь!»		"Ti drov ne rubil, kashu ne varil, mne ne pomogal: ti kasha ne poluchish!"	"You didn't help chop firewood, didn't help me cook kasha, you won't get any kasha!"

I was excited to see this, because I had been taught a version of this rhyme over the phone a few years earlier by an elderly lady named Lana Grimberg. Lana Grimberg was the mother of the rabbi of our shul, Rabbi Tina Grimberg. Lana was taught by her mother, who came from a small village in the Ukraine. Notice the difference in pronunciation to the version recorded above by Natalia:

Child is seated:

Saroka Varona
Kashku Varilla [draw a circle on the palm]
Djetak Karmela
Tamoodala
Tamoodala
Tamoodala
Tamoodala
Kashku, Kooshaw
Yakashku [this one she did not give]
Gooly Gooly
Sjeli Nagoovolichku [and then they all flew away and sat
on your little head]
Epanyee teli [birds fly away]

2. Belarusian finger game

Гэты пальчык у лес пайшоў,	This finger went into the woods,
гэты пальчык грыб знайшоў,	This finger found a mushroom,
Гэты пальчык чысціць стаў,	This finger became clean,
гэты пальчык смажыць стаў,	This finger became roasted,
Гэты пальчык усё паеў,	This finger ate everything,
Ад таго і патаўсцеў.	That's why it put on weight.

"I also asked a coworker to have a look at the Belorussian translation and she suggested some changes which I think make sense. They are really minor but I think this translation is better.

This finger went into the woods
This finger found a mushroom
This finger began to clean,
This finger began to roast,

This finger ate everything,
That's why it put on weight.

"Finally Igor got in touch with his mother – she was staying at a dacha out in the countryside without phone service, so it wasn't easy.

"She told him that there weren't lap or finger rhymes that she knew of among the Tartars. She thought this was due to the harshness of life – there wasn't time for that sort of thing, but she did have lullabies. Unfortunately she could no longer remember the words."

When Natasha told me about this, she added, "but it makes sense that she would remember still that there *had been* lullabies, because lullabies are essential."

Anyone who's had to settle a baby knows this, though I hadn't thought of it that way. To excite a baby might not be every parent's object, but every parent, every day, will come to that moment when they need the baby to stop crying, and to sleep.

What's interesting here, too, is that Natasha is Jewish, and came from a town and area directly adjoining the area my wife's grandfather came from.

But Natasha only heard Yiddish in little bits from her grandparents – Yiddish culture was actively suppressed by the Soviet government. So Natasha grew up learning the Russian infant games – no Yiddish was passed on.

Amy's grandfather on the other hand, in the small Ukrainian village of Luginy, in the Korosten district directly south of Belorussian Gomel, learned only Yiddish rhymes as a child, sixty years earlier.

IDZIE IDZIE STONOGA

Intrepid Natasha also tracked down a Polish version of the same rhyme through someone she met online named Elena Rutka. I didn't know Elena Rutka, and neither did Natasha, which didn't mean her version wasn't legitimate! But I wanted to check it out with someone closer to home, so I wrote to my cousin Jim Buck and asked him if he'd ask his wife, Agnieszka, who grew up in Lublin, Poland.

She replied, "I know the first poem, 'Tu sroczka kaszke warzyla,' very well. It is used in a similar way in Poland as the 'This little piggy went to market' poem in the USA. It is a cute little rhyme, mesmerizing to babies.

"You would typically have the baby on your lap and include fingerplay and palm stroking when saying it.

"I have never heard the other poem ('Idzie Idzie Stonoga') but I did a quick Google search and it seems legitimate. Maybe it's a regional thing and where I am from it wasn't popular?"

Tu sroczka kaszkę warzyła

Tu sroczka kaszkę warzyła,	Tu srochka kashke vazshila,	Here magpie porridge cooked,
Swoje dzieci karmiła:	Svoe dzetxi karmila:	Her children fed:
Temu dała w garnuszeczku,	Temu dala v garnushechku,	This one she gave in the pot,
Temu dała w rondeleczku,	Temu dala v rondelechku,	This one in the saucepan,
Temu dała na miseczce,	Temu dala na misechtze,	This one in the bowl,
Temu dała na łyżeczce,	Temu dala na lidzchetze,	This one on a spoon,
A temu nic nie dała,	A temu nizt nie dala,	And this one she did not give,
Tylko frrr . . . poleciała.	Tilko frrr . . . polishala.	Only frrr . . . she flew away.

"When the mom tells this rhyme about a magpie she bends the child's fingers – the first four, but not the last one – because the magpie flies away at this point."

Idzie, idzie stonoga

Idzie, idzie stonoga,	Izdie, izdie stonoga,	Here goes, here goes centi-pede,
A tu . . . noga,	A tu . . . noga,	And here is . . . your leg,
Idzie, idzie malec,	Izdie, iszoe maletz,	Here goes, here goes a boy,
A tu . . . palec,	A tu . . . paletz,	And here is . . . your finger,
Idzie, idzie koń,	Izdie, izdie kon,	Here goes, here goes a horse,
A tu . . . dłoń,	A tu . . . dlon,	And here is . . . your hand,
Idzie, idzie krowa,	Izdie, izdie krova,	Here goes, here goes a cow,
A tu . . . głowa,	A tu . . . glova,	And here is . . . your head
Leci, leci kos,	Letzi, letzi kos,	Here flies, here flies a blackbird,
A tu . . . nos.	A tu . . . nos.	And here is . . . your nose.

"In the second rhyme the mom imitates a centipede, her fingers are 'walking' on the kid's body and then she grabs the kid's leg. When the mom mentions a boy, a horse and a cow, her fingers 'jump' on the kid in the manner that a boy, a horse and a cow would. She grabs his finger, his palm and then his head. In the end a blackbird is flying by and mom gently strokes the kid and then grabs his nose."

The Baltic Sea

Lithuania

Kaliningrad Oblast (Russia)

Russia

Minsk

Zabludow

Belarus

• Warsaw

Retchitza

• Lodz

Luginy

Poland

• Korosten

Lublin

• Kiev

Sosnowiec

Shepetivka

• Berdechev

• Lviv

Ukraine

Slovakia

• Shargorod

Chernowitz

Hungary

Romania

Moldova

CHAPTER EIGHT
YIDDISH AND EASTERN EUROPE

HUSBAND OF THE TUESDAY DOCTOR

"You're the husband of the Tuesday doctor," said Naomi Bell. "I've never been sick on Tuesday, so I haven't met her." It was funny to think that my wife, who worked a Tuesday clinic at the Terraces of Baycrest Retirement Residence, was known to many people simply by her function, and the day of the week on which she performed that function.

I met Naomi early in the summer of 2016. Seven years ago I'd interviewed Chana Fish and Fela Karmiol, two other elderly residents at Baycrest. Over the course of the intervening seven years, both of them had died. There were things about the Yiddish language rhymes and songs they'd taught me that I wanted to clarify and Sofie Shleifer, a secretary who worked at the health centre, offered to connect me with other residents – those who were still knowledgeable in Yiddish – who might be able to help me.

In 1939 there were about eleven million Yiddish speakers, living mostly in Eastern Europe. Today, because of the Holocaust, there are only three million, and of those, it's a first language for a very small minority, most of whom live in Israel or the United States.

Naomi and I watched the camera films I'd taken of Chana and Fela. It was hard for her to make out what they were saying because she grew up speaking a different variety of Yiddish. "My father was a snob, and he raised me to be a snob, too. We spoke a pure form of Yiddish at home,"

Naomi laughed.

She listened to Chana Fish's song about the rabbi and the shiksa with a look of shock, and started laughing. "That doesn't sound like a folk song to me! I bet it came from the Yiddish theatre." She herself used to collect Yiddish songs and she donated her collection to the University of Toronto when she moved into Baycrest.

"Toronto used to have Yiddish theatre, shows – everything – there were people from all over the Yiddish speaking world."

I told her about Isaac Bashevis Singer's memoir *Love and Exile,* where he described eating in a restaurant on Spadina Avenue in the mid 1930s. It's quite possible that he was describing a scene at the United Bakers dairy restaurant – formerly at 338 Spadina Avenue, which moved to Lawrence Plaza (at Bathurst and Lawrence) in the 1980s. It still exists today, run by the fourth generation of the same family, the Ladovskys.

This place was a Canadian version of the Warsaw Writers' Club. Its patrons engaged in the same kind of conversations one always hears among Yiddishists: Could literature ignore social problems? Could writers retreat to ivory towers and avoid the struggle for justice? I didn't have to listen to their talk – their faces, voices, and intonations told me what each of them was: a Communist, a Left Poalei Zionist, or a Bundist. Hardly anyone here spoke with a Litvak accent. These were boys and girls from Staszow, Lublin, Radom, each one hypnotized by some social cause. I could tell from the way they pronounced certain words from which bank of the Vistula the speaker came, the left or the right. I imagined that even their gestures had unique meanings.

Singer is describing here the nuances of the language, all the way down to hand gestures, that Naomi's father would have encountered in concentrated form in Toronto at exactly the same time.

Naomi decided that she didn't know enough to help me clarify the earlier research, but she suggested that I talk to Shirley Kumove, who lived across the hall. "We were born at Mount Sinai Hospital on the same day in 1931, and our mothers shared a room. So we're like twins. Shirley's an expert – she can help you more than I can."

Before I left, Naomi gave me a manuscript copy of her father's memoir. He had spoken into a tape recorder, in Yiddish, which she had listened to, translated into English and typed out.

"He was a teacher and speaker of *reine* Yiddish – literary Yiddish," said Naomi. She encouraged me to read the first part, if I had time for nothing else, because she thought I might enjoy reading about shtetl superstitions, which she found fascinating.

THE INVISIBLE BABY

Ziscind Socol, the father of Naomi Bell, grew up in the village of Yablenke – in Polish, *Jablonka* – but which of Poland's ten Jablonka townships it was, I'm not sure.

Reading the first part of his autobiography, which Naomi entitled *My Father's Voice*, it really was fascinating to see how much the magical world, with its good and bad spirits, was woven into the lives of people in the shtetl. The first few chapters have titles like "Wrestling with the Evil Eye" and "The Haunted Bathhouse."

The following is an excerpt from "The Haunted Bathhouse," which I'm including here because of the strange, sweet connection Ziscind describes between a group of praying boys, and an invisible baby and its mother:

It was the custom in our shtetl to take Talmud Toyreh boys to recite the KRYAS SH'MA (the Sh'ma and accompanying blessings) at the homes of newborn infants. The custom arose because in those days many children died at birth, or after only a few weeks or months of life. It was believed that this was the work of devils and evil spirits who came to steal children away, and the kheyder boys' prayers were believed to offer protection from the Evil Eye.

I vividly recall the first time I was brought to the house of a KIM-PETORN, a woman who had just given birth, and discovered that she and her baby were hidden by a curtain made of sheets. (Since most of the houses in our shtetl consisted of only one large room, it was common practice to curtain off parts of that room to create private alcoves.)

Pinned to the sheets were SHIR HAMAALOS'N, small sheets of paper containing passages from the Psalms as well as selected incantations. These bits of paper were supposed to act as charms to keep the Evil Eye away. The SHIR HAMAALOS'N were also stuffed under the sheets and hung on the walls surrounding the bed, because it was believed this would give the baby further protection.

We would stand in front of the curtain and recite Kryas Sh'ma for the first week of the invisible baby's life. As a reward we would be given some nasheray (treat), usually chickpeas, but sometimes a cookie or sweet which we really enjoyed. Praying for the newborn was not such a bad thing – it was a diversion for the Talmud Toyreh boys, and relieved the monotony of studying. Once in a while the new mother would peek out at us from behind the curtain, and that always cheered us up.

The sweetness of this memory stuck with me for a long time after I read it.

Back at Baycrest, following Naomi's advice, I went back down to the nurse's station, to ask Sofie if she could put me in touch with Shirley Kumove. She did, but before we turn to Shirley, we must travel back to 2009, and my meetings with Chana Fish and Fela Karmiol.

NO ONE HERE REMEMBERS THEIR PHONE
NUMBER, BUT GOD CAN STILL FIND US

I interviewed Mrs. Chana Fish on a bench outside of the Terraces of Baycrest late in the summer of 2009. She was waiting for a shuttle to take her to Yorkdale mall, but since the shuttles came every ten minutes and she wasn't in a rush, she was willing to spend a little time with me while I questioned her about the Yiddish language children's games she'd played back in the 1920s and '30s in Poland.

A grounds worker kept walking around us using a loud, dusty leaf blower, so several times we had to stop, or start over, as she told me about her life.

Chana was born in Sosnowiec, Poland, around 1917. For readers familiar with Art Spiegelman's *Maus*, Sosnowiec is where Spiegelman's parents lived just before the Second World War, and where they hid for a time before they were captured.

Chana's father was fifteen when her parents got married, and her mother was nineteen. "To get a job, if you were poor, you had to agree to marry someone – my father was a shoichet [shochet] – he asked the owner of the slaughterhouse for a job, and the owner said, 'You marry my sister, I'll give you a job' – that's how my parents got together . . ."

She was the second of ten children. She helped her mother look after her eight younger siblings, and so she remembered the many games and songs she had learned to entertain and soothe them.

Over the next twenty minutes, Chana showed me a few of the ones she remembered. "I never taught them to my own children because at first, we were just running, trying to survive. After the war, we were in Israel, trying to learn a new language. After that, we were in Canada. Again we were trying to immerse ourselves in another language. There was no use anymore for Yiddish."

It gave me an odd feeling, knowing that these rhymes and games she was showing me on the bench outside of Baycrest she was bringing to life for the first time in seventy years – emerging from memories that predated the birth of my own mother.

Sosnowiec, close to the German border, was invaded in the very first days of the war. Hearing the guns come close, Chana, her husband and infant son ran away, staying just ahead of the Nazi onslaught. Eventually they ended up in Uzbekistan.

Back in Sosnowiec, her parents and all nine of her siblings were murdered.
This was the first rhyme game Chana showed me:
When rocking a baby, or bouncing baby on your legs, or clapping:

Olets Olets Kinderlach
Kozaman into jung
Weil fur vom dem sommer bis dem winter
Is a kaltz gesplian.

As I'll explain below, this was actually:

Hulyet hulyet kinderlach
Kolsman ir sent noch ying
Wayl fun friling bis tsum
Winter is a katsenshpring.

Chana translated this as:

Dance dance little one
As long as you're young!
Life is short, from the summer
To the winter you spring!

She explained, "You jump the child up at the end, on the word *spring*."
Next, Chana taught me this:

Zok choin kinderlach
Tirech kinderlach
Voos da rab sagt
Sagt cha nachaman
Intakya nachamoor
Kometz alafoo.

She translated this as:

Say to your children
What the rabbi said
Tell me once more
And tell me once more
The shape of the alef.

You drew the alef (or aleph) on the child's hand with your finger – see image below.

Partway through, Chana remembered something else she wanted to tell me. She said, "In Uzbekistan, there wasn't much food. I was in the market one day, and saw a man was selling a turtle. I knew Jews shouldn't eat turtles, but we were hungry – I had two children by then. I asked the man how to cook it. He said – 'First, you trick it into sticking its head out with a piece of grass. Then, quickly, cut its throat. When it sticks out its legs, it's dead. Serrate it under the shell with a knife, and then crack the shell with a hammer. Cook."

I could see, all these years later, that she was pleased at this memory of her own resourcefulness. She seemed to be thinking, "In a pinch, I could still cook a turtle."

I thought of Chana at the Yorkdale mall, thinking this. And then thought of all the other survivors of horrors from all over the world, thinking thoughts like this, as they moved through the world.

She then taught me a lullaby, to put a child to sleep:

Shlof ay mein kind	Sleep my child
Ay loo loo loo	Ay loo loo loo loo
Schlofen	Mama will buy the shoes

Die Mama koifen scheechelah	Papa will buy the socks
De Tata koifen zekalech	The child will wear shoes and
Das kind van tragen Shehech und	socks.[4]
die Zehalech	

She also remembered a song a mother would sing to her son before his bar mitzvah:

A boy went to the cheder
And he readies himself to be bar mitzvahed at the age of
   thirteen
After came a matchmaker
Who made him see a girl
He became engaged
The mother, when she took him to the synagogue
Saw him singing on the way
A chuppa! Order a wedding!
And after the wedding,

Time passed away
And he got old
And it's not too far

Life is like a dark night
Life is short, a dream
Shaking from nervousness
Now is a small kid

---

4. Translation by Shirley Kumove, who says: "This is a variation of an old familiar lullaby and should read:
     Shlof ayn mayn kind
     Ay loo loo loo loo
     Di mame vet koyfn shikhelekh
     Der tate vet koyfn zekelekh
     Dos kind vet trogn shikhelekh un zekelekh."

Moishele is in the cheder
So fast . . .
And now he waits for his grave
And now he's in the cemetery.

Near the end she suggested that I take her phone number in case there
was anything I wanted to check back about later. After giving me the final
four numbers, she said, "Those might actually be in reverse order – I don't
know. Could be this way, could be that way – no one here remembers their
phone number, but God can still find us . . ."

She laughed, then waved goodbye as she boarded the next shuttle to Yorkdale.

IN THE GRAVE WE'LL BE SEPARATE, BUT AT LEAST I'LL SLEEP ALONE

Fela Karmiol was born in Łódź, Poland. I met with her in her room at
Baycrest shortly after I met with Chana Fish. She was full of enthusiasm –
extremely expressive with her hands and eyes as she told me her story.

When the Germans invaded in 1939, Fela fled with her husband and
four-month-old baby to Russia. For two years they lived in Stalingrad (now
Volgograd), before having to flee again, this time to Siberia. She said there
were times that hundreds of people just slept in fields, out in the open – no
blankets, no toilets, no food, no water – nothing.

At a certain point, she realized that to save her son, she would have to
steal from others. Her husband wouldn't do it; he felt it was wrong. She
said, "You don't look at me, and I won't look at you." It became easier when
her husband joined the army, she said – then she didn't have to worry
about his disapproval.

"Life gave us lots to do – life taught us," she said, "if you stay in one
place, you learn nothing. Maybe it's better to learn nothing . . ." It sounded
more like a question than a statement.

Fela taught me this:

Ay gazintel zalba acht
In betten nur zwei
Es gib die nacht
Wie shclofen um zwei?
Trei mit den Taten
Trei mit dem Mama
Handlich und facelach geflochten
    zuzammen
Sag du Mama – Och, doch
    anke unteiten basinde
Enk is emlave, doch schlafe
    besande.

They had six children,
And they are two
That's eight!
Hands and face and legs twisted
    together
The mother said
In the grave we'd be separate
Tight is the grave,
But at least I'll sleep alone!

Fela also remembered this song:

An orphan is walking
He saw the sun shining so beautifully
How can you shine so beautifully
When I'm in tears?
This is all I can do
I have to do as I am made to do.

She tried also to recall a song she liked about a boy who speaks to a cloud, and the cloud is meant to be a letter to his mother, but she couldn't remember it.

Then, another song, which she sang with relish – smiling and laughing at it:

In a small village lives a rabbi with a son
Very orthodox!
Somebody called to tell him his son was with a shiksa
Between the trees

And the father was angry
He took a cane
To beat his son
But the son saw him
So he ran away

The father took the shiksa home
The religious people were angry
She'll make things unkosher!
She cooks, cleans
Soon people came to ask questions
She answered one hundred per cent
They were happy
She was smart,
She can stay with our rabbi!

This "Shiksa" song was all about challenging the norms – literally challenging the Orthodoxy. Sometimes songs and rhymes are written to put power in perspective, whether that power is exerted through religious or financial control. Robert Burns in Scotland did the same, in songs like "A Man's a Man for A' That." Here's a single verse:

Ye see yon birkie, ca'd a lord, [birkie: fellow]
Wha struts, an' stares, an' a' that;
Tho' hundreds worship at his word,
He's but a coof for a' that: [coof: dolt]
For a' that, an' a' that,
His ribband, star, an' a' that:
The man o' independent mind
He looks an' laughs at a' that.

TSEEP, TSEEP, HEMERL

Finf finger in eyn hant un zaynen oykh nit glaykh.
Five fingers on one hand, and each one is different.
[Referring to the differences of siblings.]
– Shirley Kumove, *Words like Arrows*

And now, let's turn to Shirley Kumove, whom Sofie Shleifer so kindly put me in touch with.

I badly needed Shirley's help. Not just with the video clips of Chana Fish and Fela Karmiol, but also with a little Yiddish rhyme I referred to as "Tseep Tseep," taught to me years earlier by a young woman named Amy, whom I met in a high school German class in Dundas, Ontario, back in 1984. There was no one present from the future to tell us that we would get married thirteen years later, and go on to have three children.

In 2002, when our little Sophie was a year old, I saw Amy act out this Yiddish children's rhyme for the first time. It had been taught to her thirty years earlier by her zaeda (grandfather) Harry Freedman. Harry Freedman was born in Luginy, in the Ukraine, in 1905. Later he lived in nearby Korosten. He came to Toronto in the early 1920s, after the Russian Civil War, and ran a ladies' wear store in Brantford, Ontario, for most of his life.

Amy and her zaeda were close. He liked children. And she always remembered this little Yiddish tickling rhyme he played with her, though she had no idea what the words meant. Although I say that Amy's zaeda was from the Ukraine, I should point out something important, in Amy's own words: "They were not Ukrainian! They never described themselves as Ukrainian – yes, they lived in what's now called the Ukraine, but they called themselves 'Russian Jews.'" When I say that Amy's zaeda was a Ukrainian Jew, it drives her around the bend. Also, when I say her bubbi was from Moldova – the Transnistrian part of modern Moldova – it does the same thing.

Amy has nothing against Ukrainians. Or Moldovans. Or Transnistrians. It just seems silly (even tedious?) to her that I describe her grandparents in a way that they would never have described themselves.

Jews who were born in, what was then, the Russian empire described themselves as Russian Jews, wherever in that huge empire they happened to live. If you were Jewish and born in exactly the same place Amy's zaeda was born (Luginy) after 1990, you would (or probably would) describe yourself as a Ukrainian Jew. So Amy is right to be driven crazy by me – I'm being anachronistic. Is that the right word? Maybe I'm just being irritating.

Anyway, Shirley came down to the nursing station, and asked what I needed. We sat side by side while I showed her the rhyme, written out in its transliterated form.

I questioned Shirley, and she chanted it out loud as she figured out how to write it down. While Shirley was chanting, Michael Noer, a nurse who works in the clinic, was walking past. He came right over and finished the lines out loud, adding two final lines that weren't part of Amy's memory of the rhyme.

"How do you know it?" I asked in surprise.

"How do I know it? I was raised on my father's lap, of course I know it!"

It turned out that Amy didn't know the whole thing. Either her zaeda had forgotten the rest, or he'd modified it, or she herself had only remembered the first part. As it happened, Michael's father came from a city that wasn't far from Korosten – a place called Shargorod.

Michael himself came from Berdichev, even closer, one hundred and thirty kilometres or so from where Amy's zaeda grew up. He said many of the Jews in his town survived the war because it was controlled by Romanians, who would ignore orders to murder them if they bought the soldiers off with chickens and other produce. This meant that he had a large number of older relatives after the war, which was very unusual. So Michael learned a lot from his parents and aunts and uncles, including Yiddish rhymes and children's games.

Next, Sofie Shleifer joined in. It turned out she also knew it.

Sofie's family also came from a city that wasn't that far away. She herself grew up in Chernowitz, but her grandmother, who taught her the rhyme, came from Shepetivka, close to where Amy and Michael's families came from.

"*Kemerl* is from the Ukrainian word *kamorka* – means room where you store things, like a shed, where you keep supplies," said Sofie.

"What are you talking about? That's crazy – *kemerl* is Yiddish, don't you know your Yiddish?" responded Shirley.

Sofie addressed me, bypassing Shirley. "Trust me, it's a Ukrainian word – *kamorka*."

Shirley turned to me, too, and shook her head. "No, it's not. It's Yiddish."

I did a little reading on the word and came up with a theory of my own. *Kammer* is a German word meaning little room, a cognate of the English word *chamber*. You can see the common root at once. German *kammer* to Yiddish *kemer* is the change of a vowel sound. That the word *kammer* would travel into Ukrainian as *kamorka* to describe a shed, or equipment room, doesn't seem like a big stretch.

In any case, this is the rhyme!:

[P-P-P-P – pretend or real spitting in palm. This was apparently a custom to help avert the influence of the evil eye. It was frequently done in the old days, in some areas, can be done before the "Saroka Varonka" rhyme, too.]

Tsipe, tsipe, hemerl	Tap tap [or bird sound – cheep cheep],
Kum tsu mir in kemerl	little hammer
Ikh vel dire pes vayzn	come to me in the little room
A shisele mit ayzn.	I have something to show you –
	a bowl full of ice! [iron]

I couldn't resist sending all of this information to my friend the writer Michael Joseph, who's also a librarian at Rutgers University. Michael sent it to his friend Hanita Wish, another expert in Yiddish language and folklore.

Hanita responded:

"To the best of my knowledge, *ayzn* is iron, not ice. Ice is *ayz*, but I don't believe it has any other (plural) form. And while I suppose *hemerel* could be a little hammer, I believe that the usual translation would be *gavel* (which I suppose is a little hammer), and I'm not sure why *tsipe* is translated as *tap*."

Michael Noer said the rhyme was about a little chicken – it's done as if you were speaking to a little chicken. The "little hammer" refers to the chicken's beak, tapping at the ground.

In Michael's version, there's no spitting on the palm – instead, you pinch the back of the hand when you say "Tsipe Tsipe." In Amy's version, she remembered it more as "tseep tseep."

We thought Michael Noer knowing and adding those extra lines was an amazing piece of luck, but there was more to come.

A FEW WEEKS LATER

Never generalize. The world beyond the mind consists of nothing but exceptions.
– Steven Heighton, *Workbook*

Shirley sent me an email. She said she had something important to show me, related to "Tseep Tseep." But she couldn't just tell me, I had to see it with my own eyes. So I went back to Baycrest again for another conversation about this strange little rhyme.

As we sat in her apartment, her husband returned, steadying himself with a walker. I stood up to introduce myself and to shake his hand.

Shirley said, "Aryeh, this is JonArno Lawson. He's doing research on Yiddish culture."

Aryeh shook my hand and smiled at me. "Come here," he said, beckoning me over to the windows. "I want you to come where it's light so I can really see you."

Shirley explained, "Aryeh pretends he can see, but he has macular degeneration – he can't really see you."

Aryeh used his walker and I walked by his side over to a window. He reached out and gently took my arm and turned me, tipping his own head back, so he could look right into my eyes. He smiled again. "Now I can picture you," he said. "I've burned your image into my memory." He tapped the side of his head to indicate where he'd burnt my image, and went off to work in another room. They were a sweet couple.

Shirley beckoned me back over, so I went and sat by her again.

"You won't believe this when you see it," she said.

She handed me a very old photograph – probably a hundred years old. It showed a handsome dark-haired man in a studio portrait, dressed in a South African uniform, his arm resting on a South African sun helmet placed on a table by his side. On the back of the photograph was written in Yiddish:

Tsip, tsap, hemerl	Tip, Tap, little hammer
kum tsu mir in kemerl	Come to me in my room
ikh vel dir epes vayzn	I will show you something
shiselekh mit ayzn.	Little bowls made of iron [though there's a play on the word for ice, here]
shir in di krigelekh	
kinder in di vigelekh	Dregs in the little jugs
shrayen vi di tsigelekh	Children in the cradles
meh . . . meh . . . meh . . .	Bleating like the kid goats
	Meh . . . meh . . . meh . . .

"Where did you get this?" I asked.

There it was – with an entire extra verse!

As it turned out, another resident at Baycrest's Apotex Centre, named Yankl Gladstone had heard the discussions about "Tseep Tseep," and he'd suddenly remembered an old family photograph with that very rhyme written on the back. Yankl had no idea who the relative was, or where and when the picture might have been taken.

Yankl remembered this song being used in Zabłudów, Poland, when he was a boy in the early 1930s, when his uncle (his mother's brother) was married. Zabłudów had a famous synagogue, built in the 1630s entirely out of wood, without any nails, because the builders said iron was an instrument of war. It was burned down by the invading Germans in 1941.

Yankl said the wedding ceremony was held outside the synagogue. The whole community went. The bride was walked to the courtyard of the synagogue by her parents, holding candles. There was klezmer music after, where they had special wedding songs and dances, and this was one of them.

As a last note, Yankl founded a musical theatre group at Baycrest to sing some of these old songs. He said, "The members keep dying, but we go on. It's good to remember the songs our mothers taught us when we were children. It honours their memories, and reminds us of them, which is a comfort to us."

I finally found a full text of the poem in a book called *Voices of a People: The Story of Yiddish Folksong*, by Ruth Rubin.

Hey, hey, hemerl,	Hey, hey, little hammer,
Kum tsu mir in kemerl!	Come to me in my little room!
Ch'vel dir epes vayzn,	I will show you something,
Shiselech mit rayzn,	Little bowls of rice,
Shiselech mit loyter gold,	Little bowls of pure gold,
Chosn-kale hobn zich holt.	Groom and bride love each other.
A por ferd yogn zich,	A pair of horses are racing,
Mechutonim shlogn zich,	In-laws are fighting,
Redele dreyt zich,	The little ring is turning,
Un chosn-kale freyt zich.	And groom and bride are happy.
Tsimbl, bimbl, tu a klung,	Tsimbl, bimbl, let it ring,
Chosn-kale, tu a shprung!	Groom and bride, take a jump!

And there was even the reference to a wedding at the end! Which fit nicely with Yankl's memory. Zabłudów is a good five hundred kilometres away from Korosten, and likely there were many versions of the poem if it travelled that far, and was remembered by so many different people seventy years after Yiddish stopped being actively used by the larger Jewish community.

This poem, in Rubin's book, seemed to be the last word on it [though it wasn't the last word on the journey of this rhyme through Amy's family, see Appendix 2]. Shirley pointed out that this finally explained the strange iron/ice problem – rice made much more sense – it must have been misheard at some point, or playfully re-rhymed, and the innovation spread.

Shirley Kumove also identified the source of Chana Fish's bouncing song: "This is a verse from a very famous Yiddish song which everyone knew. It was the last song we sang at our wedding." She produced the little booklet of songs that had been sung at her and Aryeh's wedding in 1949. "It was written by a very famous songwriter – Mordechai Gebirtig. The song is from the perspective of an old man missing his youth. Everyone knew this song. The interesting thing is that Chana took a single verse of it, and used it as a song to bounce a baby. It works! But I've never heard of it used that way before."

קינדערלעך הוליעט הוליעט
יונג נאָך זענט איר זמן כל
ווינטער צום ביז פֿרילינג פֿון ווייל
קאַצנשפרונג אַ איז
	Hulyet hulyet
	  kinderlach
	Kolsman ir sent noch
	  ying
	Wayl fun friling bis
	  tsum Winter
	is a katsenshpring.
		Rejoice, rejoice, children,
		As long as you are young
		Because from spring to
		  winter
		There's only an instant.

Shirley learned the next two as a small child from her parents (Tzvi Meyer and Rivka Reft), who grew up, like Fela Karmiol, in Łódź, Poland. She did it with her own children, and does it still today with her grandchildren.

Finger game: [start from baby finger]

Eygele	Little eye
meygele	little belly
keygele	[Translation unknown for this line
greygele	– possibly just nonsense]
yaykhele	[Translation unknown for this line
hum, hum, hum [Scratch the palm	– possibly just nonsense]
of the hand]	a little delicacy
	hum, hum, hum [Scratch the palm
	of the hand]
	[Tickle up and under the arm.]

Lullaby:

Patchi, patchi, kikhelekh	Pat-a-cake, pat-a-cake
tate vet koyfn shikhelek	Daddy will buy the little shoes
mame vet shtrikn zekelekh	Mama will knit the little socks
far di kleyne kinderlekh.	For the little children.

I ran Fela Karmiol's poem about the overly large family and their complicated sleeping arrangements by Shirley. Fela had it memorized – she had no idea how old it was or who had written it. Shirley didn't recognize it, but she was able to figure out some of the problems with my transliteration by referring to Fela's accompanying translation. Using her corrections, I was finally able to discover the source.

It was written by the Yiddishist Avrom Reyzen [Abraham Reisen], who came from Koidanov, Belorussia (now Dzyarzhynsk, Belarus). The poem is called "A Gezind Zalbe Akht" and was written in Warsaw in 1899.

Shirley also said that the song Fela sang about the rabbi and the shiksa was a Yiddish theatre song meant to tease the Orthodox. She could remember hearing it as a young woman in a theatre hall in Toronto, but she said it was the sort of thing no one would have recorded – it was too controversial. But for young people who were trying to break free of religious and old country traditions, it was a breath of fresh air, which might be why both Fela Karmiol and Chana Fish had it memorized, and could still sing it seventy years later.

Before I left, Shirley, finding out I was a writer, asked me what my best-known book was.

I said, "It's called *Sidewalk Flowers*, but it's wordless."

She laughed and said, "Isn't that the way! But what's worthless to you may have value to others."

Mishearing *wordless* as *worthless*, Shirley had made an almost perfect, though unintentional, homonymic pun. Which allowed her to make a wise – and to me very useful – response. It was humbling. It was what I should have said myself, so I didn't correct her.

CHAPTER NINE

EASTERN SCOTLAND

SCOTTISH NEW YEAR

The braw broun cou	The fine brown cow
Hes a cauf ti loue	Has a calf that lows
She gies it a kis wi hir mukkil mou.	She gives it a kiss with her great big mouth.

– Lallans rhyme for bairns (children)

First Foot

We can shape wir bairn's wyliecoat but canna shape thair weird.	We can shape our children's clothes but not their fate.

– Lallans proverb

The term *first foot*, in Lowland Scotland, could mean either a child's first step, or the tradition connected to how a New Year must be started.

It literally means, the first foot to cross the threshold on New Year's Day. It's one of the only Scottish customs my family continued to follow until my grandmother died, in 2001, nearly a hundred years after her parents left Scotland.

I only met my great-grandmother (Janet Lonie Robertson Wright Glen) once, or twice – there was a lot of estrangement on the Scottish side of our family. I know I once sat on her lap in Gore Park, in the middle of downtown Hamilton. This is where she liked to spend her time when she was an old lady. She was apparently very proud to have a former lady's maid as her frequent bench companion. She herself had started out as a char girl (a much lower position as a servant) in Cupar, Scotland, back in the 1890s.

It seems amazing to me now that my hand touched her hand, which had been touched by the hands of her own grandmothers, who were poor nineteenth-century Scottish women in Fifeshire towns. She had clear memories, I'm told, of one of these grandmothers smoking a corncob pipe behind a kitchen door in Cupar, sometime in the 1890s. I'm no more able to imagine their lives than they would have been able to imagine mine – and yet we were only as far away from each other as the touch of one hand.

My great-grandmother was also very proud of being Scottish. My grandmother remembered her mother saying, "Remember, Biddy, you're a Scot." And my grandmother remembered shouting back, "I'm not Scottish, I'm Canadian!" which made her mother angry.

The form of English she spoke as a young woman is called Lallans – it's comprehensible to a speaker of what we call standard English, but only just. The accent, and different vocabulary, can make it very difficult to make sense of without effort.

National history is formed out of the collective histories of thousands or millions of individual histories. A national narrative, or mythology, then becomes common to all. But that national narrative may not, in turn, coincide – it may even conflict – with many of the personal stories.

It's easy, as an Anglo-Canadian – a WASP – to ignore or forget about differences in your own background. I was aware of the varied national groups in my ancestry before I got married, but it was really because of Amy's strong Jewish identity that I got interested in religious, national and cultural differences in my own family's background. Amy had a strong sense of where she came from, but I didn't, and this made me look with greater interest at my roots.

For instance, I remembered at the funeral of my grandfather – who was half Irish, ancestrally – that his brother told us jokes and acted quite happy. He did what he remembered being done at family funerals when he was growing up, following the customs of Irish wakes. I found his good humour strange, though not unwelcome, but my grandmother – from her more severe Scottish background – clearly found it offensive.

Often people will say "I'm from a Scots/Irish background," but there are in fact a lot of differences, culturally, between the Scots and the Irish. Once I started thinking about this, it helped to make sense of some of the stresses in our family, as well.

In any case – First Foot.

A dark-haired man (fair-haired men were considered bad luck) had to throw his hat and a silver coin through the door on New Year's morning; otherwise no one could leave the house. I was the darkest haired man in our family, and so once I was twelve or so, this became my job. I remember it made me feel important. It was a serious business for my grandmother. She claimed not to be a Scot, but there was nothing Canadian about this.

I read up on it recently, to figure out the logic problem of the dark-haired men having to leave their houses without being released by other dark-haired men, and found out that many Scots got around this by having the dark-haired man leave the house just before midnight, and throwing the hat and money in right after the New Year started.

I haven't done this for fifteen years, but now writing about it, and thinking about it again, I'm going to have my children take it over this New Year's Eve.

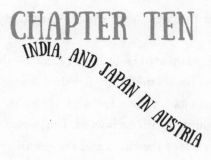

CHAPTER TEN
INDIA, AND JAPAN IN AUSTRIA

CHOO CHOO CHANDUNGA

വിരൽ വപ്പൊാനിടം
കൊടുത്താൽ പിന്നവിടെ ഉരൽ
വക്കും-

– Malayalam proverb

Give a clown your finger and he will take your whole hand.

Anushka Ravishankar has often been described as the Dr. Seuss of India. Trained as an IT specialist, she later became a writer and editor, and then, in 2012 she founded Duckbill Publishing house with Sayoni Basu in Chennai. We've never met in person, but we've corresponded many times over the past decade, mostly about children's poetry and children's books. Once, she kindly helped me track down a book I was looking for that was only available in India.

Malayalam is one of India's twenty-two officially recognized languages. It's one of the four main Dravidian languages, closely related to Tamil, Telugu and Kannada. Dravidian languages are spoken by nearly forty million people.

I wrote to Anushka when I started working on this book, to see if she had any examples of children's rhymes and games that she might want to contribute.

She quickly wrote back:

"I asked my mum for some Malayalam rhymes, and she sent me a positive flood of them! I've translated three that were interesting in the variety of the activity accompanying them.

"They're recited in a dialect of Malayalam spoken in North Kerala – the versions of these same rhymes in South Kerala might be slightly different. The one directly below is recited before a game, to decide who will be 'it.' The players stand in a circle, and are counted with each word. The person who is pointed to at the last word goes out of the circle, and the counting starts again. The one left at the end is 'it.'

"Many of the words are nonsensical and made up for the rhyme or the homophonic quality. The poem itself is purely nonsense.

Aripoo tiripoo torani mangalam	Flower-shlower wedding pendants
Paripoo pandrandu aanim kudrim	Bower one dozen horses and ele-
Cherichittum vallachittum padi-	phants
naam vallikku	Listing, twisting the thirteenth
Endamboo?	creeper
Murikamboo!	What, Amboo?
Muriki chariki kedanolle	Bigbamboo!
Arani enna kudicholle	Eat up, have fun, go to sleep
Akkarikkarulla maado pravinde	Twenty-four bottles of oil, drink
Kayyo kaalo randalonnu	deep
Chethi kuthi madangatu.	The turtledove flying to and fro
	It's hands or legs – one of the two
	Chipchop chipchop, off you go!

"2. Sung while playing with the baby's toes. The big toes are held and tapped together while this is recited. At the last line the feet are gently thrown to one side.

Choo choo chundanga	Goo goo gooseberry fruit
Kuthi parikunna naranga	Pluck the thorny lemon fruit
Aarikku vennam naranga	Who wants the lemon fruit?
Achanu vennam naranga	Father wants the lemon fruit
Ammakku vennam naranga	Mother wants the lemon fruit
Mon nu vennam naranga!	Baby wants the lemon fruit!

"3. This is sung to scare the mango tree into giving up its mangoes! The children go round the tree holding a twig with a leaf, plucked from the tree. At the last line, the mango tree is supposed to let fall a mango.

Maavay maavay maavinde appan	Mango tree, mango tree, mango tree's papa
Baapu Kannan chathinnippol-lum	Baapu Kannan, has died, they say
Oru kola maangem	With one lot of mangoes
Oru kola thengem	And one lot of coconuts
Edayelu povinna kanyakuttide	The head of the little lady in the lane
Tala kettu odakennum polum!	Has to be bust, they say!

"4. And finally, here's something I used to play with my daughter when she was a little baby:

Appavum Chuttu
Adayum Chuttu
Achchandey veetil povumbol
Ivadey Kallu
Ivadey Mullu
Ivadey Kallu
Ivadey Mullu
Ivadey Kallu
Ivadey Mullu ...

"This is in Malayalam, and it translates very roughly (appams and adas are both somewhat like pancakes, but made of rice) to:

Baking pancakes
Baking cakes
On the way to Father's house
Here a stone
Here a thorn
Here a stone
Here a thorn
Here a stone
Here a thorn . . .

"Actions:

"During the first three lines, pat the baby's palm with your own.

"During the next lines, move up the baby's arm with the index and middle finger – moving one finger at each line (simulate walking, basically) until you reach the baby's armpit and tickle her (usually accompanied by silly noises!)."

KAMISHIBAI: FROM THE STREETS OF JAPAN TO AN AUSTRIAN CLASSROOM

In the spring of 2016 I came across a review of one of my books in an Austrian newspaper online. It was written by someone named Veronika Mayer-Miedl, and, through the magic of Google Translate, I could tell that what she'd written was positive and thoughtful.

I then googled her name to see if she was a children's book writer, too, and came across something even more interesting. She was a practitioner of something called kamishibai, a Japanese form of children's entertainment, which originated as a kind of street storytelling performance, using a small handmade theatre with painted boards for scene changes.

Some think this form of entertainment has its roots in a famous set of thirteenth-century scrolls from the Kozan-ji temple in Kyoto called the scrolls of frolicking animals. In the scrolls, a group of animals seem to be wrestling, chasing each other, participating in a funeral and, in the case of a solitary frog, praying to Buddha. I've only seen the images online, but these thirteenth-century animal drawings have as much energy and interest in them as anything done by Beatrix Potter or Arnold Lobel – they're quite modern looking, actually.

I found contact information for Veronika, and we had a great exchange of emails. There were many strange points of coincidence between our lives and families. In any case, I asked Veronika if she could tell me more about kamishibai – I had a feeling it was something I'd like to try doing myself. This was her response:

"About kamishibai: There is so much I could tell you, I don't know where to start . . .

"I'm almost sure there is no English translation of *Das Städtchen Drum-herum*, by Mira Lobe, though a few of Lobe's books appeared in English. The English title might be: *Little Town Around the Wood*.

"It was important for us (I tell/perform kamishibai with my friend and sister-in-law Alexandra Mayer-Pernkopf, who founded figurentheater [www.isipisi.at] together with another woman) to choose stories we like very much. *Das Städtchen Drumherum* was published in 1970, we knew it from our own childhoods, and it was always a favourite story for both of us.

"The plot is quite simple, very accessible to children ages five and up:

"A major wants to build more houses in the city, he wants the city to become bigger . . . and to reach this aim, his glorious master plan is to destroy the woods, all the plants and trees; he doesn't care about the animals living there.

"His children, Julius and Juliane (there is no mother in this story – it was the nineteen seventies, there's no word about her . . . she wasn't required ;-)), fight for the green area, they write big signs – for example,

'Attention, a robin is living here' or 'I am 100 years old, I want to become 1000' (a sign for the tree), 'Birds nest with eggs, careful, they might break' – and they put them up in the woods.

"In the meantime the animals are crying, and the little witch-ghost Frau Hullewulle, who has green hair, performs a spell on the major, and he dreams three horrific nightmares (two in our play): he dreams of himself as a rabbit, escaping from bulldozers; then as a bird whose tree with his nest full of eggs get destroyed; and in the end he dreams a beautiful dream of himself as a butterfly (flower power made in Austria – I love the seventies!), who enjoys living in the woods.

"After awakening he sees something new on his plans – the green leaves Frau Hullewulle brought with her when she flew into his bedroom. She has created a different picture: the green leaves are now at the middle of the blueprints, and the houses are arranged around it. And this gives him a new idea for how it could work: the houses should go *around* the woods. But the old plans are already fixed, the bulldozers will roll over everything and do their work. He hurries up in order to be present at the building site . . .

"When he reaches the wood he notices all the childrens' signs, birds are singing, butterflies and dragonflies sailing through the air . . . he feels a deep peace in his heart – and then, the bulldozers and excavators approach, and he suddenly stops them: The woods will stay untouched, the houses will be built around them and everybody is happy.

"We are mindful of using a Japanese form: concentrated, slow, mindful – not digital – we do all noises, singing, sounds with several instruments, afterwards the audience of children is invited to look behind the scenes and try to do the telling (and work the props) themselves.

"Children are the same all over the world, and it's wonderful to tell an Austrian story with kamishibai!

"We also lead workshops at the college of education to speak about the possibilities for pupils to put on kamishibai-stories themselves at school. And also, we do workshops for librarians who might also want to perform simple kamishibai-stories for children at the library.

"In Austria the kamishibai is used as a tool to impart picture books. The traditional Japanese kamishibai has no connection with books, but is done using special picture boards, which are also removed slowly, laterally, and deal also with the composition of the pictures (for example, a slope in the picture gets longer and longer while removing the board . . .)

"We take the pictures out of the books and edit them with Photoshop (my colleague does this work), and we pay sideshow rights to the publisher. You can see several details in the photos at www.isipisi.at.

"It is important for us to create all stage elements on our own. We do this so that it's easy to do also for children. We've worked, too, with a school class – they told fairy tales, drew their own pictures – and also with a group of children during last summer holidays in the library of Ottensheim."

After reading Veronika's account, and looking at the pictures she sent me of the little theatres she and her sister-in-law had made, I felt quite excited to try this out myself.

But before doing that, I asked her if she knew any German lap and finger rhymes she could share. It was quite a wonderful coincidence that she knew a German version of the bouncing lap rhymes that ignited my own childhood interest in the whole subject:

Hoppa Hoppa Reiter (Upper Austrian slang!)	**Hop-a, Hop-a, Rider!** (English translation)
Hoppa Hoppa Reita wenn er fällt, dann schreit a	Hop-a, Hop-a, Rider! if he falls, he screams
Fällt er in den Graben Fressen ihn die Raben	If he falls into the ditch the ravens will seize him
Fällt er in die Müllermücken die ihn hint' und vorne zwicken	If he falls among the Miller's mosquitoes they tweak him back and front

fällt er in den Sumpf,	he falls into the swamp,
dann macht der Reiter	the rider goes
PLUMPS!	PLOP !

"Especially funny are the Müllermücken – mosquitoes of the miller – who grinds cereals – it doesn't make sense, but who cares?!

"During this rhyme the child gets tickled and pinched softly on the back (hint' = backside) and on the belly (vorne = frontside).

"This was a classic from my childhood, which is played still today."

Standard German Version	**English translation:**
Hoppe, Hoppe, Reiter,	Hop, hop, rider,
Wenn er fällt, dann schreit er.	If he falls, he will cry.
Fällt er in die Hecken,	If he falls into the hedges,
Tut er sich erschrecken.	He will get frightened.
Fällt er in den Sumpf	If he falls into the mud,
Macht der Reiter plumps!	The rider falls with a splash!
Hoppe, hoppe, Reiter,	Hop, hop, rider,
Wenn er fällt, dann schreit er.	If he falls, he will cry.
Fällt er auf die Steine,	If he falls on the stone,
Tun ihm weh die Beine.	His leg will get hurt.
Fällt er in den Sumpf	If he falls into the mud,
Macht der Reiter plumps!	The rider falls with a splash!
Hoppe, hoppe, Reiter	Hop, hop, rider
Wenn er fällt, dann schreit er	If he falls, he will cry.
Fällt er in den Graben	If he falls into the ditch,
Fressen ihn die Raben	He will be eaten by the ravens.
Fällt er in den Sumpf	If he falls into the mud,
Macht der Reiter plumps!	The rider falls with a splash!

I happened to be editing a hard copy of this book on a flight from Toronto to Jibacoa, Cuba, when I got into a conversation with the woman sitting next to me, an Austrian university student named Hedwig Knötig, who grew up in Linz.

I had to ask her if anyone teased her about sharing her name with Harry Potter's owl. She said Hedwig is an unusual name, even in Austria (it means *battle-war*), and people hadn't teased her, but they had asked her if she was named after the owl. She said that clearly made no sense, since she was obviously born before the series had started.

I pointed out that I'd also interviewed someone with the name Aslan for this book. As a children's book writer, I wondered if this might be an occupational hazard? Hedwig laughed and said, "At least they're both positive characters!" Which was true. Better to meet up with Aslan and Hedwig than the White Witch (Jadis) or Tom Riddle.

In any case, Hedwig said that she knew an alternate version of two lines to the "Hoppe, Hoppe, Reiter" rhyme.

Instead of Vernonika's lines:

Fällt er in die Müllermücken
die ihn hint' und vorne zwicken

or the standard German:

Fällt er in die Hecken,
Tut er sich erschrecken.

she had learned:

| Fällt er in die Hecken, | If he falls into the hedges |
| Fressen ihn die Schnecken. | he will be eaten by snails |

And now, back to Veronika for one more!

"This is another my mother always played with us:

Steigt ein Büblein auf den Baum	Little boy climbs up the ladder to the tree
Hooooch! hinauf! man sieht es kaum.	Up high, you nearly see it!
Steigt von Ast zu Ästchen	Climbs from branch to branch
guckt ins Vogelnestchen.	Glances in the bird's nest
Ei! Da lacht es.	Egg! He laughs
Rums, da kracht es.	No! It crashes
PLUMPS	PLOP!
da liegt es unten.	There it lies.

"The mother crawls with her fingers up the child's arm, up to the head and plays in the hair:

"Vogelnestchen: then the hand (Büblein) falls down. But he is not injured and crawls or climbs up again, immediately!! (Nobody would say 'Büblein' in our days! the old words make something of the magic of these games . . .)

"It's a bit like 'Itsy Bitsy Spider'! I sang this one also in my playing groups in the library in English!"

Natalia Grayfer also provided this Ukrainian version of "Hoppe, Hoppe, Reiter," which is used as a bouncing rhyme:

Іхав, іхав пан, пан	The master, the master was riding,
На конику сам, сам	riding a horse.
А позаду Гриць, Гриць	And behind him Gritz, Gritz on
На конику гиць, гиць!	his horse hops, hops!

CHAPTER ELEVEN
MAURITIUS AND DOMESTIC MAGIC

SIRANDANES

I met Soraya Peerbaye at Athens Pastries on Danforth Avenue in To-ronto. She had generously promised to do some research on games people play with their children while she was back in Mauritius with her family for a trip during the winter.

Soraya Peerbaye is a brilliant, modest, highly sensitive poet with a personal (and professional) interest in dance, as well. Her first book, *Poems for the Advisory Committee on Antarctic Names,* is as good as its name, and her second, *Tell: Poems for a Girlhood,* which grew out of her interest in the circumstances surrounding the murder of Reena Virk, was nominated for the Griffin Poetry Prize. Later it won Ontario's Trillium Book Award for Poetry.

Soraya was born in London, Ontario, to parents originally from Mau-ritius, an island country in the Indian Ocean one thousand kilometres east of Madagascar, which is the closest large landmass. It's best known to those interested in natural history as the sole home of the now extinct dodo. Its population, of just over a million people, comes from Africa, In-dia, Europe and Asia – the country has a very mixed and rich multi-ethnic culture.

An email from Soraya shortly after she returned informed me that she hadn't found anything along the lines I'd told her I was hoping for, but she still had something she thought might interest me.

And so, when we met to talk, she showed me a little book called *Sirandanes*, which had been collected by J.M.G. and J. Le Clézio. The book was entirely in French, aside from the sirandanes themselves, which were in both Mauritian Creole and French translation.

Soraya opened the book and showed me (translating on the spot) some of her favourites.

As far as the form goes, they are all very short – just a few lines each. The first line is always a description followed by a question mark. The point of the question mark is to ask "What do you imagine I'm describing here?" The second line is always the answer, which is invariably a little offbeat and surprising.

But I wanted to understand from Soraya's perspective, from a Mauritian perspective – what are sirandanes?

"I don't know much about the social function of the sirandanes – I've been researching this, but have found information hard to come by. I didn't grow up with them myself, but I understand that in other families they were exchanged between child and parent, between adults, became familiar, cultural reference points. When I spoke about it with my dad, he knew them, was delighted by them, but hadn't grown up with them either. I forgot to ask him how he came across them – perhaps through friends?

"The exchange seems to me playful, informal. I don't know about the heavier undertones of race, Mauritius's colonial history. I wonder if that would be something to speak of with the people who are sharing with you rhymes and games from the African continent. It seems to me that there are a number of elements being taken for granted, which I imagine makes contemporary North American/European culture uncomfortable . . . one is Blackness and Whiteness . . . these identities, these differences . . . the other is violence . . . the presence of it . . . It's funny, the sirandanes don't seem to function as warnings, of power imbalances, of vulnerability . . . they just seem to accept certain things as a fact."

Soraya agreed to translate more of them for me, and in my eagerness to start understanding them (using my very poor French) I translated some,

162

too. I've indicated which of us translated each sirandane with our initials.

Why did I love them so much, straightaway? There's the simplicity, the surprise, the careful, concrete observations, the poetic conclusions, which are much more than just answers to riddles. You are being shown more than one thing at the same time – like psychologist Joseph Jastrow's duck-rabbit picture – your perspective shifts back and forth as you see one, and then the other.

And there is a sense that a great game is beginning in your own mind – that this is, potentially, a new way of seeing, or thinking about things. You can still feel the quiet but profound excitement of the person who first discovered and used this form. Something like the feeling you get reading Mulla Nasrudin tales, which are also full of strange, funny, quiet surprises.

And here, now, is a very small selection. The first is one of Soraya's favourites:

I Break the Coffin

Mo kas sekey, manz dimun mor?	Je casse le cercueil, je mange le mort?	I break the coffin, I eat the dead?
– Pistas	– La cacahuete	– Peanut [SP]

Two Beautiful Ponds

Mo ena de zuli basin, saken ena en lilo dan milye, lerb dan bor. Kan zot borde, wu truv so dilo dule dakenn so kote, me kanal ki donn sadilo, wu napa kapav truve?
– Lizie

J'ai deux jolis bassins, chacun a un ilot au milieu, et de l'herbe au bord. Quand ils debordent, vous voyez couler l'eau de chaque cote, mais le canal qui donne cette eau, vous ne pouvez le voir?
– Les yeux

I have two beautiful ponds, each has an island in the middle, and grass at the edge. When they are outside, you see the water run from each side, but the channel that gives this water, you cannot see it?
– The eyes [JL]

Put in a Straw

Mo basin li sek, met en lapay, liborde? – Lizie	Mon bassin est sec, mettez-y une paille, il deborde? – Les yeux	My pond is dry, put in a straw, it overflows? – The eyes [JL]

Never Turning Back

Mo mars dan en piti simin, zame mop u pose, zame mop u turne? – Larivier	Je marche sur un petit chemin, jamais je ne me reposerai, jamais je ne reviendrai en arriere? – La riviere	I walk a little path, never resting, never turning back? – The river [JL]

The Birds Who Come to Drink, Drown

Mo ena en basin, to zozo ki vinn bwar dadan noye? – Lalamp av papyon	J'ai un bassin, tous les oiseaux viennent y boire se noient? – La lampe et les papi-lons de nuit	I have a basin – all the birds who come to drink, drown? – The lamp and the moths [JL]

A Gold Drum

Tambur lor anba later? – Safran	Un tambour d'or sous la terre? – Le Safran	A gold drum under the earth? – Saffron

[I think they mean turmeric, which grows as rhizomes under the earth; saffron is generally the pistils of the crocus flower. SP]

164

A Ball of Blood

Bul disan anba later?	Une boule de sang	A ball of blood under
– Betrav	sous la terre?	the earth?
	– La betterave	– The beet [SP]

When the Black Grandmother Sings

| Kan gran manman nwar santé, tu piti blan dansé? | Quand le grand-maman noire chante, tous les petits Blancs dansent? | When the Black grandmother sings, all the little Whites dance? |
| – Marmit duri lao difé | – La marmite de riz sur le feu | – A pot of rice on the fire [SP] |

A Gate in the Corner of the Mountain

| En vann dan kwin montagn? | Une vanne dans un coin de montagne? | A gate in the corner of the mountain? |
| – Zorey | – L'oreille | – The ear. [Ahhhh ... SP] |

This last one might help to elucidate what it is that's so appealing about the sirandanes. They are like a small opening, an unexpected gate into something as enormous and monolithic as habitual thought.

Soraya sent me many more, but I'm hoping she'll do a book on them herself, and don't want to ruin that future book!

I was reminded of riddle exercises I did with children in poetry workshops. In fact, I found sirandanes described in one place as "a little quiz." I nearly always use a page of riddles Jamaican/English poet James Berry included in his book *When I Dance* as models for what I want students to try.

This is one of them. And its similarity to one of those above makes me wonder whether there was a West African original for both:

Riddle my this, riddle my that –
guess my riddle or perhaps not.
Little pools
Cluster in my father's yard
A speck in one and it overflows –
What is it?
– Somebody's eye
with dust in it.

Here's another:

Riddle my this, riddle my that –
Guess my riddle or perhaps not.
Rooms are full, hall is full, but
You can't use a spoonful –
What is it?
– Flames and smoke
of a house on fire.

This riddle exercise never fails to elicit amazing work. I'm surprised again and again by how much children love riddles. As a child I had no interest in them. The living oral culture of riddles is remarkable among children, down to this day – most of them still know the Sphinx riddle. When I told my own children about how surprising this was to me, they all produced riddles for me on the spot. They learn them from other children.

In any case, the sirandanes of Mauritius are something different again – related somehow to riddles, but not quite the same thing.

They're a quiz, but, from Soraya's understanding of them, a quiz that isn't meant to be solved – you are given the answer with the question. They're more of a contemplation exercise. An exercise in making the usual unusual. They conjure up odd, sometimes grotesque and upsetting contrasts. But sometimes not – sometimes it's a surprise that's meant to be savoured, and not just once, but over and over.

In some way they seem to provide the same slight jolt, or subtle (but definite) shift of attention, that emerges when engaging with other traditions of startling gnomic brevity, like landays, a form of Afghan women's oral poetry.

Come and be a flower on my chest
So that I can refresh you every morning with a burst of laughter.

Or:

At night the verandah is dark, the beds too numerous.
The tinkling of my bracelets will tell you where to go, my love.

As well as the vacanas written in India's Kannada language – this is an excerpt from one by Basavanna:

Does it matter how long
A rock soaks in the water:
Will it ever grow soft?

The editor of *Sirandanes* wrote the following in the introduction to the book: "Are they really riddles? They are, rather, keywords, allowing the memory to open and reveal a treasure."

To me they seem like an exciting avenue, a different kind of poetic form with which to re-explore everyday life.

GRABBING STEAM

Once, when JoJo was very small, he tried to grab the steam rising off a heap of hot pasta sitting in a sieve in the sink – he couldn't understand why it wouldn't stay in his hands. A few weeks later I saw him doing the same thing with the water streaming out of the tap into the tub – he tried, unsuccessfully, to hold onto it as it rushed through his fingers.

He looked more surprised and impressed than frustrated, as if he was encountering some kind of magic. And of course, if you slip outside of your habitual ways of experiencing things, you can see again that that's exactly what he was encountering.

CHAPTER TWELVE
THE PHILIPPINES AND TORONTO

EXTRA HELP

Ako ang nagbayo, ako ang nagsaing, saka ng maluto'y iba ang kumain.	I did the threshing, I did the cooking, but once served, someone else eats it.
Ang tunay na anyaya, sinasamahan ng hila.	A sincere invitation is accompanied by a pull of the hand.

– Tagalog proverbs

Even before our third child, Joseph, was born, we realized – after years of knocking people who relied on nannies – that we'd need extra help, and more specifically, and embarrassingly, the help of a nanny.

We found Amalia Tomangong through Craigslist – the family she was with didn't need her five days a week anymore. We called her up and made an appointment. She came over, and right away we could tell she was kind-hearted and easygoing, and most importantly, she was also smart. She would be a good fit. As soon as my wife, Amy, went back to work, she started to work with us two days a week. Being home at the same time – and wanting to be about and involved while she and the children got to know each other – I asked a lot of questions.

Straight off I found out that she was not from Luzon or Visayas, like most Filipinas in Toronto, but was instead a Manobo from a place near

Cotabato City, in Mindanao. This seemed like a great stroke of luck to me, though I wasn't sure why. Probably I was excited simply because Mindanao was a place I'd never heard of, and the Manobo were a people entirely unknown to me. Later I discovered that the Philippines is a multi-ethnic region with dozens of different nationalities and several hundred different languages.

There are currently only about twelve thousand speakers of the Manobo language. Amalia said that she rarely heard it used in daily life, the exception being certain Manobo prayers or chants that were used by older people at funerals.

Amalia had a university degree in economics. She'd been working, as well as going to school, since she was eight years old. Like many of the women who come to Canada as nannies from the Philippines, she had worked first in Hong Kong (where she became proficient in Cantonese), was university educated and multilingual.

She had also grown up in a rural area, without electricity or any of the machines electricity brings with it, and so she was full of fascinating stories. Her early life was, in many ways, not unlike that of my nineteenth-century farm-raised grandmother.

I never met my paternal grandmother as she was born in 1888, and grew up in Arlington, New York, outside Poughkeepsie, but my father told me she could whistle the calls of twenty different types of birds. When she died, they found several scrapbooks she'd made that were full of magazine and newspaper pictures of trees. She'd ended up on a bleak street in inner-city Albany, but at heart she was always a farm girl.

Amalia had also grown up with this kind of intimate connection to the natural world. Which inevitably meant closer contact with, and a different sense of, the supernatural world. She told me, one day, about a creature called the aswang – whose upper body separates from the rest of itself, allowing it to fly at night. According to her grandmother, one of their neighbours was an aswang. Her grandmother had seen the upper half of the neighbour's body stuck in a tree early one morning and the family had

had to come quickly before the sun rose to retrieve her. I wondered about the affect of the sun on the aswang, but Amalia said this wasn't the point. The sun wasn't dangerous to it; the family just didn't want anyone to see. For this reason Amalia's grandmother forbade her to interact with these neighbours anymore.

I could see my son Ashey listening to this with an indecipherable expression on his little face. I was tempted to cover his ears, but it seemed at this point that this was more likely to draw attention to what she was saying, and I didn't want to worry or insult her.

She told us also about the kapre (giant), the duwende (little people) and their front yard tree that had been jealous of suitors who came to see her pretty aunt. Her grandmother, using a mix of spells, as well as hotheaded speeches designed to shame the tree, had finally put a stop to the tree's sulky and aggressive behaviour.

I told her about my maternal grandmother's belief that our dog was her father reincarnated. She instantly understood this. My grandmother, who came from a Lowland Scottish background, had believed that her father had come to life again in our now-deceased standard poodle named Teddy. She fed him from her kitchen plates – the same meals her father had loved. Teddy enjoyed these meals – he liked meat and potatoes. And he looked at her, my grandmother claimed, with what could only have been her father's same sad, brown, deeply grateful eyes.

Personally, at the time, I believed Teddy was an opportunist when it came to my grandmother. I briefly searched for traces of reincarnation in his eyes, but all I saw was a manipulative poodle. I sensed that he knew it, too – he often looked guilty when I stared at him, and averted his gaze while wagging his tail slowly.

Nowadays, though, I wonder – why was I so quick to dismiss what my grandmother saw? Even if it was a misunderstanding on her part, it allowed her to feel close to her father again. It increased her sense of intimacy with the world around her. One of the most lethal side effects of over-rationalization has to be alienation. We can be so busy not believing something that we forget to imagine, and the power of what we might have drawn from that imagining is lost to us.

Skepticism may ground us, and that's great, but our feet should be firmly planted on the ground, not on our dreams, or on other people's beliefs.

Amalia also told me how she had once apologized to some trees in Toronto, near Steeles and Bathurst. I asked her why. She said that she and her friends had been laughing under them, having a picnic, but when they looked up they saw that the trees looked very serious, and they felt they'd disturbed and offended them. Though she didn't really believe, at a certain level, that the trees could understand her, she couldn't help feeling that it was safer to say something. To make things up to them, just in case.

For those growing up in monotheist traditions, it's worth remembering that Moses spoke to a burning bush, Jesus cursed a fig tree that didn't provide figs when he hoped it would and Muhammad once soothed a weeping date palm.

This reminded me also of something the Palestinian author Mourid Barghouti wrote about in his memoir *I was Born There, I was Born Here*: "The voice of the tree seduces me into listening to my voice, which is hidden at a depth of which I am aware only when I make it a written voice."

Shortly after Amalia told me the story of the trees, I was standing outside my children's school, waiting for the bell to ring. When Sophie joined me I shared the story about the trees at Steeles and Bathurst. Sophie wasn't surprised. In fact, Sophie had names for the trees we were standing under – Shake-a-mon and Branches, even expressing a preference for Shake-a-mon, who had a better personality.

It suddenly occurred to me that Sophie and Amalia shared what seemed to me to be a supernatural world. I understood it just a little, maybe, from reading Tolkien's books, and from C.S. Lewis, J.K. Rowling and Rick Riordan. Trees with agency, with a will of their own, aren't uncommon in children's books, when you think about it. In *Prince Caspian*, Lucy wanders through woods that have fallen silent, and remembers the voices of the trees: "She knew exactly how each of these trees would talk if only

172

she could wake them, and what sort of human form it would put on."

In biblical stories, important moments are often linked to oaks or other strong trees – Jesus, too, was a carpenter, and died nailed to a piece of timber.

I was even told a story once in Sunday school that the cross was made from dogwood, which used to be a large type of tree, but because of the dogwood's shame at its role in the crucifixion, it asked to be cursed so that it would never grow tall again. Jesus agreed, but he also gave it red flowers with four petals, shaped like a cross, and a centre like a crown of thorns, with dents in each petal resembling nail marks.

In any case, I was tempted to show Sophie and Amalia each other's trees, to see what they made of them.

Sophie also talked to the trunks and branches. But she pointed out that while you may ask them questions, "You never really get a straight answer from a tree."

One day, Amalia was telling me about a movie she'd seen that had touched her deeply. She said it was a true story. In the movie, the main character was so upset about the death of his son that he invented a clock that made time go backwards.

She was so sure the movie was based on a true story that I, too, started to feel it was possible. Trying to shake myself out of it, I questioned her: "You really believe that? That someone could build a clock like that?"

She was surprised that I was surprised. "If you were sad enough, you could build that kind of clock," she said.

When the writer Tahir Shah was in Toronto, he spoke about living so long among people in Morocco who believed in djinn that he started to behave as if he believed in them, as well. Skeptical though he was, he would address the djinn he had been told lived in the elbow drain under his sink, just to be safe.

My conversations with Amalia and with my children brought back suppressed magical, and by magical I mean unexplained supernatural-seeming phenomena, childhood memories of my own. They also made me wonder how much I'm filtering out because of an overactive, and maybe unnecessary knee-jerk skepticism. What else am I missing when I don't notice the personality of a tree? What am I not seeing in the branches, in the early morning, before the sun fully rises? Would there be any limit on the things I might see, or, from another angle, invent, if I wasn't so quick to pigeonhole and dismiss everything that I don't quickly understand?

I've gone a long way from the Philippines now, but here are a few of the songs Amalia remembered from her childhood. Between university semesters she would go home to help her family with their farming, so the first had very concrete meaning for her. She only knew the first verse, though there are five verses in the song:

Magtanim ay di biro, maghapong nakayuko, di man lang makatayo, di man lang makaupo, Magtanim di biro, maghapong nakayuko, di man lang makaupo, di man lang makatayo.	Planting rice is not a joke, bending all day long You can't stand straight, you can't sit down Planting rice is not a joke, bending all day long You can't stand straight, you can't sit down.

Amalia said it was a folk song that everyone knew, but searching for more information on the Internet I discovered that the author was Felipe Padilla de Leon, one of the best known Philippine composers and scholars of the last century. He was, apparently, intent on keeping Filipino traditions alive, and on "Filipinizing western music forms" not the other way around!

Below is another that Amalia said was very popular when she was growing up:

Ang Lobo Ko

Ako ay may lobo
lumipad sa langit
di ko na nakita
pumutok na pala

Sayang ang pera ko
pambili ng lobo
kung pagkain
sana nabusog pa ako.

My Balloon

I had a balloon
That flew into the sky
I watched it rising
Then it popped.

I wasted my money
Buying that balloon
If I'd bought food instead
I'd be full now.

And this is one of the most popular folk songs in the Philippines. As in the Venezuelan lullaby earlier, men are definitely in for some ribbing here:

Leron, Leron, Sinta

Leron, Leron, sinta
Buko ng papaya
Dala dala'y buslo
Sisidlan ng sinta
Pagdating sa dulo'y
Nabali ang sanga,
Kapos kapalaran
Humanap ng iba.

Leron, Leron, My Love

Leron, leron, my love,
Seeds of the papaya!
He took a bamboo box
to pick the fruits that ripened.
Then as he neared the treetop,
The branch he stood on broke up.
"What bad luck –
I must find another love!"

Ako'y ibigin mo,
lalaking matapang
Ang sundang ko'y pito,
ang baril ko'y siyam.
Ang lalakarin ko'y
parte ng dinulang.
Isang pinggang pansit,
ang aking kalaban!

I love all men of valour
Who carry seven knives,
In addition to nine guns.
"I make heroic journeys
To the table,
And battle with my foe –
A plate of noodles!"

And this last song, my favourite, is for the very small. It's about frogs:

Mga Palaka

Mga Palaka
Mga Palaka
Sila'y masasaya
Malaki ang mata
Maliit ang paa.
Magaling kung kumanta
Oh – kak, kak, kak,
Oh gali gali gak
Oh – kak, kak, kak,
Oh gali gali gak.

Many Frogs

Many frogs
Many frogs
They're happy –
Big eyes
Small feet.
Great at singing
Oh – kak, kak, kak,
Oh gali gali gak
Oh – kak, kak, kak,
Oh gali gali gak.

Some adults act this one out, as well – popping their eyes, pointing at their feet and making a frog face for the frog sounds.

THE SEVERED HEAD

I was driving Sophie to a day camp once when she was about eight, along with her best friend, Vivien. Sophie started to glance at me in the rear-view mirror – I could see she was going to say something to Vivien that she didn't want me to overhear, and so I avoided making eye contact with her and maintained a distracted, bored expression.

After a moment, Sophie told Vivien that she kept picturing Vivien's severed head, and it bothered her. Vivien asked what *severed* meant. Sophie told her. Vivien wanted to know if her head was just hovering in the air, or on the floor. Sophie said it was on the floor. Vivien wanted to know if the floor had any pattern, or if it was just a plain floor. Sophie said it was just plain. They both looked uncomfortable.

Then Sophie said, "I have an idea, I'll make a poem out of it."
She said:

Your severed head is on the floor
I throw it out the open door
your body follows it, and then
puts its head back on again.

Vivien liked this. They went over it a few times together to memorize it. Then five minutes later Vivien had made up a tune for it, and they were singing it together . . .

Sophie had taken a static image, an image that had become a barrier or burden to her, and set it in motion – she didn't just try to get rid of it, which she probably sensed wouldn't be possible, and so instead she made use of it. I had never told her that saying something aloud, or making a poem out of something that disturbed her, might help her to get rid of some of its burden – she came to this on her own, and by the age of eight she was no doubt doing it from experience – because it'd worked for her before.

The desire to repress violent thoughts, thoughts that seem disturbing in some way, is natural, but at the same time, it can be wasteful and fairly pointless. Sometimes the attempt to transform is a better and more effective use of the mind and imagination than blunt (and usually ineffective) attempts at mental repression.

DEATH OF A HULA HOOP

When Joseph was two or so, he and I were playing in the park one day by Cottingham Junior Public School, waiting for Sophie and Ashey to be dismissed.

A little girl named Abby asked if she could play with us. I said sure. Joseph was making cakes out of sand, with twigs for candles, trying to relive his birthday glory. Abby suggested using a frond to make sprinkles. She went and got one, and put the same number of frayed fronds on each cake. Her nanny called her before she could finish, so she gave me the last few fronds with a couple of instructions, asking me to complete the task, and disappeared. I nearly threw the leaves away, but decided that wasn't nice, especially since she'd taken such care over the numbers and the instructions. I finished the task.

Over by the play structure, we were joined by a little girl named Ariel. Ariel showed us her badly bent purple hula hoop. She asked if we knew of a hula hoop doctor. I said I'd never met one. She said she'd met one once, in the hula hoop forest. Suddenly she dialed her own hand, and started talking into it. "Hello? I need a hula hoop doctor." She wandered around a bit, muttering into her hand. Having sorted this out, she came back. Joseph offered her a pinch of sand saying, "Cake?" She said, "Okay, I like cake." I said, "Are you hungry? Joseph can probably make you a whole meal. What else are you making, JoJo?" JoJo was happy to oblige. He offered, "cone!" (corn), and "penny!" (penne pasta), and more cake. Ariel accepted all, and even paid with twigs.

The next day I was back in the park with Sophie, Ashey and JoJo. I told Sophie and Ashey the story of Ariel's search for a hula hoop doctor. The bent hula hoop was still lying in the sand. Ashey said, "I think she needs a hula hoop undertaker."

THE MOONFLOWER

One day, on our way to school, Sophie said, "Tell me the story of the moonflower again."

She was talking about a story I told her once about a time when I was house-sitting for a couple from Hong Kong. They had in their home a moonflower (*Ipomoea alba*) – a fascinating large and fragrant flower that opens very quickly – over the course of a few minutes – and then fails within a few hours. I worked all sorts of crazy shifts at a group home in those days, and had no way of knowing whether or not I'd be home when it bloomed, but one evening I suddenly smelled a powerful fragrance, and ran down the stairs to see the flowers literally popping open – I had been able to smell the early opening blooms within moments, a floor away. That's how powerful the fragrance was. I was delighted, because I could easily have missed them. By the time I got up the next morning they had all wilted.

I asked Sophie why she'd liked the story – I had told it to her months before, and was surprised she remembered it.

She said, "I like it because it has more than one meaning."

"What are its meanings?" I asked, expecting her to say what I might have said – that beauty is fleeting, or that I was amazingly lucky to see such a rare phenomenon. Instead she surprised me with the following:

"That it's a mistake to become obsessed with something you may never see, because if you do manage to see it, it might only be by luck. And also that it's a mistake to become obsessed with something beautiful just because it's rare – like this flower – you might become blind to the more common flowers that are just as beautiful, and then you'd miss opportunities."

How, at eight, could she be so much wiser than I was at forty? But I remember, too, listening to less-intelligent adults when I was small. Of course I never thought then that the time would come when I'd be one of them.

CHAPTER THIRTEEN
CHINA, CAMBODIA AND KOREA

STRANGE OR NOT STRANGE?

輪車跑得快 | Strange or not strange.

Under the direction of the ubiquitous and talented poet and publisher Beth Follett, Sherwin Tjia and I collaborated on two books together. I wrote the poems, he drew the pictures – though Sherwin is a poet and author, too, known for his sensitive, humorous and surprising books, such as *The World Is a Heartbreaker* and *The Hipless Boy*. He's also a well-known organizer of social events for the shy and socially reluctant who want to be more daring, like the Toronto Queer Slow Dance (with designated dancers for the shy, whose job it is to "seek out wallflowers and turn them into 'perennials'"), as well as strip spelling bees and crowd karaoke.

I don't see Sherwin often, because he's based in Montreal and I live in Toronto, but we've stayed in touch over the years. When I wrote to him to ask if he knew any Chinese nursery rhymes, he responded quickly and helpfully.

Sherwin's mother, Judy Tjia, is Chinese by background, but she grew up in Malang, Java, in Indonesia. Sherwin remembered his mother singing him the rhyme below when he was little. He asked his mother about the history of the song for me. She told Sherwin that when she was a child living in Malang, she had to go to school to learn Mandarin and this was one of the songs they used at the school to introduce the language.

Sherwin only knew about the first two verses. Later I discovered there was a third:

三輪車

三輪車跑得快 上面坐個老太太
要五毛 給一塊 你說奇怪不奇怪

小猴子吱吱叫 肚子餓得不能跳
給香蕉還不要 你說好笑不好笑

城門城門 雞蛋糕 三十六把刀
騎白馬 帶把刀 走進城門敲一敲

Three-wheeled cart goes real quick
On top sits an old lady
Wants fifty cents, but gives a dollar
Don't you say it's weird? Isn't it weird?

Small monkey keeps shouting out
hungry now so doesn't cry
given banana, he won't take
you say this is very weird, isn't it?

According to the only Internet source I could find about this rhyme in English, *Castle of Costa Mesa*, there are many variants, and children often change the last lines, on their own, for fun.

The full translation might be something like this:

Three-wheeled cart, goes real quick
Some old lady sits on top
Costs fifty cents, she pays a dollar . . .
Do you think it's strange or not?

Little monkey, cry and shake
He's so hungry he can't jump
Offered a banana he won't take
Do you think that's funny or not?

City gate city gate, chicken egg custard . . .
Thirty-six swords, I ride a white horse,

I wield a big sword
I walk up to the city gates and knock!

After printing out a draft of this book at St. Clair Printing & Graphics
on Vaughan Rd., I showed this section to the owners, Chris and Ellen,
who come from Singapore. Ellen had a big laugh when she saw the poem
– she said, "It doesn't matter where you're from in the Chinese-speaking
world – Mainland China, Hong Kong, Singapore – every Chinese kid
learns this."

HE'LL NEVER GET WELL

Haichao Ren was a student my friend Lourdes Zelaya put me in touch
with. We met at a Starbucks at Yonge and Wellesley one winter evening.
She got herself a tea, but it was only to keep her hands warm. She didn't
sip from it, but held the cup in both hands, warming up her fingers during
our half-hour conversation.

Haichao came from Jinan, the capital of the Shandong province in
Eastern China.

The first thing she showed me was a lullaby for a baby. Her mother
had done it with her, but she had forgotten about it until she watched her
mother do it with her daughter. You rock the baby, and pat its back, and
sing:

乖宝宝睡，	guai bao bao shui,	Good little baby,
乖宝宝睡，	guai bao bao shui,	good little baby,
妈妈来梦里陪。	ma ma lai meng li pei	come with your Mom-
		my to dream

There are a number of different versions of this. Another version, for
when the first one isn't working:

guai bao bao,   Good little baby,

shui jiao jiao,   just sleep,

yan jing bi bi hao.   and with your eyes closed!

Another very popular song for small children is the song of the small donkey:

	Xiao Mao Lu	**A Small Donkey**
我有一头小毛驴, 我从来也不骑。 有一天我心血来潮, 骑着去赶集。 我手里拿着小皮鞭, 心里正得意。 不知怎么哗啦啦啦摔了我一身泥	wo you yi zhi xiao mao lu. wo cong lai ye bu qi. you yi tian. wo xin xue lai chao. qi zhe qu gan ji. wo shou li na zhe xiao pi bian. wo xin li zheng de yi. bu zhi zhen me hua la la la la. suai le yi shen ni.	I have a small donkey I never ride But one day I went to the market Riding on my donkey Holding a whip in my hand Proudly – too proudly! I don't know what happened I fell to the ground – now I'm covered in dirt.

But the song Haichao felt most attached to was a song she and other small children sang to taunt rich people when she was little. She said it was an act of defiance against the party bosses.

"In those days, in China, there were very few rich people. Not like now. When money suddenly started flooding in, there were people who started wearing their pyjamas in the street, just because they could, because they were rich. Then things calmed down again. But before all of that, only the party bosses had money, and they were resented. So we had a song we taunted them with. If one of them passed us in the street, this is what we'd chant. It's called 'Bia Ji.' We were too small to be afraid of them":

Bia Ji

San San Si Si
Bia ji bia ji bia

"It's a wordplay poem, and it means (or would be understood by the rich, taunted man, as)":

Three Three, Four Four
A rich man caught a "bia ji" disease
Then got a "bia ji" injection,
Then took a "bia ji" medicine
But the treatment didn't work after three days . . .
[This final line literally means, he'll never get well – he'll die.]

STRAWS, STICKS AND A LIME

I met Ly Chhour and Kimny Lo on a Forest Hill playground, as I did so many other parents. Their daughter, Sophia, was in my son JoJo's class. After I got to know them a little, I told them about my research. Ly and Kimny said because of the very difficult circumstances in Cambodia when they were growing up, the aftermath of several decades of war and genocide, there hadn't been time for things like lap games and finger rhymes.

The Khmer language is spoken by about sixteen million people, most of who live in Cambodia, though there is a considerable Cambodian diaspora in North America and in Europe.

Kimny, a year or so after I first asked them about the games, came back to the subject and asked if I also meant games children played with each other. I said yes. She then told me about a game called Tres:

"I played this game with my friends during school day in the 1990s. Usually we took ten pens/straws/sticks and a lime. This game doesn't need a big group to play, two people are enough, but if there are more, you just take turns. If a player drops the ball, the next person gets to take their turn. I don't think it's popular anymore.

"The ten sticks are arranged in a row on a table. The lime is thrown up in the air with one hand, and then – with the same hand – a stick is grabbed up before the lime is caught (again, with the same hand). This stick is passed to the other hand, and this is repeated until all ten sticks have been picked up and passed to the other hand. After this, the same thing is done again, except now two sticks are grabbed at once. On the next round, three at once, and on the next round, four.

"Another game I remember is Bos Angkunh – a game played by two groups, separated by gender. Each group throws its own 'angkunh' to hit the top 'angkunh,' which belongs to the other group and is placed on the ground. The winners knock the knees of the losers with the 'angkunh.' *Angkunh* is the name of a fruit seed (it's an inedible fruit), which looks like the knee bone.

"Sometimes, the losing side has to sing and dance their way over to the winning side as a punishment for losing."

There are similiarities to the Persian Haft Sang game. Angkunh seeds are only sold just before the Khmer New Year, which is April 13 to 15.

"There is also a New Year game called Leak Kanseng. It's played by a group of children sitting in a circle. Someone holding a 'kanseng' (Cambodian towel) twisted into a round shape walks around the circle while singing a song. The person walking secretly tries to place the 'kanseng' behind one of the children. If that chosen child realizes what is happening, he or she must pick up the 'kanseng' and beat the person sitting next to him or her.

"Boys and girls will play this popular game to welcome (and honour) the arrival of the Khmer New Year Angel-to-be.

"The song for this game is 'leak kanseng, kama kam keng ous loong ous loong' – it's a fun game.

"The seven possible New Year Angels are all female, and the upcoming Angel is determined by the weekday that the New Year falls on. Each has her own special characteristics, and animal that she rides:

Sunday brings Tungsa Tevy, who rides a garuda.
Monday is Koreak Tevy who rides a tiger.
Tuesday: Reaksa Tevy, rider of the horse.
Wednesday: Mondar Tevy, rider of the donkey.
Thursday: Keriny Tevy, rider of the elephant.
Friday: Kemira Tevy, rider of a water buffalo.
Saturday: Mohurea Tevy, rider of peacocks."

WHEN TIGERS USED TO SMOKE

One last note from Korea. According to my friend the writer Dan Bar-El, in the Korean mode of storytelling "when tigers used to smoke" is the equivalent to "once upon a time" in the West European tradition; a phrase that allows the audience to infer that a magical or supernatural tale is about to be told.

CHAPTER FOURTEEN

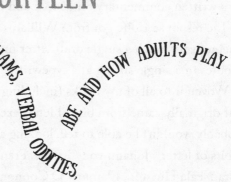

WILLIAM CARLOS WILLIAMS, VERBAL ODDITIES, ABE AND HOW ADULTS PLAY

DANCE AMONG THE WORDS

Despite vastness of frontiers, which are as it were the fringes of a flower full of honey, it is the little things that count! Neglect them and bitterness drowns the imagination.
– William Carlos Williams, *Kora in Hell*

But why dissect destiny with instruments
more highly specialized than the components of destiny
   itself?
– Marianne Moore, "Those Various Scalpels"

From 1956 through 1958, my cousin Rolfe Lawson was an editor of the *Trinity Review* in Hartford, Connecticut. He and his co-editor decided to put together an issue of the journal in honour of Marianne Moore, to be published in conjunction with her visit to Trinity College, where she would also give a reading and lecture. Rolfe wrote to William Carlos Williams to ask if he would contribute something for the issue.

Marianne Moore was one of the most important and influential American poets of the last century, winning the National Book Award, the Pulitzer Prize and the Bollingen Prize. She was an active mentor of younger poets, as well, including Elizabeth Bishop, Sylvia Plath, Ted Hughes, Allen Ginsberg and James Merrill. William Carlos Williams was a poet of the same generation and stature as Moore, which is why Rolfe sought him out for a written commentary on Moore and her work.

The response Rolfe got from Williams is lovely – cheeky and spontaneous, very much a single draft letter fired off in the course of a few minutes in a single sitting at a typewriter.

Woven into all of my books (including this one) are passages or poems that originally came from bits of letter exchanges with good friends. You probably wouldn't be able to tell, looking at them, which bits started out as bits of letters. Johann von Goethe, Franz Kafka, Rainer Maria Rilke, Zora Neale Hurston, Flannery O'Connor, Doris Lessing – the list goes on and on – all these writers and many others used letters as a way of trying out their thoughts – of making things up. But this isn't just something for professional writers to do – it's a chance for anyone at all to play with language, and to say something about their lives, or to catch thoughts on the fly.

Williams sent the following letter and tribute back to Rolfe:

April 9, 1957

Dear Lawson:

If you can make anything of this you're welcome to it/

Yrs
WCW

Marian [*sic*] Moore

Taking her at her own estimation, she's no poet, just a rhymester or worse. What justification is there for such an evaluation? And you may be certain that she'll not seek to avoid such a decision if it seems to her justified.

Take alone her poem, Those Various Scalpels. Go into it. No nit wit has let himself into the pitfalls that such alert stepping implies. There is deftness and an inclination to dance as well as a dance accomplished among the words. The keenest of wit, a disdainful scorn of the prevalent novel or short story reader, which the young woman of those early days kept all within herself, those days of the heavy braids, those twin heavy braids curled about the head or they would reach far below the waist and make a mock of her stringent virginity.

Or take the one, A Talisman, the image of a gull or other bird flying, transmuted to sculpture. But these are comparisons which no one saw at the time of the writing. Marianne Moore was writing for herself, passionately secluded, living her own secret among her intimates and perhaps never hoped or thought to transcend them and was satisfied with just that and the flights of imagination on her meager librarian's salary.

Who was she? Nuts to you. Though the vulgarity of such a phrase must have offended her then and must continue to offend her to her death. She has no patience with me when I use such terms and is not backward in saying so.

Meanwhile I love her and have always loved her through her convoluted wrestlings with the words, gaining and failing, to the end.

She has never disappointed me.

William Carlos Williams

It's fascinating to look at (and listen to) the playfulness of the language in this letter. Rolfe sent me a picture of it – you can see it was typed up in a moment, off the top of his head. Williams is teasing Moore here as one sibling teases another. By 1957 Williams and Moore were both major, and also elderly, figures in the world of American poetry. In 1957 Williams was also finishing up the last volume of his long poem *Paterson*. Williams incorporated several letters that had been written to him in the final volume of *Paterson*, including several letters from a young and openly gay poet named Allen Ginsberg.

I point out that Allen Ginsberg was openly gay in 1957 because even thirty years later, in the mid 1980s, that still took incredible courage. Even today, in 2017, it takes incredible courage – and really, should it have to take any courage at all to be open about your sexuality? The fact that it does doesn't say much for the times we live in. Things are changing, of course, but this isn't something our society should be struggling with anymore.

In book two of the same long poem, Williams also included a highly critical letter of himself (and his WASPy male self-centredness) from the poet Marcia Nardi.

Instead of posturing as a grand old man of American letters, he continued to experiment – to take risks. Poetry at its best questions and undermines authorative voices. But Williams showed that it wasn't all serious work – this undermining could be approached playfully. If other people wrote brilliant critiques of him, and of his poetry, wasn't it the best sort of play to insert those critiques directly into his own work?

I'm including this letter not only because it isn't collected anywhere else, but also because I think it shows a way of working that should be thought more about as a method: letter, or email, writing.

My good friend the writer Michael Joseph has enriched my working life in all kinds of ways with his emails over the years. I once wrote to Michael about lullabies, and children's poetry, trying to make connections, and this is what he wrote back:

"'When did children's poetry begin?' Lullabies, lyrics sung to babies to induce them to fall asleep, might lead us in the direction of the answers. The first recorded lullaby in English dates to 1372: John of Grimestone's 'Lullay, lullay, litel child, / Softë slep and faste' [as noted by Iona and Peter Opie in their introduction to *The Oxford Dictionary of Nursery Rhymes*]. Doubtlessly, English or Anglo-Saxon lullabies are older than that – we just don't have any before Grimestone. We know lullabies as a genre are older. S. N. Kramer in his work on ancient Sumer, which arose around the Tigris and Euphrates Rivers in what is now southern Iraq, observed lullaby texts on cuneiform tablets that date back to 3100 BCE: that's from the beginning of written language, about forty-five hundred years before Grimestone.

"Can we go any farther back than that? F.J. Harvey Darton writes, in *Children's Books in England*, that lullabies are 'as old as the hills where the first human mothers bore children.' Darton is just being poetic, but he could claim scientific support, of a kind. In *The Singing Neanderthals*, Steven Mithen says that lullabies originated as part of an early protolanguage he calls 'Hmmmmm' – holistic multi-modal manipulative musical and mimetic – around the time hominids stood upright. Upright mothers gathering food in the fields were able to use their hands and therefore required a new means to soothe and pacify young babies lying restless and cranky on the ground (Mithen, 202). That would place the origin of lullabies approximately two million years ago, and suggest that lullabies were not an outgrowth of literature or language, per se, but rather language was an outgrowth of the lullaby."

This was a casual email for Michael. But for me, there was a great deal to think about here – a lot of profound ideas that took me a long time to consider and digest.

Recently, I came across a quote in Brian Boyd's *On the Origin of Stories* that fit well with Michael's ideas. It seems obvious, in a way, once you read it, but I've never seen this idea articulated so clearly before: "Mothers and others provide a social entertainment system for infants, apparently because evolution has selected for both adults and children who can turn childhood dependency into mutual delight."

And Mary Catherine Bateson describes this in a memorable passage of her book *Peripheral Visions: Learning Along the Way*, as well: "What interested me about these 'conversations' was that whereas the mother was speaking sentences to the infant, using the words and grammatical patterns of adult language, the infant was responding with little coos and gurgles. The internal structure of the infant's behaviour was quite different from the internal structure of the mother's behaviour, but together they were collaborating in sustaining a joint performance. That capacity, and the delight it gave them both, preceded the differentiation of linguistic structure – learning words of grammar or rules of sentences."

ASHEY'S VERBAL ODDITIES

A child has a difficulty in achieving the miracle of speech, consequently we find his blunders almost as marvellous as his accuracy.
– G.K. Chesterton, *The Defendant*

To be a child is to be on the receiving end of power, to have one's voice denied, one's language corrected, one's will thwarted. *A Hole is to Dig* [by Ruth Krauss] grants children agency by showing their particular voices and allowing them to define the world on their own terms. As Sendak said, Krauss was "the first to turn children's language, concepts, and tough little pragmatic thinking into art."
– Philip Nel, *Crockett Johnson and Ruth Krauss*

My son Ashey approximated (or reinvented) words all the time, from the very beginning of his talking life. Ashey called Piglet "Pliggit," basement "baintit," girls "gwills, grills or goi-ells." "Cobby Nannies" for froggy jammies.

Gra-Lilla – gorilla
Krill – coral
Lello – yellow
Peatrix Potter – Beatrix Potter
Valentimes – Valentine's
Cookie Montair – Cookie Monster
Twildren – children
Kinepones – pine cones
Toucan Datoes – Froot Loops
Pryminjet – prime minister

From a rhymes point of view, he came up with the compelling "Eenty Peenty Pidah!" for "Eensy Weensy Spider" – we started to prefer Ashey's version, and that's the one I still sing when I have the chance. He also called the "dirty rascal" the "the dickle dackle" in the "King of the Castle" rhyme (I'm the king of the castle / and you're the dirty rascal).

He often got the vowels right, and the syllable count was often right, too, but his consonants often seemed to be the product of wild guesses.

When toddlers are learning to speak, their mispronunciations and approximations are often a matter of both stress and entertainment for parents and older siblings, and even for the child who's trying the new words and sounds out. My wife, for instance, called cucumbers "Boombungies" as a toddler. We knew that because her mother still, twenty-five years later, liked to remember this comical approximation-word and laugh about it.

One of the hardest sounds to get at first is the *ssss* sound. Toddlers often either drop the letter altogether, or make a *duh*, *tuh* or *ffff* substitution. Our youngest son, JoJo, called his sister Sophie "DoDo," "Ophie" or "Dophie" for a long time.

A certain similarity to this kind of "wordplay" struck me in Richard Wilbur's "S" poem in his book *The Disappearing Alphabet*:

What if the letter S were missing?
COBRAS would have no way of hissing,
And all their kin would have to take
The name of ERPENT or of NAKE.

Ashey, when he was only five or so, taught me the value of giving some history to a poem before reading it – when he was small, and I would give readings to children, he often came along and he'd sometimes stand up and explain to the audience a bit about where the poem came from – he gave it a context. It was something I thought wouldn't interest small children, but they were often fascinated by Ashey's commentary. I think they saw creative potential for their own "mistakes."

As a writer for children, it doesn't surprise me that Maurice Sendak, Ruth Krauss, Margaret Wise Brown and many other children's writers spent a great deal of time watching and listening to small children play.

ABE'S SENSE OF HUMOUR

When Amy went to medical school, she made friends with a fellow student named Andrew Hyman, but everyone called him Abe. Abe always made us laugh. He was one of the funniest people I'd ever met. Almost everyone who knew him felt the same. But there was something mysterious about it – he didn't tell jokes, he just came up with funny things to say on the spot.

One evening, when a group of us got together, I decided to pay close attention to what Abe said. I wanted to understand how he did it. What I discovered that evening was completely unexpected. What Abe did was pay close attention to what everyone was saying, and as the evening went on, he would weave details from earlier in the conversation back into the present conversation, but in surprisingly funny ways. It was all situational humour – taken from life and talk on the spot. He never made fun of anyone; he never put a negative spin on what had been said. And so everyone laughed, and the atmosphere was lightened, again and again. It was a real gift. And he worked only with the material at hand, which I found fascinating. He was like someone spinning gold out of straw.

TABLE TALK

Could the art of conversation be taught from an early age in elementary school?

It is often used as a means of teaching a second language, but rarely as a means of learning how to use a first language well. Robert Graves pointed out that much English university teaching used to be done in casual conversation over breakfast between tutor and student. There are many collections of "table talk" from the Arab world, where a table conversation between a teacher and students was a method of education. The Last Supper itself might be taken as an example of this.

Robert Chenciner records the following about teaching in Daghestan, the immediate neighbour of Chechnya: "To develop a healthy mind there were a variety of board games, learning and reciting poetry and tongue twisters, guessing riddles, explaining proverbs, finishing a story started by another, and composing fables. Much time was also devoted to singing and dancing to music."

This way of teaching language/conversation arts encourages sociability and spontanaeity. Why couldn't the same thing be done in our schools?

In the United Kingdom, in 2001 at Oxford, Theodore Zeldin founded an organization called the Oxford Muse: Conversation, Dining and Dancing, which arranges conversations and dances between people who don't know each other at all, or only know each other vaguely. It started as a local initiative, but now they organize events all over the world. It aims to create richer intercultural, professional and cross-generational relationships. As Zeldin writes: "When two people talk with mutual respect and listen with a real interest in understanding another point of view, when they try to put themselves in the place of another, to get inside their skin, they change the world, even if it is only by a minute amount, because they are establishing equality between two human beings."

Zeldin goes on to discuss how dance is also a conversation:

Dancing is like a carnival, freeing you from what you normally are; dancing together creates harmonies between people with different tastes. That is also what conversation seeks.

The Muse places great importance on reviving conversation between the generations. It is not just for those who call themselves adults. On the contrary, it reveals the danger of thinking that one ever is adult, which sadly means fully grown, with no room to grow any more.

JONARNO LAWSON

OCCUPIED HANDS, RELAXED MIND

Does having something to do with your hands enhance conversation, and maybe even suggest ideas and help memory?

Let's go back to Robert Chenciner in Daghestan again: "Their immobility (like that of academics) was not at all what it seemed at first glance. Men often gathered at the *godekan* [like a market square, or piazza] in their spare time to do light work in company, such as carving utensils, twisting rope or preparing sheepskins. At other times the revered old men sitting in the *godekan* would instruct the young in morals and customs, passing on legends and folk tales, or teach manual skills."

Might people knit, hook rugs, whittle wood or draw as a way of taking some of the weight off the words. Sociability would be preserved, and words could have more fun since they wouldn't be doing all the work.

Alison Gopnik mentioned something related in her book *The Gardener and the Carpenter* when talking about a study done by the anthropologist Polly Wiessner who was researching conversational content among the Ju/'hoansi.

Some old men and women in particular, no longer so productive by day, became master storytellers by night. Their enthralled listeners, including the children, laughed, wept, sang, and danced along until they drifted off to sleep. . . .

This nighttime talk engaged some of our most distinctively human abilities: imagination, culture, spirituality, and "theory of mind." Over the fire, the Ju/'hoansi talked about people and places that were far away in space and time and possibility; they transmitted cultural wisdom and historical knowledge to the next generation; and they explored the mysterious psychological nuances of other minds.

Gopnik goes on to talk about this specifically in terms of children's culture: "Children are enthralled by stories but they also create stories themselves, and that ability also seems to be both ancient and fundamental. From the time children are eighteen months old, they spontaneously immerse themselves in the fantastic, imaginary worlds of pretend play. Exactly why this ability emerges at this age isn't entirely clear, but it's probably connected to the beginnings of language."

In other words, it appears that the beginning of the ability to speak, and to tell stories, and to imagine oneself into stories (which we might also act out, or act out with the help of puppets, toys or other props) all seem to happen pretty much simultaneously, at the same developmental moment.

To me, it seems worth considering the imagination and storytelling part of this in connection with how Walt Disney worked to develop his films, which were so appealing to children and adults alike. What follows is a description of Disney's work methods, quoted from Neal Gabler's 2006 biography of Disney: "Everyone at the studio marveled at his acting – how Walt, who was usually fairly reserved now, would get up at the story meetings, enter his trance, and suddenly transform himself uninhibitedly into Mickey or Donald or an owl or an old hunting dog . . . 'And as Walt acted it out, it became funnier and funnier,' Frank Thomas and Ollie Johnston wrote. Then, as his audience began to respond, Walt would dive deeper into the character, finding more comic possibilties. 'He would imitate the expressions of the dog, and look from one side to the other, and raise first one [eye]brow and then the other as he tried to figure things out' . . . This became his chief means of communicating his ideas and the foundation for the studio's cartoons."

Apparently George Lucas sometimes worked in a similar way. This description comes from Brian Jay Jones's 2016 biography of Lucas: "As post-production [on *Star Wars*] kicked into overdrive during the spring, Lucas was still overseeing as many of the details himself as he possibly could, even acting out each of the holographic monsters that would fight one another on the *Falcon*'s chessboard."

We really shouldn't underestimate the importance of play – how it connects us to ourselves (and to each other) and how it helps us to find and tell stories.

CHAPTER FIFTEEN

ITALY AND NONSENSE

E CHE FA BEHEEHE

At the opening for an exhibit of "silent books" at the North York Central Library in 2015, I met the spry and remarkable Mariella Bertelli. She had helped put the show together – the exhibited books were destined to go to a library for refugees and local people on the island of Lampedusa – and she had travelled back and forth several times already to work with the local children and the refugee children living on the island.

We had a good chat, and then by luck a few months later we crossed paths again at one of Toronto's great annual events – the Toronto Storytelling Festival, which takes place over several days at venues all over the city.

Mariella helps to organize events, and she participates as a storyteller, as well. Over two evenings I got to hear Tahir Shah, TUUP, Ivan Coyote and Chirine El Ansary – each one completely different, and all of them remarkable.

El Ansary told a story from the Banu Hilal story cycle, a set of stories that aren't well known in the West. She strongly recommended that the audience find out more about these stories. It's possible, come to think of it, that she even commanded the audience to find out more.

I spoke with Mariella about this afterward. As Chirine El Ansary was staying with her, she promised to find out what she could about the Banu Hilal cycle – she wanted to know more about them, too – and to get in touch with me. We exchanged email addresses.

In the end, we were both stumped. Nothing much about or from the Banu Hilal had been translated into English. But finally, after a lot of searching, I found a book called *Ten Thousand Desert Swords*. I ordered two copies – one for each of us – and invited Mariella to meet me for coffee.

The book was a bribe, of course – a bribe that was totally unnecessary. Mariella was incredibly generous with her knowledge. As soon as I told her about my research, and asked if she had any ideas for Italian games, she produced half a dozen on the spot.

Mariella had just returned from working with the local children on Lampedusa. She had gone, at first, to help with the integration of Syrian refugees, who were arriving there in large numbers, but for bureaucratic reasons, volunteers weren't allowed to interact with the refugees after the first year or so. The Italian government did, however, allow volunteers to help the Italian inhabitants of Lampedusa who were also underserviced, so Mariella kept going back. She explained to me, "I told the children. 'It's up to you – you have to pressure the adults for a library.'"

We talked a bit more and I found out she came from a mixed Armenian/Italian family, born in Egypt, but brought up in Italy. The story of her family would be a book in itself.

I could have listened to more, but she finally said, "Let me tell you what you came here to find out! First, this is a tickling rhyme I know from my childhood:

Questa è la bella piazza
Dove passa la pecora pazza
Che vien dalla montagna
Per andar alla sua capanna
E che fa beheehe.

Here is a piazza [Hold hand of the child]
In the middle of the town [Tap on the palm of the hand]
And here is a woolly sheep [Tap again on palm and]
Going round and round [Go round and round]
Down from the mountain [Use finger to come down the arm]
Looking for her hut [Again finger going around the palm]
And she goes baahaa. [Now all the fingers climb up the arm and tickle]

"This one is from a mother, her name is Letizia, originally from Modena but living in Bozen [Bolzano], in northern Italy. She told it to me after my rhymes program at a storytelling festival there in 2014:

Lap Rhyme

Lava lava le scodelle
Per mangiare le tagliatelle
Lavale bene lavale male
Butta l'acqua nel canale

Take your bowls
And wash them clean
For the pasta will go in
How you wash them doesn't matter
Throw the water down the gutter!

[Actions: For the first four lines, hold baby on lap and move her around in a circle in a washing motion. For the last line, throw the baby up in the air.]

"This one I collected recently [in May 2016] from a child in Lampedusa, his name is Pietro and he knows many many rhymes. He is about eight years old:

Clapping Rhyme

Traisì	Traisì [Two children face each other and
Digulì	slide hands together once for each of the
Questo qui	first four lines]
Traisì	Digulì
Questa è la storia	This is the one
Di una cameriera	Traisì
Acqua salata	This is the story [Now they clap own hands
Zucchero filato	in the middle]
Boom boom yè	Of a certain maid [Now they clap partner's
Boom boom yè.	hands with hands up]
	Salted water [Now they clap own hands in
	the middle]
	Sugar candy [Again they clap partner's
	hands with hands up]
	Boom boom [Clap own hands in the
	middle] yay. [Raise hands bunched in fists,
	thumbs up toward shoulders]
	Boom boom [Clap own hands in the
	middle] yay. [Raise hands in fists,
	thumbs up toward shoulders.]

"Instead of a clapping rhyme I would do it with babies as a bouncing rhyme, first four lines moving baby back and forth, then bouncing baby up and down during the middle portion and finally dropping baby in the middle while saying *Boom Boom yè*.

"So much of the world is nonsense – so nonsense has great power.

There is an element of nonsense to everything we think, and do. Nonsense is essential – it's part of everything."

Mariella brought up a story she once heard Sheree Fitch tell. She said, "This story tells you something of the importance of early rhymes, and it tells you something, too, about the important role of nonsense. Get in touch with Sheree, ask her about it!"

So I did. Sheree graciously agreed to let me include it here.

THE SHEREE FITCH STORY

This comes from Sheree Fitch's book *Breathe, Stretch, Write: Learning to Write with Everything You've Got.*

Before I went off to university to study children's literature at the graduate level, a well-intended friend – in a very friendly manner – challenged my decision to study children's literature. "Why study children's books when you could study great literature?" he asked. To me, children's literature was the most important literature. After all, wasn't that where children developed their love of books? So I got a tad upset. Actually, I started ranting about my belief that children's literature was worthy of scholarly study, even though at the time it was still called "kiddie litter" in some academic circles. When my pal saw how upset I was, he backed down a little. I had to take a few more deep breaths.

"Okay," he said. "I get your point, and maybe after you've studied children's literature at the Masters level you can come back and answer a question I've had for a long time."

"What's the question?" I asked.

"Well first I have to tell you a story," he said. (See, everyone is a storyteller!)

"I'm all ears," I said. We sat at my kitchen table and this is the story he told.

Several years ago I was returning home from doing research in Ireland. Halfway over the Atlantic the plane started experiencing engine difficulty. Now, it's a funny thing, when people are in a time of crisis. You start to see how different everyboy is. Some people began to pray. Some people began to cry. Some people wanted a drink. Others wanted information. And some people like me got very, very quiet and still. Unfortunately, the woman sitting next to me decided to use me as a pinching pillow. She kept kneading the flesh of my arm between her fingers until my skin turned white, and whimpered every time we hit a bump. I tried to remain calm, even though I realized my research was in my briefcase under the seat and all my efforts in my wee quest for truth might possibly end up in the Atlantic Ocean. Obviously we finally made it all the way to Newfoundland. And when they got us to the airport they herded us into a bar. I pulled up a seat and ordered a whisky. Unfortunately, the arm grabber pulled up the seat next to mine. "I just wanted to say thank you," she said, "for being so nice to me. I know I really lost it there for a while." At these words of praise I puffed myself up and said to her, "Well, yes, I never knew I could remain calm in such a time of crisis." At this, the arm grabber threw her head back and laughed. Laughed hysterically. For a second, I thought she might be in a state of shock, and then she said to me, "Don't you know what you were doing?" And I said, "Yes, I was reading my magazine." In between fits of laughter she told me, "First of all, that magazine you were reading was upside down. And this is what you were doing. You were rocking your head back and forth a little like this." She showed me. "And all the while, you were saying 'hey diddle diddle, the cat and the fiddle, the cow jumped over the moon' and 'James James Morrison Morrison Weatherby George Dupree.' The whole time," she said, "You were reciting poems and Mother Goose."

My friend looked at me that day and asked me with great seriousness, "So what I need to know, when you're all done studying children's literature and have your Masters degree, is why, when I was closer to death than I've ever been in my entire life, I started to recite Mother Goose and A.A. Milne."

I was smiling by this time. "I don't need my degree to answer that question. You went back to the poetry of your childhood because it took you to a safe place." In the moment of the telling of the story or the poem there is the creation of a safe place.

Primo Levi talked about the same phenomenon in his book *Survival in Auschwitz*. In conversation with another inmate, he suddenly remembered some rhythmic rhyming lines of Dante he'd had to memorize, reluctantly, when he was a schoolboy. Now when he needed them, there they were – waiting in his head. And he badly needed them. Analyzing the meaning of the lines, and trying to discuss them with his friend helped him to survive.

I mentioned my notion of a possible connection between children's poetry and war experiences to the poet Richard Wilbur in a letter many years ago, and in response he wrote, "It interests me that you find or sense a connection between the writing of children's verse and military experience in wartime, because it was during active service that I began to write and illustrate light poems which, if not addressed to children, were at any rate done in the manner of Hilaire Belloc's *Cautionary Verses*. I expect that they were, in a sense, comic relief."

When the mind is highly stressed, it seems that a reversion to rhythmic sound (whether remembered, or invented, or both) might be a natural response.

I can think of several instances where I reacted in this way under duress. Once when my father had a bad leg injury, and I was rushing to get a bus to Hamilton to see him, I started to chant in my head, "Mike's more a Mike than a Michael, Michael's more Michael than Mike," which eventually (a few weeks later) turned into the first line of a poem.

Another time we were lost at night, driving around Miami looking for our hotel, and by mistake I drove over a small concrete barrier in the middle of the road in our rental car. (The chassis of a rented car scraping over concrete – a horrible sound and feeling!) Into my head popped: "A nanny in a van drove a ninny to an inn," which also later became the first line of a poem.

I was creating a mental puzzle for myself to solve, a distraction – a verbal game to funnel my stress into. And it worked.

SOME FUNCTIONS OF NONSENSE

He would never dare to consider himself a poet, because he wasn't anything like that; he just loved rhymes. Anything you said out loud, he rhymed it inside. Sometimes the rhymes made sense, sometimes they didn't. Fezzik never cared much about sense; all that ever mattered was the sound.
– William Goldman, *The Princess Bride*

When we speak of nonsense, and its uses, we are sometimes also speaking about surprise, or confusion, or the unexpected.

If you live among children, you soon become highly aware of their seemingly odd shifts of attention, their attempts to get the attention of adults hypnotized by adult routines, their strange repetitions, mispronunciations, bizarre perspectives – sometimes they seem overly logical, at other times their surreal babble is almost impossible to follow.

If, like me, you write for children, all of this can become extremely useful material.

Tom Bombadil, in J.R.R. Tolkien's *The Fellowship of the Ring*, is, among other things, a nonsense poet. He loves singing and making up silly verses. For instance:

Hey dol! merry dol! ring a dong dillo!
Ring a dong! hop along! fal lal the willow!
Tom Bom, jolly Tom, Tom Bombadillo!

Is it just a coincidence that he's also the only character in *The Lord of the Rings* over whom the Ring of Power has no power?

In Beatrix Potter's *The Tale of Ginger and Pickles*, the Dormouse family sells bad candles to customers who become very disgruntled. How does Mr. Dormouse deal with his customers? "When Mr. John Dormouse was complained to, he stayed in bed, and would say nothing but 'very snug;' which is not the way to carry on a retail business."

Remember, also, the behaviour of Mole in Kenneth Grahame's *The Wind in the Willows*:

"Hold up!" said an elderly rabbit at the gap. "Sixpence for the privilege of passing by the private road!" He was bowled over in an instant by the impatient and contemptuous Mole, who trotted along the side of the hedge chaffing the other rabbits as they peeped hurriedly from their holes to see what the row was about. "Onion-sauce! Onion-sauce!" he remarked jeeringly, and was gone before they could think of a thoroughly satisfactory reply. Then they all started grumbling at each other. "How *stupid* you are! Why didn't you tell him –" "Well, why didn't you say –" "You might have reminded him –" and so on, in the usual way; but, of course, it was then much too late, as is always the case.

"Very Snug" and "Onion-sauce" in the face of reprimand and confrontation seem like very clever ways of muddling the issue in what might otherwise have become more difficult (even dangerous) situations for Mr. Dormouse and Mole ... but was it also just their way of putting things back into proper perspective?

In Robert Chenciner's book *Daghestan: Tradition and Survival*, he writes about what almost became a violent confrontation between groups of Kumyks and Laks back in the 1990s. A policeman, who was trying to keep the two groups apart, finally said, "If you're going to beat somebody, why don't you beat me?"

This is nonsensical, of course, and it put an instant end to the tension –

the two sides stopped, thought again and finally decided to resolve things by negotiating.

This reminds me of a psychologist my mother told me about, who advised parents with children who wouldn't listen to them to behave in a bizarre manner. For instance, let's say Michael's mom has come to pick him up and says over and over, "Come on, Michael, we have to go," but Michael never listens. Michael's mother, instead of shouting, should start to tap dance and sing loudly. Michael, baffled, and possibly embarrassed, now wants to leave as quickly as he can.

To me, writing nonsense poetry has always been very much about playing with (or being played with by) words. For instance, two sets of words with a similar sound start to repeat over and over in my mind, like *bare knuckles* and *barnacles*. Any sensible person might notice this for a moment, and then forget all about it. But my mind, for whatever reason, refuses to let it go. It has to be more than just a coincidence. Why are they suggesting themselves to me over and over again? There must be a reason. They refuse to see it as a chance meeting in my mind, and my task is to find out what their relationship is – what do they mean to each other? A character emerges, a woman who swims to the bottom of the sea in search of treasure, who "barks her bare knuckles on bevies of barnacles." Now, joined by other words in that sentence, the words are satisfied, and I can forget about them. They end up in a book, which could also be seen as a set of formulas to neutralize my word obsessions, and now my mind can move on to other things.

This kind of work renders me harmless, in general, and I suppose that's one of the valuable aspects of it. While I might be doing some sort of large-scale world-damaging work, instead I'm playing about with, or being played about with by, words.

WHAT HAPPENED AT SCHOOL TODAY?

One day, when JoJo was four or so, I picked him up from daycare, and I asked him what happened at school that day. He said, "We were playing outside. I was standing still but the wind was blowing – a leaf landed on my hair. I went to touch it, but before my hand reached the leaf, the wind blew it away again." He had no other news. This was the most interesting thing that had happened, and really, even now, it still seems very interesting to me. A little poem, almost, about a leaf in the wind, that captures a psychological reality.

How many times have you gone to retrieve or touch something that's just landed – a feeling or a thought – and then, before you can reach it, it's gone?

Is this what he was describing? Did the encounter with the leaf seem so poignant to him because it perfectly described something that he already experienced all the time in the workings of his mind?

PAY ATTENTION THE FIRST TIME AROUND

One morning seven years ago I was interrupted early in my workday by Joe, a spry and friendly old Italian man, who had shown up again to look after my garden. Amy answered the door, and came down to get me from my office in the basement.

When Joe showed up, as he did once a year, he pruned the grapevines and the rose bushes – he was a perfectionist, and he clearly couldn't stand my messy garden – even the idea of it must have bothered him, because he wasn't a neighbour. But wherever it was he lived, it must have eaten away at him – maybe he noticed the overgrowth spilling out onto the sidewalk when he was driving by one day? I have no idea how he ended up making his yearly pilgrimage to our yard. He wouldn't take any payment for what he did – not even a bottle of wine. He wasn't doing it for me; he was doing it for his own peace of mind.

He was late that year, so I was worried about him. When he finally showed up, I asked him where he'd been, and he told me he'd been down with the flu for six weeks.

He was always full of interesting tips, like how to cook the garden snails we have everywhere (pick two or three pounds, put them in a cov-

208

ered pot with a little bit of air, let them eat cornmeal for two days, which cleans them out and makes them tastier, boil them out of their shells, peel off the skin, fry up with a little red pepper). My young son Ashey was listening with a look of horror on his face when he told us this. "I'm a vegetarian," he announced. Joe said, "You like their little eyes, don't you? They're funny, how they move – and very tasty, too." Ashey wasn't impressed. He frowned at Joe and left to do something else.

Joe told me had two children. "One isn't enough, two is too many."

He entertained me with little sayings like this as he snipped and clipped. I had to get back to work, but didn't know how to leave him politely.

Then I thought – relax, be patient. It occurred to me it might even be possible to get a bit of information out of him about rhymes for children or children's games from his part of Italy, but he resisted. Joe pretended not to hear me when I asked him, and instead he told me the story of how St. Francis came to his village – he learned the story from a painting in the niche of a wall in the local monastery.

He said, "You go there someday and look at the painting, and maybe you'll see a different story. Maybe I'm full of shit, for all you know. You have to go see for yourself, like everything in life. Never take anyone's word for anything."

According to Joe, St. Francis wanted to journey from France to his town on the bottom of the Italian boot, near Eboli, but the fishermen he asked for a lift wanted money to take him.

He didn't have any money, so the fishermen wouldn't help him. Finally he said, "Don't worry about it," and he laid his cloak on the water, put his staff in the middle of it and attached his handkerchief to the top of the staff as a sail. (Joe pulled a handkerchief out of his pocket at this point and waved it at me, to demonstrate.) His little cat joined him, and they sailed away. "Come back!" yelled the fishermen. But St. Francis shook his head. "No, I don't need you anymore." Then St. Francis sent a terrible storm to afflict the greedy fishermen, and all the fish went away from that part of the sea, and the fishermen suffered. They never recovered.

St. Francis then arrived in Joe's village, where he ordered a monastery to be built overtop of a stream. "Everything's gone well there ever since – even a big half-ton bomb dropped during the Second World War didn't explode when it landed on the monastery lawn. The explosives experts came and took the fuse away, and it sits there to this day.

"By the way, was that your wife who answered the door?" asked Joe.

"Yes," I said.

"Not a babysitter?"

"No."

"Your wife used to be . . ."

He jumped backwards and spread his arms out wide on either side of him. He was grinning. "Hmmm . . ." I said, as I struggled to understand what he was talking about. "Oh, yes!" I said, suddenly remembering. "She was pregnant when you were here last spring. We had another baby in June."

"No," said Joe, "*No.*"

He was definite about his *No.* He flapped a hand dismissively at me. He was frowning – I had offended him somehow.

What did he mean by "No"? I tried to figure it out, but he wouldn't elaborate. What had I missed? This strange exchange illuminated again the tough areas that have to be navigated sometimes when you don't share the same first language.

We never saw Joe again. He must have died. But I just now remembered something else he told me.

When he was little, his father only showed him how to do anything once. "I had a single chance to learn," he said, "and this was the most important lesson he taught me – pay attention the first time around. Remember that, because I'm only going to show you once how to prune these grapes!" Trying to fix in my mind his instructions about the importance of paying attention, I stopped listening as he showed me where it was best to put a stop to new growth.

CHAPTER SIXTEEN

SAUDI ARABIA, HUMAN APPENDAGES, TOUCH, ERITREA AND SOUTH AFRICA

BUT THIS IS SO SILLY!

Baraa Alghalyini and her husband, Abdulaleem Alatassi, came to
Canada from Riyadh, Saudi Arabia, to finish their medical training, which
is how Baraa met my wife, Amy. Amy and Baraa worked together in the
same family medicine site at St. Michael's Hospital.

Our families were at the same stage of life – our eldest children were
even born on the same day – and we had a lot of other interests in common. It was our good fortune to get to know Baraa and Abdulaleem
socially, before they returned to Riyadh.

I questioned them a lot about Islam, because most of what I knew came
from books. However useful books are, they're no substitute for a personal
oral account of anything, in my experience anyway. One of the most interesting discoveries for me was that the Quran contains many stories that appear
in the Torah and the Gospels – and the stories are very similar, though they
differ in many details. Some stories are completely different. One detail
that intrigued me (Quran 5:31) was that after Cain murdered Abel, a crow
arrived and scratched the ground to show Cain where to bury the body. It's
a powerful image . . . Cain is ashamed that even the crow knew enough to be
ashamed of the murder.

Baraa gave us a book, in English, of stories from the Quran retold for
children.

Amy and I, along with the children, were fascinated to discover that in the Quran version of Noah's Ark, Noah's wife, Waliya, and his eldest son, Kanaan, don't believe God's warning, so they ignore the need for the Ark. They refuse to come aboard, and perish in the flood.

Doris Lessing suggested in the preface to her novel *Shikasta* that it was "an exercise not without interest" to read the Torah, the New Testament, the Gnostic gospels and the Quran as a single epic. Talking to Abdulaleem and Baraa, I began to see the point of what she was saying.

But back to playing with babies! When I explained to Abdulaleem and Baraa what I was after, Baraa told me the rhyme below, and then asked, "Is that the sort of thing you're after?" "Yes, exactly!" I responded. She laughed and said, "But this is so silly!" Both she and Abdulaleem come from Syrian backgrounds (specifically, from Homs), so this was learned from their parents and grandparents who knew it from Syria, though they said variations of this are known all over the Arab world.

	My Grandma Ayesha
بعتتني ستي عيشة	
وقع الكوز و انكسر	im taimshih. im naimshih,
لتعلقني بالشجر	batetni setti Aishi
	la ishteri basael
	waiaa el kooze
مطيمشي منيمشي	wa inkaser
لأشتيري بصل	halfet malimte
حلفت معلمتي.	la talini belshajer
	wa el shajer aroosh aroosh
	khabi idek
والشجر نقوط نقوط	ya aroos
خبي إيدك يا عروس	imm el halah
ام الحلقة و الدبوس	wa el daboos

My adaptation (which takes into account, but doesn't strictly follow, Baraa's explanation of the words' meanings):

Imteesha Nameesha
My Grandma Aisha
Sent me for onions
I broke my cup
My teacher
Warned me
About a tree
Where someone
Was planning
To tie me up
A tree full of coins!
Go and hide
Your hand, pretty bride
Wearing your jewellery
An earring, a pin
And other tomfoolery.

Baraa then explained how to do it: "You take the child's hand, pinch each finger gently with each syllable, travelling along in a line over and over, and at the end of the last word fold down one finger. Do the rhyme on the remaining fingers, until all the fingers are folded down – when the last finger is turned over, run your fingers up the child's arm to tickle. This is how it's done in the original."

This methodical elimination of fingers isn't something that happens in any of the rhymes I'd come across, but seems like the kind of action that could be easily transferred to almost any of the others.

THE ROLE (AND PERCEPTION) OF HUMAN APPENDAGES

The very smallness of children makes it possible to regard them as marvels; we seem to be dealing with a new race, only to be seen through a microscope. I doubt if anyone of any tenderness or imagination can see the hand of a child and not be a little frightened of it. It is awful to think of the essential human energy moving so tiny a thing; it is like imagining that human nature could live in the wing of a butterfly or the leaf of a tree. When we look upon lives so human and yet so small, we feel as if we ourselves were enlarged to an embarrassing bigness of stature.

– G.K. Chesterton, *The Defendant*

Baby fingers and toes are very, very cute. The nails, too, are paper-thin. For some reason, it's hard to believe they exist even as you hold them close and look at them – they don't look real. How can a human being be so small? Some baby hands are chubby, they look and feel like little puddles of dough. Some are exactly like adult hands but tiny – you notice more the bones. While the rest of the body is quite serious and compact, fingers and toes are like its comic fringe. Noses, ears, hair, penises, breasts – among adults and children, these are common grist for the joke mill. If it's a part of us, but apart from us, it seems we're more tempted to joke about it.

Fingers and toes are also our "first responders." They create a safe, though not a passive, fringe – and our hair does, as well. But it's with our fingers and toes that we sample the world, all our lives. Our fingers, especially, remain forever fascinating.

It may help that they're asymmetrical and idiosyncratic. Similar, but different. There is no such thing as a standard finger. Each finger is recognizably a finger, and yet has its own relative size and place on the hand. Most of us also have two copies – one being the mirror of the other. But they aren't stuck in a rigid, mirrored position, like our nostrils. We can turn them and twist them, do so many things with them. But also just wiggle them around, twiddle our thumbs, make different shapes. They're like a little workshop that's always available, right under our noses. We can't see our faces, unless we look in a mirror, but our hands are nearly always visible.

This may be part of why our appendages are so interesting to us – they're us, but not entirely us.

Why do we play with them so much? I would say most of all because it's pleasurable – one of the nicest things to feel in your hand is another hand. And one of the first things a baby holds is its own hand – one hand clutches the other. Our earliest tactile self-exploration is of our two hands discovering each other And one of our next big self-discoveries, as infants, happens when our fingers find our toes. I would guess that infants find the active nature of fingers and more restricted possibilities of toes a fascinating contrast.

To link language to fingers and toes seems like a natural progression – the hand or foot becomes a sort of visual (and/or touch-based) memory device. It's also a fun new way of knowing or reimagining the toes and fingers. The fingers are now little birds, or the toes become piglets. A dramatic scenario takes place – a small, quick bit of theatre. And it usually involves the very pleasurable sensation of a hand or foot being held by adult hands.

NAMING TOES

This is one that my mother-in-law, Sheila (Kirsh/Kirshenbaum), taught my wife. You take each toe in turn and tell the child what their names are, for instance:

The jelly bean,
the cucumber,
the gentleman,
the hydrant,
the Big Guy . . . (one of my children, I think it was Ashey, objected to
    calling the big toe "the astronaut")

You can also give them person names – once one of my kids wanted to name them after relatives.
Anything goes! You could say

215

The pebble,
The postman,
The debutante
The dandelion
The bulldog.

SNIFFING EARS

This is a lot of fun with children, and you can get them to do it to you, as well. This is one my wife, Amy, made up. Sniff each ear and tell the child what it smells like. The two ears should always have different smells, for instance:

[Sniff sniff at left ear] – Popcorn!
[Sniff sniff at right ear] – Fresh mown grass!

Or:

[Sniff sniff at left ear] – A cloud!
[Sniff sniff at right ear] – A gymnasium!

Or:

[Sniff sniff at left ear] – An old book!
[Sniff sniff at right ear] – A strawberry!

THE SHAPE AND FEELING OF A FACE

Touching people I would never have otherwise touched while doing this research brought back an important childhood memory. My mother, who's a psychologist, had taken me to the university one day when I was around seven or eight. She had to do an errand, so she left me for a few minutes in a room next to her office where a little blind girl was sitting by herself. My mother said, "JonArno, this is Kathy, Kathy this is JonArno. JonArno, Kathy is going to feel your face because that's her way of seeing you."

I sat close to Kathy and Kathy's hands reached out and gently ran over my face. It felt lovely. It made my shoulders tingle. Then the spell was broken, she sat back in her chair, and we talked. I can't remember what we talked about. All I remember now is that I found it amazing that she really couldn't see. And that it was nice to be known by the shape and feeling of my face. I would have liked to touch her face, as well – if I had been blind, I wonder if that's what I would have done? But because I could see her, there seemed to be no point. I wonder, now, if she found that odd – if she wondered if I was capable of really understanding what *she* looked like without touching *her* face?

TOUCH

Once, when we were up at Wasaga Beach for a day off as a family, we walked into the outdoor playground of the local YMCA where we discovered a woman who'd hurt her leg while playing with her grandson. She couldn't stand up.

She had managed to pull herself onto a plastic crocodile, but her knee was swelling. The YMCA sent someone out to see what was happening – and then he went straight back in again to call for help.

I took the woman's keys and drove her pickup truck around to block the sun and give her shade while we waited.

I could see she was going to slide off the crocodile, so I asked her if she wanted me to get behind her and brace her back with my back. She said yes. She was very worried about her grandson, but he didn't seem that fazed. He continued to play (he was about seven). I remembered how helpful I'd found it when I was in pain, before my appendix was removed, that the nurse chatted with me, so I asked her questions and chatted.

The paramedics arrived, and just then she started to slide off the crocodile. She was in terrible pain. She started to scream. I tried to hold her bottom, but I had my back to her back. I felt very uneasy about grabbing her bottom – but I had no choice if I was going to stop her from hitting the ground. It was hard work. The paramedics held her arms while I let go and turned around, and then it took four of us to lift her up onto the stretcher, because of the awkward spot she'd found herself in among the playground structures.

While all of this happened, I was remembering something my great-aunt Mae told me once. She fell one day in the street, when she was old and very heavy, and she said no one seemed to know how to help her. Anglo-looking people stood about trying to comfort her with words, calling an ambulance, but not knowing what to do in any practical sense. Then she said an Asian man arrived on the scene, got down and put his arms around her and pulled her up, and held her till help could come. She asked him how he knew how to do that, and he said, "It's easy – in my country people aren't afraid of touching each other."

I'm not sure what country he was from, but without this story in mind, I'm not sure I would have helped the woman in the playground in the way that I did. My inclination was to avoid touching her.

PEEKABOO!

While most of us have many inner selves, we really do have only one face. Hiding, and then suddenly revealing the face to a baby or very small toddler seems to be a human universal – something you find almost anywhere you go in the world. Most languages have a special word or sound that goes along with this simple baby favourite. And because it's a baby favourite, it's inevitably an adult favourite, too.

Similarly, mooning someone by waving or waggling your bottom at them also appears to be a human universal. It was noted by Captain Cook's expedition when they encountered the Maori for the first time that one of the Maori expressed his contempt for the newcomers by mooning the English sailors.

Below are a few (of the many) verbally wonderful peekaboo translations from other languages, provided by the website WordHippo:

Dutch: Kiekeboe
Danish: titte bøh
French: Coucou!
Finnish: kukkuluuruu
German: Gugus? Dada!
Zulu: Bheka lab
Italian: Bao bao cette!
Japanese: いないいないばあ (inai-inai . . . bā!)
Korean: 까꿍 (kkakkung)
Vietnamese: ú òa
Welsh: Peekabook
Mandarin Chinese: Duǒ māo māo
Thai: (Ćaxě)
Croa ʒ̃ːːɵ žmurke
Serbian: жмурке (žmurke)
Marathi: एक अरेरे पहा (Ēka arērē pahā)
Scottish Gaelic: Giog Ort

GOD, WHO SPENDS THE EVENING WITH YOU

ሓደ ቋንቋ ኡኹል ኣይኮነን።
Hade qhwaniqhwa 'ikxul 'iejikonen.
One language is never enough.
– Eritrean proverb

One day, walking down St. Clair after I'd dropped my son Ashey off at nursery school, I noticed what looked at first like an empty storefront – I peeked in and saw a few empty desks, then looked up at the sign above the plate glass. It read Eritrean Canadian Community Centre. I had no idea that there was an Eritrean community, let alone an Eritrean community centre, in the neighbourhood. It moved to another part of the city a year or so later, so my timing was lucky.

I wasn't even entirely sure where Eritrea was – next to Ethiopia, but on which side? A few days later I went back when they were open, and told them about my research.

A friendly man named Menase told me to come back in a week and he'd have some information for me. The three Eritreans who were there that day exuded an incredible sense of quiet welcome and friendliness. I went home and googled Eritrea, and discovered that though it was geographically small (and *north* of Ethiopia, not east or west as I'd guessed), it was home to nine different peoples and several dozen languages, though Tigrinya and Arabic were dominant.

The country had a long complicated history; most recently they'd had a war with Ethiopia, during which they'd become independent. It was because of this war that many Eritreans now found themselves in Toronto, and elsewhere in the world.

When I returned to the centre a week later, Menase took me to the cubicle of an older woman named Sadia Aman. You could tell at once, somehow, that she'd had a hard life, and also that she'd worked hard to make the best of it. She was good-natured, and helpful.

We spoke a little about my research. As usual, I had trouble expressing what exactly it was I wanted. But she bore with me, and soon she was demonstrating things she'd learned fifty years ago from her grandmother, in Asmara.

She taught me children's rhymes in Tigrinya, which is a cousin language to Hebrew, Arabic and Maltese – twelve of the extant fifteen Semitic languages are spoken in Eritrea and Ethiopia. Tigrinya today has about seven million speakers. My favourite rhyme was one just for little girls: you bounce the girl (one to two years old) on your lap holding her arms up in the air saying:

> You – especially you –
> God has given you a great chance –
> God, who spends the evening with you –
> you of the [family or tribe name, e.g., Hadrasee]
> are very beautiful –
> the very best –
> is You.

She said you do it in a way that will make the girl laugh, and lift her arms a little higher at the end to emphasize the final word – *You!*

In Tigrinya, this sounds like:

> Essoorchasee, Essoorchasee –
> Ezgeeheeboowah Mezarchee Zemaschee [insert name of tribe]
> Z'purchattee gualatrasee
> Zblaztchret Ehree S'charee!

Another finger rhyme she taught me changes depending on what's happening in the child's life on any given day. As you say it, you run your finger down one finger (starting at the pinky), and up the next, then down, then up, then down the thumb, travelling up the arm to the armpit, to tickle. You are treating the hand as if it was a topographical map!:

> This way you go to the well [down pinky]
> and this way you go to school [up the ring finger]
> and this way your father goes to work [down the middle finger]
> and this way your mother goes to see her friend [up the pointer finger]

and this way Grandma goes to market [down thumb]
and this way you are running, running, running!

It's all improvised – you could make up anything at all for the fingers –
except for the final part where you say "and this way you are running, running, running" as you run your fingers up their arm and tickle their armpit.

The biggest hit, once I taught it to my own children, was the Tigrinya
version of "Eeny, Meeny, Miny, Moe":

Sana, Mana, Boortookana, San- dal, Jow – Boof!	Firsty, secondy, one orange, sweet-smelling sandalwood, sweet-smelling Jow – Boof!

For a while my children started to use the Tigrinya version instead of
the English – mainly because they loved the "Boof" at the end.

Several months after meeting with Sadia a friend of mine was collecting pieces for an anthology of non-English nonsense rhymes, and I told
him about this one. He asked to use it, so I dropped in on Sadia to see
if she'd mind; if it was okay with her, he would credit her, too. She gave
her permission. I could tell she was also pleased when I told her that the
Tigrinya version of this popular deciding method had supplanted the
English one in our home.

She taught me one last rhyme, then, to put a baby to sleep:

Nome ta Al, Ya Nome ta Ali Nome ta Al, Sakateh Ajohal.	Sleep, come sleep Sleep makes innocence, quiet.

TAMATIE SAW

In 2006, while doing research for a book on English language children's
poets from around the world (*Aloud in My Head*), I wrote to Jacana Media
in South Africa. A young woman working there responded soon after –

her name is Karabo Kgoleng – and though we've never met, we've been writing each other for a decade now.

Karabo, over the past ten years, has sent me links to artists, writers and thinkers that I never would have come across otherwise. She's a fine poet herself, though I don't think she's tried to publish her work.

She grew up in Mafeking (now Mahikeng, South Africa) and in Botswana. She says that the games she played as a child in both Botswana and South Africa were similar.

"There's only one word that's indigenous in this one (the first word, it's like a local word for knock knock), but only native kids played it . . .

"Hold hands together as if praying. With each line, tap corresponding fingers together, beginning with pinkies. When you reach middle fingers you cross them over each other four times, then return them to original position. Then resume with the tapping for index fingers and thumbs. (I hope this will make sense in the end!)

"Words are as follows:

Koko!
Come in!
Hello darling, hello sweetheart!
Mwaa [like kissing sound]
Bye bye!

"There was a similar one about churches and steeples, but that's an English one . . .

"I remember another one.

Tamatie saw,	**Tomato sauce . . .**
Tamatie saw-saw, so-so so so	Tomato sauce-sauce, so-so so so
tamatie saw-saw, so-so so so	Tomato sauce-sauce, so-so so so

O bitsa mang?	Who are you calling?
Nna?	Me?
Ha ke batle!	I refuse!
O bitsa mang?	Who are you calling?
Nna?	Me?
Ha ke ho rate (prn: raa-ti)!	I don't love you!

"Played it as a little girl, clapping hands and shaking booty with hands on hips. Showed 'virtue'; a 'good' girl responds in the negative when a boy calls her in the street (sigh).

"When my younger sister and I got bored with 'koko come in' we'd do it backwards: Bye bye mwaa hallo darling hallo sweetheart come in koko."

CHAPTER SEVENTEEN
LOCAL PLAY

PAW-SEE-BA-LAY

We work so hard to get children to understand us – and they want so badly to understand, at least, when they're first learning – and to say things *properly*, and to interpret *correctly* the meanings we're trying to convey. It's a very serious business. But we're made to laugh, even when we're tiny, when we can still barely speak. And this allows us some relief.

Spontaneous wordplay with children is something that children themselves suggest to adults through the oddity of their pronunciations and experiments with grammar. The surprised adult is sometimes inspired to try out the experiments with similar words, or different but similar sentences. A playful back and forth around these linguistic novelties can be highly pleasurable for both.

A similar thing can happen with stories. Children will often tell stories that seem highly surreal because they're just starting to explore possibilities with different characters and plots. Sometimes a child will want an adult to tell many stories about one character. In our family, there was a huge demand for extra Star Wars stories – we simply made more up to satisfy the demand. If we hit on what seemed like a good scenario to the children, we might have to retell it many times.

I remember one in which Count Dooku hit Obi-Wan Kenobi in the face with a frying pan. This upset Anakin because he had just cooked the eggs, which were still in the pan, and Dooku's attack had ruined a perfectly good breakfast, in more ways than one! And he'd hit his best friend, which made it worse! It was completely foolish, but we ended up having to tell this little piece over and over again in exactly the same words . . .

I remember, too, my father making us guess what he was saying when he'd mispronounce something deliberately. He would say, for instance, "Paw-see-ba-lay." We'd make one guess after another. I remember that one in particular because he went into a store and left us in the car in the parking lot thinking about it – I said it to myself over and over and over again. I couldn't get it. When he got back in the car he said, "Did you get it?" We all said no. "Possibly!" he said, laughing.

All of this to say, playing with language (and with stories) is a way of helping to affirm our need for and enjoyment of language and stories, and simultaneously a way of undermining our overreliance on (and seriousness about) both.

I USED TO BE A HOUSE

This evolved one day when I was taking my son and two of his friends on a long drive somewhere through the city. One of his friends asked me if I was a teacher. I said no. Then he said, as a joke, "Were you ever a house?" I said, "I was, you know, but I got tired of standing in one place, and of people always leaving my windows open, so one day I decided to become me instead." After that the three of them took turns asking me what I used to be, and then they tried it out on each other. Each time you had to agree you'd been whatever it was, but then you'd stopped being that because of . . . whatever it was that had been hard about being a – highway, cat, sink, horse, toothbrush, seat belt, cloud . . .

A STORY TWO WORDS AT A TIME

This evolved spontaneously during a rainstorm at Centre Island four or five summers ago. My brother-in-law, Mark Freedman, started it, and then

226

we all joined in with our own lines.

Up until we started doing this, the whole day had seemed like a miserable mistake – but this activity completely lightened the mood:

Clouds – grey
Ferry – crowded
Kids – sad
Day pass – really?
Rides – cancelled
Tickets – wasted
Marital relations – strained
Clothes – wet
Cold drinks – unnecessary
Children – shivering
Popcorn – soggy
Good time? – Not really

This could be used for any tedious or miserable occasion – a long car trip, during turbulence on an airplane.

GROCERY LISTS

This is another game my children liked playing. When we went to the supermarket, inevitably people would leave their grocery lists behind in their shopping carts, or arm baskets.

We would study the lists, and then guess at the personality (and back-story) of the person or family the list was for. We first invented it in the summer of 2009, at the Wasaga Beach Real Canadian Superstore. This store is one of those massive supermarkets that sells anything and every-thing, so the material in the lists was particularly rich.

Unfortunately, more and more people are putting their grocery lists on their cellphones, but it's still not uncommon to find a scrap of paper with a list of items to consider. A receipt could be used in the same way, but then you miss out on the person's handwriting.

Here's a sample list:

Fan
Pork chops
Celery
Orange juice
Eggs
Jam

We decided this was a single, middle-aged man. He lived in an apartment, or small house, without an air conditioner. He was bald, and spent most of his time at home wearing an undershirt (it was important to picture the person, in this game). He was a card player and he liked his car. He was divorced. Celery was the only vegetable he liked – mostly because of the crunching sound it made. He only ever bought one type of jam – probably strawberry. (There was a bit of disagreement here – one of us thought he might like experimenting with different types of jam, but he never admitted this to anyone.) His orange juice didn't have pulp. His eggs were scrambled, and he oversalted them. Eggs for breakfast was one of the great pleasures of his day. But he also liked his meat-heavy dinners very much.

He had a son named Karl who never called him. (There were objections to this – Karl did call him, and came for dinner once a week. They ordered pizza, and once in a while they walked by the bay together. Karl had happy memories of going to the beachfront fair with his father.)

And so on – the grocery list was just a departure point, but all the items had to have a role in how we conjured up the person.

USING WHAT IS FOUND THERE IN A PICTURE BOOK

When my son JoJo was in kindergarten, I went into his class one day to read a book.

He asked me to bring in a book called *It's My Birthday*, by Helen Oxenbury. It wasn't a book I knew well – it was about a boy who has a birthday and a bunch of animals help him make a cake. Looking it over, it seemed like an odd choice to me.

But JoJo's plan with the book was completely different than mine – I had a passive relationship to the story – I had no imagination about how to use the book, but I didn't realize this until later.

As I started reading it, JoJo stopped me, and shouted out to his classmates, "The first animal is a chicken – everyone make the noise of a chicken!"

They all made the noises of a chicken.

"Now," he said, "get up and move like a chicken!" They all got up and started jumping around, then they all sat down again.

He did this for each animal, and his classmates loved it. He was like a very experienced children's librarian conducting storytime, and I was like someone who'd never spent time with a child before.

He also made an extra illustration to show the class, after the last page – he wasn't satisfied with the way the book ended. This, too, made me think about our usually passive relationships with books as objects. Why shouldn't we add a page to a book, or even alter a picture if it makes us happy?

My son Ashey, who's older than JoJo, often had us change words in picture books if they weren't to his liking. For instance, he strongly disliked the word *dinner*, and if it appeared anywhere in a book, he'd have us scribble it out and write *lunch* over top. Until my children suggested that I do otherwise, I always treated books – cover, pictures and text – as permanent and inviolable.

Now I think that altering a book so it's more to your liking is actually a way of treating the book with respect. This is how it always was with stories, when stories existed only as oral literature.

I don't feel that way about a manuscript – I think if there's only one copy of something, you shouldn't alter it however you like. Unless, perhaps, you're the author, and even then, it's probably best to have someone supervising you in case you're unable to see the value or destructiveness of what you're doing.

But any book that has a large print run – why not? You don't just have to think "how would I have done this differently?"; you can actually, all on your own, do it differently.

TAPE TAPE TAPE

For four years I lived in Montreal. One of the years that I was there, I worked at a Coles bookstore at the corner of Rue Sainte-Catherine and Rue Stanley. Today, in 2017, it's a large Victoria's Secret. I loved this job, not because of the work, which was dull, but because of the staff. They were a lively, interesting, artsy group, mostly young students like myself at the time. This was a long time ago, in 1991.

For an Anglo from Ontario, the stylishness, easy eye contact and physical immediacy of Quebeckers came as a shock – in my case it was a happy shock. I once spoke with a Montrealer who'd moved to Vancouver, and she told me about an awkward interaction in her new workplace, after she'd grabbed the leg of a male co-worker while laughing at one of his jokes. She said an hour or so later, another co-worker came over to tell her that the man whose leg she grabbed wanted her to know that he was happily married, and not interested in her *that way*.

She found it funny – and a little embarrassing, of course – but she knew that it was a misunderstanding emerging out of cultural differences. I understood, because I remembered thinking in my early days at the bookstore that I was being flirted with all the time – I couldn't believe how attractive I'd suddenly become! My arms and legs were squeezed affectionately, people kissed both my cheeks during greetings and farewells, there was a lot of intense and lingering eye contact. And then it became clear – that was just how people interacted in French Canada!

It wasn't that it didn't mean anything – it meant closer physical contact among people, which was really nice, and a whole other level of nuanced communication. It just didn't have the meaning it had in English Canada, where there's a very heavy reliance on words.

There were, of course, many parties held by the bookstore staff, and these get-togethers had almost equal numbers of English and French Canadians. At one of these soirees, I remember a young mother playing with her baby; she was saying something that sounded like "Tapa tapa tapa." I wasn't that interested in babies at the time, so the memory almost faded away completely.

But as I gathered material for this book, I wrote to the illustrator Josée Bisaillon (we collaborated on the book *Leap!*) to ask her if she had any French-Canadian baby games she could suggest, and right away she sent me a video link to this exact game.

Tape Tape Tape
Pique Pique Pique
Roule Roule Roule
Cache Cache Cache
KooKoo!

Josée played it with her children when they were babies, but said in her version the *Pique* and *Roule* are reversed. Literally translated it would be:

Tap Tap Tap [or Clap Clap Clap]
Peck Peck Peck
Roll Roll Roll
Hide Hide Hide
KooKoo!

To play this with a baby, you face the baby and you:

> *Clap clap clap* your hands.
> Then when you say *Peck peck peck* you tap the palm of one hand with
> the pointer finger of the other,
> then you *Roll Roll Roll* your hands over each other,
> then you cover your face with your hands and *Hide Hide Hide* your
> face
> and finally, you open your hands and say *KooKoo!*

LEELY LEELY HOSAK

Golnaz Fatemi had grown up in Tehran. She left with her family after the Iranian Revolution in 1979. She found it hard to believe that I was interested in this sort of thing – ephemeral children's entertainments – but she remembered many, and was extremely helpful. Like many of the immigrants I spoke with, she'd never taught them to her own children because, when they came to Canada, she was busy trying to immerse her children in English. You could see it gave her great pleasure to revisit them, these old childhood memories, after all these years.

Golnaz placed her closed fist on its side on the table, and indicated that I should do the same. Overcoming a short moment of panic, I placed my closed fist on top of hers. I'm not sure where this panic came from – probably it was the oddity of the situation, because you don't normally touch other adults you don't know well, unless it's to quickly shake hands.

My panic disappeared as quickly as it came, I think, because it is, in fact, very pleasant to be taught in this way – which is one of the reasons these games persist. As I mentioned earlier, it's nice to be touched, and to touch. We wobbled our hand-tower about as required by the game, and she chanted the words. Our tower was supposed to represent an unstable minaret.

Golnaz laughed over her translation – "It's too silly!" she said. "It's embarrassing – I'm embarrassed to translate it. I'd never really thought about the words." I tried to reassure her by telling her this was exactly the sort of thing I was in search of:

	Jom Jomak	Something moving
	Badegeh Hazum	autumn leaf
جمجمک برگ خزون	Modarash Zainab	Mother Zainab
- مادرش زینب خاتون	Hatun	her hair is like a bow
- گیس داره قد کمون	Geesderah Atechka-	[bow and arrow]
- ها جستم	mun	even longer than a bow
- واجستم	As kamun balandterah	more black than a kanga-
- تو حوض نقره جستم	As shabaq mishkee-	roo's afterbirth, or night
- نقره قلمدونم شد	tarah	I jumped here and I
- هاجری به قربونم شد	Johastameh Vojasaam	jumped there and I
	Tuhosa nogrejestam	jumped into a small pool
	Nogreh alam doonam	The swimming pool
	shod	became my ink pot
	Haji Ali Behgoorbu-	and Haji Ali will die for
	namshod	me.

I think of it now as "The Wavering Minaret" – which, as she said, is what the wavering stack of fists represents:

Something that by moving,
moves,
An autumn leaf
Mother Zainab
Her hair is
Like a bow, a bow and arrow,
Even longer than a bow
More black than a kangaroo's afterbirth
Blacker than night

I jumped here
And I jumped there
And I jumped into the small pool
And the pool became my inkwell
And Haji Ali died for me.

At this point everyone pulls their fists away and tries to tickle each other. Any number of people can play, not just two, though I would guess more than eight fists at a time would be tricky.

Golnaz told me about her life in Tehran as a girl. "We'd go to help my grandmother, and while we washed clothes or did kitchen tasks, she would tell us stories to pass the time. Even when I was a college girl, I would still call my grandmother up at night and say, 'Grandma, tell me a story.' These are very special memories for me." I asked her if she remembered any of the stories in particular. She told me she'd think and get back to me, but as it happened, we never spoke again.

When I went to find her again, I was told she'd moved to Los Angeles.

After the wavering minaret, she taught me a last favourite of hers – a finger game, not unlike "This Little Piggy," or Sadia Aman's improvised finger game from Eritrea, or Natalia Grayfer's "Saroka Varona":

Leely Leely Hosak Gonjikeh Umat ob bokhereh Ofdot to hosak	Leely leely little birds came to drink water and fell into the fountain
Een goft berimdoseh Een goft chichi be- doseh Een goft ongoshteteh talor ro Een goft ki mideh javobeh khodahro Maneh maneh chaleh gondeh	let's go and steal something steal what? the gold ring who's going to answer to God? Me, with my fat head.

ی لی لی لی ی حوضک
جوجو اومد آب بخوره افتاد تو حوضک

این میگه بریم دزدی
این میگه چی چی بدزدیم؟
این میگه طشت
طلای پادشاه رو!
این میگه جواب خدا رو کی میده؟
این میگه من من کله گنده

Each finger dips toward the palm, starting with the pinky – the palm of the hand is the pool.

My adaptation:

Leely Leely
Little birds
Came down from the mountain
And fell into the fountain

Pinky – I'm ready to steal anything
Ring – What can we carry away on a wing?
Middle – I say grab the King's gold ring
Pointer – But who's going to answer to God?
Thumb – My fat head will nod to God.

KING, THIEF AND MINISTER

I met Nahid Kazemi through Facebook. Nahid is a prolific Iranian children's book illustrator who grew up in Shiraz, Iran, and now lives in Montreal. While writing friendly notes to each other about our work, Nahid suggested that we collaborate on a book together. We have (and are), and she even gave me a drawing for the cover of *this* book.

I was honoured that Nahid wanted to work with me. I asked her if, at the same time, she'd clarify some of the information Golnaz had given me years before. Nahid was willing, and she offered to tell me about some of the games she'd played growing up, as well.

These were her favourites:

King, Thief and Minister game

"This is usually played with four people.

"In this game you must select four small pieces of paper and write on each of them one of these words: king, thief, minister, executioner. You then fold the sheets, and shake them in a bowl, or hat. Each person takes one piece of paper. At the beginning of the game no one but the king reveals their identity. Then the king calls for their minister to make themself known, and so the minister introduces themself.

"Now comes the critical moment of the game. The minister has to choose which is the thief from the remaining two players. If they guess right, the king orders the executioner to punish the thief. If the minister guesses wrong, the king orders the executioner to punish the minister.

"The king tries to devise and then order funny and interesting punishments.

"The type of punishment in this game depends on the level of the king's creativity, and the relationship of the king with the players. For example, once, at home, we punished the thief by making him wash the dishes, or sometimes the thief had to buy a little treat for the others ... or something similar.

"The other old game is Flowers or Null – it's one of the interesting (and simple) games that Iranians played a lot at parties in the past.

Flowers or Null

"In this game players are divided into two groups, and a few in each group hide something small, like tiny flowers, in their hands. Then the second group has to guess which hands (of those in the other group) are empty and which are full. In this game the number of players is very important. The more players there are, the more exciting the game is.

"In my opinion, this game and almost all Iranian games are punishment based rather than prize oriented :) The punishments are usually very funny . . .

"In 'Flowers or Null,' one player is chosen from each team to guess which hands of players on the other team hold flowers. If you fail to guess properly, you get punished, and someone else takes over the guessing.

"The possibility of fraud is always high, because the players use tiny things such as pea grains, or little flowers, and it's easy to empty your hands without anyone noticing. But fraud is part of the game, and the attempt to detect and avoid fraud adds to the game's excitement.

Haft Sang (Seven Stones)

"'Haft Sang,' which means 'Seven Stones' in Persian, is also played in India, where it's called 'Pitthu.' There are versions played elsewhere in the Middle East and Central Asia, including Turkey. Different regions have slightly different rules – this was the version I played in Shiraz, Iran.

"Seven stones is one of the most popular Iranian games.
* Number of players: four to sixteen people
* Age of players: six to fifteen years old
* Tools: A single tennis ball
* Play area: a place like a schoolyard

"Players are divided into two equal groups and each group selects its own ringleader and head.

238

"To start, both groups stand facing each other, at an equal distance from a small stack of seven stones, while a member of one group starts – throwing a tennis ball, trying to knock the small stack over. Sometimes each player of the group has one chance with the ball, sometimes each person is given three chances. If no one from the first group hits the stone-stack, the second group gets to try.

"If the ball hits the stones and knocks them over, members of the first group (the ones who threw the ball) run in as quickly as they can, supporting the one who knocked over the stones, who has also run in to set them up again. This is the most difficult and exciting part of the game.

"The second group now gets hold of the ball as quickly as possible, and tries to hit the player who threw successfully (while that player tries to set the stones up). The player who goes to set the stones should avoid being hit by the ball, and the other members of their group are supposed to protect this player. If this player does get hit by the ball, another player of this group should take over the task of setting up the stones. But if all the players get hit by the ball before succeeding, the round is over and the roles of the groups are reversed.

"The first team to get seven points wins."

THE MOTHER IS SOOTHING HER OWN HEART, TOO

I met with Mrs. Hameeda Khan, mother of Canadian writer Rukhsana Khan, in the summer of 2015.

I had discovered Rukhsana through one of Elizabeth Bird's book reviews, where she spoke in glowing terms about Rukhsana Khan's *Big Red Lollipop* (illustrated by Sophie Blackall). I tracked it down – it was every bit as good as the review said. Curious about Khan, I looked her up on Wikipedia.

According to her biographical details, she grew up in Dundas, Ontario. How strange! So did I. This was a very unexpected coincidence! Dundas is a small town of about twenty thousand people, tucked into the edge of the Niagara Escarpment on the western edge of Hamilton – essentially the westnernmost edge of Lake Ontario.

I found her contact information, and we ended up having a wonderful phone conversation shortly after. Rukhsana is six years older than I am, but we went to two of the same schools at the same time (at one of them, Dundana Elementary School, I was in grade one and two when she was in grade seven and eight. Her book *Dahling, If You Luv Me, Would You Please, Please Smile* is based on her experiences at Dundana – it's very strange to think I was there at the time, just down the hall).

I told Rukhsana about the research I was doing, and she recommended that I call her mother.

I got in touch with Mrs. Khan, and she invited me over to talk.

The Khans lived in a modern condominium on the site of what had been the defunct Orenstein & Koppel factory when I was growing up. The factory was closed and boarded over through most of my childhood. I had passed it every day on my way to school – so there was a sense of renewal in seeing the area brought back to life like this.

I was offered tea, fruit, a comfortable chair. I could tell that our visit was going to be pleasurable. A thoughtful happiness permeated the room, and it wove like a golden thread through everything Mrs. Khan said.

When I told her I was looking for lullabies, children's games, anything related to children's culture, she said, "When the mother sings to the baby, she is soothing her own heart, too." I had never thought of it that way before. Though Amy and I had sung many hours to our three children when they were babies, it hadn't occurred to me that we were also doing it for our own good ... but it made complete sense. It shouldn't have been a new idea to me, though it was, that the soothing went both ways.

And this applies, as well, to what we call children's games – they are often just as much adult games, because adults play them with children. We think in terms of the impact they have on children, not as much about the impact they have on us, as adults.

"For babies, spirituality begins on the first day," she said. "When a baby is born, a prayer, the Adhan, is whispered in its ear:

Allahu Akbar	God is The Greatest
Allahu Akbar	God is The Greatest
Allahu Akbar	God is The Greatest
Allahu Akbar	God is The Greatest
Ash-hadu allā ilāha illallāh	I bear witness that there is no lord
Ash-hadu allā ilāha illallāh	except God
Ash-hadu anna Muham-madan rasūlullāh	I bear witness that there is no lord except God
Ash-hadu anna Muham-madan rasūlullāh	I bear witness that Muhammad is the Messenger of God
Hayya ʻalas-salāt	I bear witness that Muhammad is the
Hayya ʻalas-salāt	Messenger of God
Hayya ʻalal-falāh	Make haste toward prayer
Hayya ʻalal-falāh	Make haste toward prayer
Allahu akbar	Make haste toward success
Allahu akbar	Make haste toward success
Lā ilāha illallāh	God is greatest
	God is greatest
	Lā ilāha illallāh

"*Allahu* – this word, all on its own, will calm a child. But when it comes to speaking – a child begins with 'lip' words – words like *Papa, Mama – Allahu* is a tricky word to say – the tongue has to hit the roof of the mouth."

Mrs. Khan's emphasis on the contrast between hearing this soothing word as a baby, and the effort required in learning to say the same word properly yourself, as a child, seemed like an important metaphor for development in general.

She grew up in Samanabad, a district of Lahore in Pakistan, and her first language was Urdu.

"My father was different than many men of his time – he loved his daughters – he wanted the best for us. He once made me look into a panther's eyes at the zoo, because he wanted to take the fear out of my heart.

He liked to contemplate the smallest things. He made me look closely at the remarkable Mughal architecture of Lahore – all of this built imagination in me."

At fifteen Mrs. Khan was married.

"My mother taught me to be a woman. Not a depressed girl, but a woman who was loved. My husband and I had three girls. And my husband said, 'We have to go somewhere where they like girls.' And that's why we came here, to Canada. Our eldest daughter even joined the armed forces to show her appreciation to her father."

I was enjoying the conversation so much that I almost forgot why I was there, but in the last bit of time we had, Mrs. Khan told me about some of the games and songs I'd come for. And also some poems that had been very important to her – that she felt had shaped her life, and so she wanted to be sure I'd include them.

When she was little, in Lahore, she liked to play a game of bottle caps with other children in her street. Four or five kids would get together, and each had two bottle caps. There would be one bottle cap that had tar in it – this was the shooter, and belonged to no one.

The caps would be assembled on the ground, and the child opposite you (there might be four or five kids playing) would tell you which cap you had to hit (with the tar-filled shooter cap). If you hit it, you got to keep the cap you hit. If you missed, someone else tried.

As Mrs. Khan told me about this game, I remembered Chana Fish telling me about a similar game she played in Poland as a girl, with pebbles in the dust.

And I remembered a young woman from China telling me about a game, not terribly different, played with the knee bones of goats.

Another game Mrs. Khan liked to play with her own children she had to demonstrate to me. She twisted and bunched all of the fingers of one hand into the fist of her other hand, so that only the tips of her fingers appeared, poking out of a circle created by the thumb and pointer finger of the hand that was fisted up around the twisted fingers of the first hand.

Now a child had to guess which of the tips was the tip of the middle finger. It's actually hard to tell. If the child guessed right, they got to go next. If they guessed wrong, they had to try again.

Next she told me about "Chichu Chichu Chacha," the Urdu version of "Hickory Dickory Dock":

> Chichu Chichu Chacha
> Ghari Pe Chuha Nacha
> ghari nay aik bajaya
> chooha neechay aya.

This is another popular Urdu nursery rhyme, called "A Fish's Child." It's about the circle of life:

Machli ka bacha ande se nikla,	A fish's child
Abbu ne pakada didi ne kata,	Came out of the egg
Ammi ne pakaya hum sab ne	Swam in the water
khaya,	Father caught it
Bada maza aaya bada maza aaya!	Brother cleaned it
	Mother cooked it
	We all got together and ate it
	It was delicious.

And the following two poems are poems Mrs. Khan learned as a child (they were written for children), and she felt they shaped her daily life afterwards. Both are by Allama Iqbal, one of the major Pakistani poets of the twentieth century. These translations are quite inaccurate – I've cobbled them together from two anonymous translations I found on the Internet. I present them here with my apologies to those who know them in the original Urdu:

243

JONARNO LAWSON

The Bird's Complaint

I am constantly reminded of the past
The spring garden, and its music
Gone are the freedoms of our former nests
Where we could come and go as we pleased
My heart aches the moment I think
Of the buds there, and the dew
The beauty, the happiness from which
I made my own nest
I do not hear those lovely sounds in my cage
May I regain my freedom!
How unfortunate I am, reminded of my homeland
Where my companions still live
While I wait in this prison
Spring has come, and the flowers are laughing
But I am in this dark house, crying
Oh God! To whom should I speak?
I fear I will die of grief.
Since I left the garden, my heart is such
That it causes my grief to grow, and
My grief causes my heart to grow
O listeners, listening to this music
Do not be happy
This is my crying heart
Oh you who have confined me,
Free me,
I will be a silent prisoner
Earning my blessings for free.

A Child's Prayer

My wishes, my prayers come to my lips
O Allah, make my life a light
To drive away the world's darkness
Enable me to enlighten each corner of the world
May my life honour my homeland.
Like a flower graces a garden

May my life be like that of a moth, O Lord,
Enlighten me through a love of learning, O Lord
My work revolves around my empathy with the poor
Sharing my love with the destitute and the old
O Lord, save me from evil
And show me the right path.

When we were finished, Mrs. Khan wished me well, and asked me to let her know what happened with the book. She was so proud of all of her children.

It was restorative, somehow, talking with her. I felt like I'd only just scratched the surface of her knowledge about the lives of infants and children.

YOU CAN'T HAVE AN AUDIENCE OF BABIES

But before this meeting, when Rukhsana and I talked on the phone, we compared notes on our childhoods in Dundas. Being dark-skinned and a Muslim from Pakistan, she'd been bullied by the lighter skinned kids from Christian European backgrounds. Dundas, especially in those days, was a very small WASPy place, where the majority of the inhabitants were descended from English, Scottish, Irish and Welsh immigrants. I had been bullied sometimes because I was chubby, and because I didn't play sports, but I still grew up taking a basic level of acceptance for granted, and hearing about what happened to Rukhsana made any problems I'd had in Dundas seem like nothing.

Mrs. Khan, appreciative as she was of the opportunities the family had found in Canada, acknowledged that Rukhsana had been badly bullied. She said of her four children, she thought Rukhsana had been the most hurt by it.

It made me wonder if this was at the root of Rukhsana's sensitivity to, and brilliant elucidation of, power dynamics in the books of hers that I've read.

On the phone, Rukhsana and I talked about the workshops we'd done with children. Rukhsana asked what was the youngest audience I'd presented to. I told her four year olds. I told her I wasn't sure I could do a decent presentation with a group younger than that.

Rukhsana then pointed out something extremely obvious, but it was so obvious I'd never thought about it. She said, "Well, babies are one-on-one – aren't they? You can't have an audience of babies!"

All of these little games and rhymes were for an audience of one! Of course! They were games of intimacy. The earliest forms of education and entertainment are completely one-on-one.

At what point do we become able to slip more into the background? We start to learn that from the beginning, as well – there is always pressure to take a step back. But it's a skill, like any other. Nearly everyone enjoys being, or having, an audience of one. Of having someone else's full attention, and of giving attention that's noticed. There is an intimacy that comes with giving someone else your full attention. Becoming *part* of an audience is a skill. But because it's a skill that involves being still, and quiet, we don't think of it as a skill.

And the ability to be intimate is something many of us have to relearn later in life, as well. But how much easier that is if we've already experienced it in infancy, and childhood. Rukhsana also made the interesting point that if I were ever to teach people the things I was learning for the sake of this book, it would be parents or caregivers I'd be teaching, not children themselves.

Her favourite song as a child, which her mother sang to her (and to her children), was an Urdu song, with some Punjabi vocabulary, about God and a well. It was often sung as a lullaby, while rocking a child:

Allah	(Oh) God
Allahu	(Oh the one) God
Allahu lawadai coo	(Oh) God give us a well
Coo dei chalkei namaz paryey	We'll go to the well and pray to
Coo dei chalkei Allah ko yaad	you
karyey.	We'll go to the well and remember
	you.

Rukhsana was able to give me a transliteration of this lullaby, and a translation, but she had no way of providing its original text. I asked the owner of the local post office, Sami Qurashi, whom I knew from previous conversations was originally from Karachi, if he could put it into Urdu script. He was able to work with most of it, but he said there were some Punjabi words he didn't recognize, and he couldn't be sure of the spelling.

So I wrote to my friend the Pakistani journalist Qurat Ul Ain Siddiqui. She was able to put it into the Urdu script, along with an interesting note. She said that the language of the lullaby was Seraiki. Seraiki (or Saraiki) is understood by some as its own language, and by others as a somewhat different form of Punjabi. It has almost twenty million speakers, as well as four or five distinct dialects.

I wrote to tell Rukhsana, and she was surprised by this. She thought the lullaby was originally from the Punjab, but no one had mentioned the Seraiki language before. It was also spoken by some people in Kabul, and she did have a great-grandfather from Kabul, so maybe that branch of the family was the source? "Learn something new every day!" said Rukhsana.

CHAPTER NINETEEN
SRI LANKA, GHANA, GREECE AND ALBANIA

MOOTU MOOTU

My wife always spoke warmly, and with high regard, for Sivajini Jegatheeswaran, a nurse who worked for many years in her clinic. Sivajini is a Tamil, from Colombo, Sri Lanka. She was a survivor of the riots and massacres of Tamils during what's now called Black July, in 1983.

When my wife told Sivajini about my research, she invited me into her office, which was across the hall from Amy's office in those days. She then told me some delightful and surprising things about adult-child interactions in Sri Lanka.

She told me about a game called "The Elephant Takes a Bath," which is used to amuse and distract a child who doesn't feel like bathing. You simply pretend the child is an elephant, and say things like "Now we wash the elephant's toes – the elephant has great round legs, and it's very difficult to lift its foot," while pretending to have great difficulty lifting the child's foot.

She said children are often fed by adults, fork or spoon into mouth, until the child is five or six years old. She said some of these customs may have changed since she was little, but that's how she raised her own children. Very close, loving, personal attention is given to the child's needs.

Children are taught to cook once they are eight or so, and there are songs that accompany the cooking, that help them remember what to do, and just for simple enjoyment.

Sivajini then loaned us a book of Panchatantra tales. I had never heard of the Panchatantra. She said her own children had enjoyed the stories greatly. Adults and children have been listening to (and telling) these tales for at least twenty-five hundred years, probably longer.

Those interested in an overview of their history couldn't do better than to read Ramsay Wood's monograph *Extraordinary Voyages of the Panchatantra*, which I discovered a few years later. Wood has also published two volumes of translations of the tales (*Kalila and Dimna*).

My children all enjoyed the tales. They really liked "The Monkey and the Crocodile" – which tells of a crocodile and a monkey who become good friends. But the crocodile's wife becomes jealous of the monkey, and she convinces the crocodile that he should bring the monkey home so they can eat him. The crocodile tricks the monkey into coming out into the water on his back, but feeling badly, he reveals his plan to the monkey. The monkey tells the crocodile that if he'd known the plan, he would have brought his heart along, because his heart was his tastiest part! The crocodile agrees to let him return to the tree to get his heart, and, of course, all goes well for the monkey after that.

I liked this story, too, but my favourite was "The Thief's Sacrifice," because it had a twist in it that I didn't see coming at all. In this story, a thief intends to rob and kill three brothers he's travelling with. The brothers don't realize this, but before the thief can rob them, all four are taken captive by other thieves. The original thief realizes that he can save the three brothers if he sacrifices his own life, and so he does. The brothers always remember this man with the greatest gratitude.

The biggest surprise of this story, to me, was that the brothers remain in ignorance. They have no idea that this man had befriended them in the first place with the intention of robbing them. You, as the reader, know it, but they are never suspicious of the man, and in the end, he is the greatest hero to them. It's a fascinating story about trust, ignorance, good intentions, bad intentions and gratitude.

A few years passed, and I got in touch with Sivajini again to ask her a few more questions. I went out to meet her at her home, near Don Mills subway station. Sivajini was curious about what we'd made of the Pancha-tantra tales, so I filled her in. She was pleased we'd enjoyed them so much.

Sivajini had prepared a full lunch – daal, paneer, vegetables, white rice – it couldn't have been more delicious. As we ate, and spoke, I looked at the art on the walls around us.

On one wall of her living room there was a picture of Krishna with his milkmaids. On the opposite wall was a picture of Krishna with his favour-ite wife, Rukmini. Sivajini gave me a very brief account of the stories about Krishna. We talked also about his chariot.

"The chariot represents the body," Sivajini told me. "Krishna is the higher mind, and his passenger, Arjuna, is the soul. The reins are the workings of the mind, and the horses represent the senses: hearing, seeing, smelling, tasting." It was easy to get caught up in the rich and complicated symbolism of the stories.

It was actually fun – not just interesting, but fun – to analyze Krishna, and all of the visual imagery that captures, and helps bring to life, the ener-gy of the stories.

I was telling Sivajini about the bar and bat mitzvah ceremonies, and she said there was no equivalent coming-of-age ceremony for boys, but for girls there was a puberty ceremony. Not everyone did it – she said about seventy per cent of parents do – she herself didn't do this with her own daughter, but she said many of her relatives still do it. She said the custom was that after a girl's first period she wouldn't go to school for a week. Af-ter that there would be a party, and people would bring gifts, and the girl would come out dressed for the first time in a sari. It's called the Manjal Neerattu Vizha (Turmeric bathing ceremony). Traditionally it was meant to indicate that the girl was ready for marriage.

She had been thinking, too, about infant games, and she'd remembered one. A simple one her mother had played with her, and she could remem-ber her mother playing it with her little brother, too, when she was six or so. It was this:

Nandu urru thu Narri urru thu	Crawling crab, Fox crawling
Chika chika chiki chi!	Coochy coochy-coo!

"You do this by walking your fingers up the child's arm, then, at the end, tickle them under the arm."

Another very dear one she remembered is played with a small baby.

You lean closer and closer to a baby's forehead, until your forehead touches the baby's forehead. You do it to make the baby bring its head forward.

While you do this you say:

Mootu Mootu Mootu.	Closer closer closer.

A STOIC ON THE BEACH

And there is one more Sri Lankan story to tell.

Fifteen years ago, I taught an ESL writing course at Humber College, and one of the assignments I gave was for the students to write a page about a personal hero.

A young woman in my class (I have no idea what her name was, after all these years) wrote a lovely piece about her grandfather.

When she was a girl he would take her on his bike to school, and he also picked her up every day on his bike. But they didn't go directly home after school – he would take her first to the beach.

At the beach, there were many entertainers, but her favourite was a man who stood very still, without showing any emotion, while people tried to make him laugh. They told him jokes, and brief, funny stories. And the people all around, listening, would laugh. But the man himself had to maintain his stony expression. If he didn't laugh, the person who told the joke, or story, had to throw some coins in his hat.

What I found so interesting about this story was the way in which this stoic man's stoicism allowed for the transmission of funny stories – of good humour – to a wide audience. Everyone was listening and had the opportunity to pick up some humorous jokes and stories, as they watched the stony-faced man. It was a brilliant, and probably unconscious, method of spreading good cheer. On the other hand, who knows? Maybe it wasn't unconscious at all – maybe he knew exactly what he was doing.

TINKO (AND THE GOLDEN STOOL)

Obi nkyere akwadaa Nyame
Nobody teaches a child God.
– Twi proverb

Esther Biney, a nurse who works with my wife at Baycrest Health Sciences, offered to tell me about Ghanaian games and lullabies during one of her breaks.

We met in the television room on her ward one morning, where she kindly, and with great cheer, spent her twenty minutes off showing me some of the things she remembered from her childhood in Akwatia, the main diamond-mining town of southern Ghana. Esther radiated a kind of huge optimism that must be extremely good for her patients, and appreciated by the people she works with.

There are eleven different state-recognized languages spoken in Ghana – the dominant ethnic group are the Ashantis. Esther herself grew up speaking Twi, which is one of several mutually intelligible languages, the others being Ashanti, Akuapem and Fante.

Esther gave me a quick history of Ghana, much overshadowed by the horror of slavery during the colonial period. It meant a great deal to her that the Obamas had made a point of visiting the Cape Coast Castle, where the ancestors of so many Americans had been held before being sent to the United States as slaves.

Many Twi speakers ended up in Jamaica in the days of the slave trade, and it was through them that the rich story cycles surrounding the figure of Anansi arrived in the Western world. Others ended up in the Caribbean, in the American South, in Colombia, in Mauritius – in places all over the world. One of the fascinating discoveries for me was how wide-ranging and pervasive the influence of West African traditions and cultural practices are, globally. In Alan Lomax's book *The Land Where the Blues Began*, he states that "the error in African-American studies had been to look to print and to language for evidence of African survivals. For instance, musicologists discovered that American blacks performed many European-like melodies, but failed to notice that the whole performance context – voicing, rhythmic organization, orchestration – remained essentially African." Further, "in a sense, African-American singers and dancers made an aesthetic conquest of their environment in the New World. Their productions transfixed audiences, and white performers rushed to imitate and parody them in the minstrel show, buck dancing, ragtime, jazz, as nowadays in rock, rap, and the blues."

It's harder to put the history of sound and movement into words! Though over the past hundred years new audiovisual technologies have made it possible to study the spread (and influence) of sound and movement more broadly and carefully.

Esther and I decided to start with babies. What better place? "This is one we do when a baby or small child is crying," she said. "And when you get to the end – to 'nana naaa!' – you toss the baby up, or hold it high.

Baby da, wope su,	Baby sleep – you love to cry!
se osua ekom na edeno.	But when she is crying, she is hungry.
Moma no kooko,	Give her porridge,
Moma no nofuo,	give her breast milk,
nana naaa!	nana naaa!

"The whole time you do this, you lift the baby up and down."

Esther also remembered playing the following game often on her grandmother's large verandah with friends in the evening. A group of children sit

253

in a circle, facing each other. One child has the ball.

The child holding the ball at the beginning of the game repeats this phrase three times: "Atowa Nkyire" (this is a nonsense phrase, but it's based on *Antoakyire*, which means "it was not put behind you").

"Tinko," the rest of the group responds (also three times).

The person holding the ball then says, twice, "Se wohwe wakyira," which means "If you turn your back."

"Tinko," the group responds.

"Ye bebo won ne," the ball holder says twice, which means "I'll beat you today!"

"Tinko," the group responds.

The person with the ball keeps on going around until they drop the ball behind one person, unnoticed. If the person sees it then he or she will get up quickly and grab the ball and will sing the same song, chasing the person who put it down. If the person doesn't see it and you get around to him or her again, you hit that person (not hard – just a tap) to draw their attention to the ball at their back, and they become the one who circles.

It's similar to the British game Duck, Duck, Goose, the Japanese game Kagome Kagome (pattern of holes in a basket) and the Chinese game Diu Shou Juan (Drop of a Handkerchief). How the game spread, and where it might have originated, doesn't seem to be known. Games involving children sitting in a circle, while one child actively moves about behind them, or of one child sitting (or standing) still in the centre of a circle while being circled by the other children playing seem to be found almost everywhere in the world.

Esther said that in Ghana, dance is very important:

"If you're Ashanti, you learn the 'Adowa' dance from the very beginning of your life. There are some who do it professionally, but everyone learns it – men, women and children – everyone knows the movements, and all the movements have meaning.

"When important visitors come from other countries, the Ashanti do this dance for them. It has symbolic meaning. And a symbolic offering has to be made to the dancers. If the offering isn't made, then the dancers block the person from passing with their dance."

The last thing Esther told me was the fascinating story of the Golden Stool of the Ashanti. This Golden Stool, the divine throne of the Ashanti, was taken out of the sky by a prophet (some call him a priest) named Okomfo Anokye. He wasn't valued by his own people (the Akuapem). The Ashanti heard he was powerful, and invited him to be with them. It was then that he took the stool out of the sky for them.

Some say the Golden Stool contains the spirit of all the Ashanti, past, present and future. Esther said it was guarded by specially trained priests, called Nsumkwaa, and also by ghosts called Saman. The ghosts would make a normal person go crazy. No normal person can approach the stool.

One of the reasons I found this story fascinating was because I had just been reading that according to current understanding, the gold we come across on the upper layers of the earth (the only layers we have access to) arrived out of the sky during asteroid impacts millions of years after our planet had formed. Gold is likely created during the collisions of dead stars, and afterwards it goes soaring about in space, landing wherever it lands, or not landing at all – billions of tons of gold are still rocketing about through the universe.

The story of the Golden Stool captures something of the magical oddness of gold and its airborne arrival here . . .

It's also interesting that though the actual stool is rarely seen, and no one has ever sat upon it (it is the seat of the entire nation, not of its king), it's okay for functional copies of it to be made.

YOU LIKE IT; I LIKE IT; WHO DOES NOT LIKE THE SNAIL?

Akoss Ofori-Mensah is the founder and publisher of Sub-Saharan Publishers in Legon, Accra, Ghana. A member of the Council of Management for the African Books Collective based in Oxford, UK, she was also an executive member of the International Board on Books for Young People from 2012 to 2016.

I came across one of the books Akoss published, Jackee Batanda's *The Blue Marble*, and wrote to tell her how much I liked it. I also wanted to find out more about what was happening in children's books in Ghana, and in West Africa.

Akoss is an interesting figure in African children's books. She went to primary school in Sekondi on the west coast of Ghana, and to middle school in Kumasi, the capital of the Ashanti Region. She attended Aburi Girls' Secondary, in the Eastern Region, and the University of Ghana, majoring in English. Living and studying in so many different parts of the country, she was able to develop a broader perspective on the country's publishing needs. She also studied at the University of Nottingham in the UK and the University of Chicago.

Over the past year we've emailed and sent some books back and forth, and when I wrote to tell Akoss about my research, she sent the following:

"I learnt this rhyme in primary school in Sekondi on the west coast of Ghana. Fante is the language there. But I am an Asante [Ashanti]. The Asantes are in the central part of Ghana. The Fante and the Asante speak variations of the same language, which is Twi, but are written differently.

"I shall give you this nursery rhyme for your collection. It goes:

Whana na ompe nwaba?	Who does not like snail?
Owo epe; moso mepe	You like it; I like it
Whana na ompe nwaba?	Who does not like snail?
Se oda dokon do a,	If on kenkey
Oye anigye de!	It is very delightful:
Se oda nkwan mu a;	If it is in the soup,
On hwehwe atser.	Then find a spoon;
Se inya nitsir no a	If you get the head
Ono nsem pa!	That is good luck!
Owo epe; moso mepe;	You like; I like it,
Whana na ompe nwaba?	Who does not like snail?

"Kenkey is one of the staple foods of the Fante. It is made from fermented corn. Snail – nwaba (scientific name is *Achatina achatina*) – is a delicacy among the Akans in Ghana.

"The rhyme is in Fante. Fante is the language of the Fante people found along the southwestern coast of Ghana, spoken by approximately two million people. There are also Akan people there, like the Asante."

I did an image search on these snails, picturing something like our local (Toronto) garden snails (*Helix aspersa*) – the type that Joe liked eating. But the Snail-nwaba is something completely different. They're large, and long, with beautiful shells, and can weigh over a pound.

For the shell alone, it's hard not to like this snail.

KOO-PE-PE AND THE MOTHER OF CLEOBULUS

One June day JoJo had me call his friend Isabella to see if she felt like going to the amusement park at Centre Island.

By luck, Isabella was free. Isabella's mom, Kathy Rispoli, offered to drive us to the ferry, and to come along, too, so a little while later we were on our way down Bathurst Street.

I didn't really know Kathy, but we had the day to chat. Her Greek background came up, and I told her about the research I was doing. "I actually don't have anything from Greece yet . . ." I told her.

Straight off she started to move her hands back and forth by the sides of her face, her fingers pointing straight up and her hands swivelling at the wrist. Basically, the same motion someone would make with their hand if they were screwing in a light bulb. She chanted:

Koo-pe-pe

Koo-pe-pe, koo-pe-pe
Etsi kanoon ta bebe
Etsi ekana kee eyo
Otan eemoona moro.

"You mean that sort of thing?" she asked.
"Exactly that sort of thing!" I responded.
She said her mother did this with her, and she had done it with her own three children. It means, essentially:

Κού-πε-πε	Turn your hands
Κού-πε-πε, Κού-πε-πε,	Turn your hands, Turn your hands
Έτσι κάνουν τα μπεμπέ	That is what little babies do
Έτσι έκανα κι εγώ,	That is what I also did,
Όταν ήμουνα μωρό.	When I was a baby, too.

Though *koo-pe-pe* itself is just a nonsense phrase, Kathy translated it to keep the sense of the meaning, and to maintain the rhythm and rhyme.

She said, "The koo-pe-pe song is a song I relearned as an adult from a very dear family friend; my 'Canadian aunt,' all my other relatives are in Greece. She sang this song to her grandchildren and all the first generation 'grandchildren.'"

I asked Kathy if she had any more, and she came up with the following. Before that, I asked where her family came from, just to place the rhymes geographically.

She said, "My parents are from a small village in Ελλάδα (Greece). The village is Μοσχάτο (Moshato), in the province of Θεσσαλία (Thessalia). The closest major city is Καρδίτσα (Karditsa). My maiden name/parents' last name is Αργυρίου (Argiriou).

"And now the rhymes! In this one, you (as an adult) are acting out the actions and facial expressions of the bunny.

Κουνελάκι	Koonelakee	Little Bunny
Έιμαι το κουνελάκι σου, Τ'αυτάκια μου κουνώ. Και σας παίζω το κρυφτό, Μέσα στο λαχανόκηπο. Δεν σας κρατώ λογαριασμό.	Eeme to koonelakee soo T'aftakia moo koono Ke sas pezo to kreefto Mesa sto lahanokeepo Dhen sas krato loyariasmo.	I am the little bunny I wiggle my little ears And I'm playing hide-and-seek In your cabbage patch And I don't have a care in the world.
Αχ κουνελάκι, κουνελάκι Ξύλο που θα το φας! Μέσα σε ξένο περιβολάκι Τρύπες να μην τρυπάς!	Ah koonelakee, koonelakee Kseelo poo tha to fas! Mesa se kseno pere-evolakee Treepes na meen treepas!	Oh little bunny, little bunny A spanking you will get! You're in a stranger's garden Holes you should not make!

Μη μου τα κλίνεις τα ματάκια,	Mee moo kleenees ta matakia,	Don't you wink your eyes at me,
Μη μου κουνάς τ'αυτιά,	Mee mou koonas t'aftia,	Don't you wiggle your ears at me,
Μη μου ζαρώνεις την μυτούλα,	Mee mou zaronees teen meetoola,	Don't you scrunch your nose,
Έισαι μια ζωγραφιά!	Eese mia zografia!	You are so picture-perfect!

"This little bunny song is one I remember my aunt singing. I would also sing this to the kids when they were babies and close my eyes, and wiggle my nose and ears. Then I would repeat the song and close their eyes and wiggle their nose and ears in unison with the words of the song.

"The next is a clapping song, or poem:

Παλαμάκια Παίξετε	Palamakia Peksete	Clap Your Hands
Παλαμάκια παίξετε	Palamakia Peksete	Clap your hands
Και ο μπαμπάς του έρχεται	Ke o babas too erhete	And your dad is coming
Και του φέρνει κάτιτι	Ke too fernee kateetee	And he's bringing something –
Κουλουράκια στο χαρτί.	Kooloorakia so hartee.	Cookies in a paper.
Παλαμάκια Παίξετε	Palamakia peksete	Clap your hands
Και η μανούλα έρχεται	Ke ee manoola erhete	And mommy is coming
Να το πάρει αγκαλιά	Na to paree agalia	To take you on her lap
Το μικρούλι της παιδιά.	To meekroolee tees pedhia.	Her little one, oh children.

Παλαμάκια, παλαμάκια Παίζουν όλα τα παιδάκια Παλαμάκια και χορό Ντάχ ντιρντί και ντάχ ντιρντό.	Palamakia, palamakia Pezoon ola ta pedhakia Palamakia ke horo Dah deerdee ke dah deerdo.	Clapping, clapping All the children play Clapping and dancing Dah dirdi and dah dirdo.

"The 'Clap Your Hands' song is the song I remember most. When all my kids were infants, we went to Greece to visit my only living grandparent. My mom's mom would sing this to all the kids and then would add her own verse. I tried to look it up and it seems to be a verse from an old song . . . this song, with my grandmother's special verse gets sung by my kids, it gets added to the end of the main verse

Μαύρα μάτια και μεγάλα, ζυμωμένα με το γάλα.	Mavra matia ke mey-ala Zeemomena me to yala.	Black eyes that are so big, Fermented with milk.

"And this last one is a lullaby:

Κούνια, μπέλα	Koonia, Bella	Swing, My Little One
Κούνια, μπέλα Έπεσε κοπέλα Χτύπησε στο πόδι Και στο καλό πόδι.	Koonia, bella Epese kopela Hteepise sto pothi Ke sto kalo pothi.	Rock, my little one My girl fell down She hit her leg Her good foot.

"It doesn't sound so endearing in English but my parents would rock us and sing this softly until we slept. If we were wide awake, then they would sing it while we were on the swing or my dad would swing his leg up and down and get us all excited. I especially remember this with our kids; their grandchildren!

"And finally, the moon:

Φεγγαράκι μου Λαμπρό	Fegarakee moo Lambro	My Bright Little Moon
Φεγγαράκι μου λαμπρό, Φέγγε μου, να περπατώ, Να πηγαίνω στο σχολειό Να μαθαίνω γράμματα, Γράμματα σπουδάματα Του Θεού τα πράματα.	Fegarakee moo Lambro Fege moo, na perpato, Na peeyeno sto sk- holeeo Na matheno gramata, Gramata spoodhamata Tou Theoo ta pramata.	My bright little moon, Shine on me, so I can walk, So I may go to school To learn my lessons, My important lessons And God's wishes.

"This moon song is one I remember learning during Greek school in preparation for the celebration of Greek Independence Day (March 25). It is this one simple poem that symbolizes so much and is remembered acutely, when so many others are forgotten. A testament to the enduring desire the Greeks, during the Ottoman Empire, must have felt in order to maintain their Greek heritage."

Reading the texts of the ancient Greeks you can find a precedent, or first record, of almost any idea later explored in the Western world, and so I wasn't surprised when I came across this reference to what must be one of the earliest recorded stories told specifically for a child: "The mother of Cleobulus the Wise is said to have made up a story about the moon for his little brother. The moon asked her mother to weave a little dress to fit her because she felt so cold; but her mother replied: 'How can I make it to fit? – today you are at the full, soon you'll be a half-moon and after that just a sickle.'"

Cleobulus the Wise, who lived in the sixth century before the Common

Era, is credited with the well-known aphorism "Moderation is best in all things." In any case, it's interesting that Tomi Ungerer used exactly this plot device for his *Moon Man* picture book, published in 1967, twenty-five hundred years after the time of Cleobulus.

LITTLE CRAB

And a last look at Greece. This one comes from Margarita Lam-Antoniades, a family doctor who works in the same clinic as my wife. Her family came from Limassol, Cyprus.

Paei to kavouraki na piei nero,	The little crab goes to drink water,
mes tis Sophia's to lemo.	In Sophia's neck!

You walk your fingers slowly up the child's stomach, and then at the end you race your fingers up to their neck for a little tickle.

After Margarita sent this to me, I forwarded it to Kathy to see if it was familiar, and she said she also did this with her children, but in their version it was a spider.

PATA PATA – BE BE BA

When I was little, my father brought home a wall-sized German map of Europe and hung it up in my bedroom across from my bed. As I lay in bed every night before falling asleep I studied the huge map, and thought about the countries and the seas surrounding them.

Many of the countries I heard about frequently, but some were completely mysterious to me, and the most mysterious of these countries was Albania. In the 1970s Albania was one of the most isolated countries in the world.

My father knew, somehow, that it was the only country in Europe to liberate itself from the Germans without outside help. Otherwise, no one in my world knew anything about it.

I wrote a letter to the Albanian embassy once to ask for information – I can't remember if it was to the embassy in Ottawa or in Washington – but either way I never heard back.

I didn't meet anyone who actually came from Albania until almost forty years later, when we hired a local teacher to help us with some tutoring, and Gledia Shani came to our house.

The moment she told us she was born in Vlorë, a southern Albanian coastal city, I told her about my research, and she sent me an email later that week with the pieces below.

Albanian is an Indo-European language spoken by about five million people. Just as with Greek and Armenian, it lacks related languages in its lonely branch of the language tree. Not only was it one of the most isolated nations in Europe for many decades, it also has one of Europe's most solitary languages.

Pata	Goose
Pata pata, qafë gjata	Goose goose, long-neck goose
I ka kembet si lopata	Her legs long like a shovel
Dhe ne ujë ajo kur futet	And when she goes in the water
Si vapor i vogël duket.	She looks like a little ship.

"This is the first nursery rhyme that I learned and sang. It is the only one that I fully remember and it is one of my first and fondest childhood memories. This is one of the first rhymes that young children will learn and recite themselves.

"The rhyme below ('Qingji i Vogel') is a popular children's song about a small sad lamb. This is also a nursery rhyme that most parents will sing to their babies, who will eventually learn the rhyme and sing it (for many it is one of the first, if not the first nursery rhyme they learn).

"The main idea behind it is that a child is singing to a lamb, asking why it is sad and trying to comfort it. Below are the Albanian and English translation of 'Qingji i Vogel' or 'Little Lamb.'

Qingji i Vogel

Qingji vogël pse mendueshëm be
be ba
pse m'shikon ashtu trishtushëm be
be be
eja eja bashkë në arë tring tring
tring
unë mbledh lule ti ha bare tring
tring tring
unë mbledh lule ti ha bare tring
tring tring

Shih në livadh fatos i dashtun be
be ban
shokët e tu në tufë janë mbledhur
be be be
unë i vetëm u mërzita tring tring
tring
zilet thonë unë të vija tring tring
tring
zilet thonë unë të vija tring tring
tring

Little Lamb

[Child sings this]

Little lamb, why are you so sad, be
be ba
why do you look at me so sadly, be
be ba
Let's go together to the fields, tring
tring tring
I'll pick flowers, you eat grass, tring
tring tring
I'll pick flowers, you eat grass, tring
tring tring

[The lamb sings this]

Look in the meadows, a little child,
be be ba
your friends are together, be be ba
I am alone and bored, tring tring
tring
When the bells ring, I have to
come, tring tring tring
When the bells ring, I have to
come, tring tring tring

265

	[child sings this]
Babi tash më ka premtue qingji im	Dear lamb, my dad promised me
stallë të re me të ndërtue qingji im	a new barn built for you
do të jem bari i fshatit tring tring	I will be the shepherd of this vil-
tring	lage, tring tring tring
do t'kullosim n'brigje të shpatit	We will herd on the green hills,
tring tring tring	tring tring tring
do t'kullosim n'brigje të shpatit	We will herd on the green hills,
tring tring tring	tring tring tring
Do të jem bari i fshatit tring tring	I will be the shepherd of this vil-
tring	lage, tring tring tring
do t'kullosim n'brigje të shpatit	We will herd on the green hills,
tring tring tring.	tring tring tring.

"The main thing that I remember about being taught/hearing the rhyme are the endings of every line, especially because it has the same rhyme/beat repeated. For example, 'be be ba,' 'tring tring tring.'

"The most appealing part is a specific part of the song – 'be be ba' – because it is the sound that the lamb makes. I remember that it was my favourite part of the song to sing because I would try to imitate the sound of a lamb. The song itself was reminiscent of something cozy, warm and cute, which made it very comforting.

"One very popular ritual around the holidays is that children dress up fancy, and together with their parents/grandparents, go for visits to relatives, as well as neighbours. The children are given gifts from the adults and traditionally also given sweets/treats such as baklava.

"Also – in Albania, New Year's is a very popular and huge celebration. Many people go to the farmers' market and buy a live turkey two weeks before the New Year. Children enjoy being around the turkey, and parents often include them in feeding the turkey for the two-week period leading up to the celebration.

"Similar to here, children and their parents will put up a Christmas tree, however, we call it a New Year's tree. Parents will tell children about Santa Claus, but we call him 'New Year's Old Man.' And bedtime rituals are very similar to those in Canada – parents read their children books and sing nursery songs together."

CHAPTER TWENTY
CIRCASSIA, LATVIA AND NORTHWESTERN SCOTLAND

YINEMIQWE

Amjad Jaimoukha and I have been corresponding for almost twenty years. I became fascinated by the literature of the Caucasus in the late 1990s, after discovering the dark, comic novels of the Abkhazian writer Fazil Iskander.

The Internet was in its early days, then, and Amjad, a polymathic Circassian-Jordanian, living in Amman, Jordan, was already busy putting together a website to make information about Caucasian culture more widely available to the Western world. Amjad invited me to help with some chapters of a book he was assembling on Chechnya, and through Amjad I learned an enormous amount about the complicated, diverse and incredibly rich cultures of the Caucasus.

I asked Amjad about Circassian children's games, and he sent me this:

"I have transliterated the piece into Latin letters, and inserted what is known of the meanings of the phrases.

"The game was played with children seated in a circle with their feet also making a circle. The patter was said and the 'foot' that received the last phrase was taken out of the game, so to speak. It is basically a game of survival. My father played the game in his early childhood in Jerash, during the 1930s.

"The Circassians had a great number of nursery rhymes, in most of which mixed rhythm was used. The classic 'Yinemiqwe' serves both as a nursery rhyme and a children's game. The meanings of many of the phrases in the piece have been lost. I will insert the meanings that are still known."

Инэмыкъуэ	Yinemiqwe	Yinemiqwe
Инэ-инэ,	Yine-yine,	Yine-yine,
Инэмыкъуэ,	Yinemiqwe,	Yinemiqwe,
Мыкъуэ щхьэл,	Miqwe schhel,	Hay mill,
Щхьэл къутэ,	Schhel qwte,	Mill breaker,
Къутэроу,	Qwterow,	Breaker of things,
Щомыхъу,	Schomix'w,	Schomix'w,
Щохъурзэ,	Schox'wrze,	Schox'wrze,
Хъурзэ натӏэ,	X'wrze nat'e,	Anchor forehead,
Хьэ натӏищ,	He nat'iysch,	Dog's three foreheads,
Лӏищ зыукӏ,	L'iysch ziwich',	The killer of three men,
Зызукӏыж,	Zizuch'izh,	Kills himself,
Лъэрыгъагъ,	Lherighagh,	Lherighagh,
Лъэрыгъыпс,	Lherighips,	Strap of stirrup,
Хьэнтхъупсафэ,	Hentx'wpsafe,	Feast of millet soup,
Псафэ егъу,	Psafe yeghw,	Malevolent watering place,
Хъурей накӏуэ,	X'wrey nak'we,	Go in a circle,
Накӏуэ тӏыс,	Nak'we t'is,	Go and sit,
Тӏыс, Аслъэн!	T'is, Aslhen!	Sit, Lion!
Аслъэныкъуэ,	Aslheniqwe,	son of Lion
Лъакъуэ кӏыхь,	Lhaqwe ch'ih,	Long legs,
Кӏэн къэхьи,	Ch'en qehiy	Bring the knucklebone
Дыгъэджэгу,	Dighejegw,	And let's play,
Шатэ къэхьи	Shate qehiy	Bring the sour cream
Дыгъэшхыж.	Digheshxizh.	And let's feast on it.

The use of the circle in children's games comes up over and over again, in every part of the world. There is an inclusiveness to the circle, but at the same time, it creates a perfect template, or setting, for games of elimination. And the children can watch a whole range of faces at once, to see how the game is being experienced by their playmates.

When my own children were small, I noticed this in the imaginary games they played. Sophie, who's the eldest, organized Playmobil figures in a circle facing inward when playing with them. My middle child set up the figures more randomly, but often had two face-to-face, in conflict. My youngest made a circle, similar to the eldest, except in his case, all of the figures faced outwards, away from him.

I'm not sure what any of that means, but my wife and I enjoyed speculating about what this said about their imaginary worlds, how they experienced their interactions with others and how they saw themselves.

INCIS THE CAT

Taking one look at Liga Miklasevics, the principal of Victoria Village Public School, I said, "You must be Estonian."

Normally I would never guess at a person's ethnicity out loud, but my mother had a close Estonian friend who could have been Liga's double. Of course I was wrong . . .

"Not quite – but you're close . . ." she said, "my background is Latvian."

Up until seven or eight hundred years ago, the Baltic region was as linguistically diverse as areas of the Philippines are today. Latvian is one of only a few languages (and Latvia is one of only a few nations) that survive in the region from its more multi-ethnic period, when there were also Skalvians, Selonians, Semigallians, Curonians and Galindians. This was in addition to Poles, various groups of Lithuanians, Germans, Russians, Scandinavians, Estonians and Prussians – and in those days, Prussian referred to a member of a non-German Baltic nation, not to a resident of the modern German province. Latvian is currently spoken by about two million people.

I was at Liga's school to do a poetry workshop, not to do research, but I told Liga about my amorphous game-and-rhyme gathering project, and she offered me one on the spot.

It was taught to her when she was a child, by her aunt Silvija Klavins.

Silvija was born in 1934, and grew up near Riga, the capital of Latvia, but was evacuated to a German work camp during the Second World War. It was possible, Liga thought, that her aunt might have picked up the rhyme in a displaced persons camp, either in Lübeck or Bergen-Belsen, after the war.

Liga loved the rhythm and the sounds of the words, which is why she'd always remembered it. When she did it with her own children, she made up gestures and hand motions to go with it. "What were they?" I asked her.

"The words explain the actions," she said.

I found this interesting, because I couldn't see it. I must have seemed very dense to her, but she showed me.

"One hand can jump the other – one hand being Incis the cat, the other being the rung. Then you can make your hands into a basket.

"Clap when the eggs break.

"Make it up as you go along!"

"So," I said, "you could make a begging or praying gesture with your hands, and a shooing gesture at the end?"

"Exactly," said Liga, "whatever works for you. And just so you know, the *sh* is really an *s* with a little *v* on top to make the *sh* sound.

Bingu Bangu Bungu

Bingu bangu bungu
Incis lec par rungu
Olas grozam prieksha
Incis olas ieksa
saplesh visas olas
samaksat tas solas
Kas tev Incit tic?
Peles medit skits!

Liga's translation:

Bingu bangu bungu
Incis is jumping over a rung
in front of a basket of eggs
Incis falls into the eggs
breaks all the eggs
promises to pay
Who believes your promises?
Mice hunting – scram!

Using Liga's translation I've recreated it this way, though it loses all those great endings:

Incis the Cat (Bingu Bangu Bungu)

Bingu Bangu Bung
Incis jumps the rung
In front of a basket of eggs
She loses control of her legs
Falls back from where she's sprung
Breaking them all she begs
Trust me – I will pay!
Who believes you?
Go away!

ÒRDAG SGEALBAG

And finally, a little more Scotland for sentimental ancestral reasons. These come from Mairi Kidd, formerly the managing director of Barrington Stoke in Edinburgh. I was put in touch with Mairi by Aoife Murray, programme manager of Children's Books Ireland.

I told Aoife I was looking for Gaelic children's rhymes, and she said Mairi would be the best Scots Gaelic source.

I was thinking more in terms of Ireland and the Irish language, so this was a surprise. There are only about fifty thousand speakers of Scots Gaelic in the world today. Of Irish Gaelic speakers, in contrast, there are more than a million.

Mairi wrote back straight away:

"I can tell you a couple off the top of my head (see below) but I reckon your best bet is to get in touch with the School of Scottish Studies at Edinburgh University who would, I'm sure, point you in the direction of a lot of resources.

Huis, huis air an each	Giddy-up on the horse
Cà 'n tèid sinne nochd?	where will we go tonight?
Huis, huis air an each	Giddy-up on the horse
Ruigidh sinne Bhàlaigh.	We'll get to Vallay. [A tidally accessible part of North Uist.]

"There are loads of versions, a different one is here, from the Scottish government's education site:

"Little songs used as dandling songs were quite common in the oral tradition, although there are relatively few still in existence. They were sung by anyone bouncing a child up and down on their knees. This cheerful little song from North Uist is a good example of this type:

Huis, huis air an each

Huis, huis, air an each,	Gee up on the horse,
An t-each a' dol a Bhàlaigh.	The horse going to Vallay.
Beiridh a' muir-làn oirnn,	The high tide will catch us,
Beiridh e air chasan oirnn,	It will catch us by the legs.
Beiridh e air chinn oirnn!	It will catch us by the head.
Huis, huis, air an each,	Gee up on the horse,
An t-each a' dol a Bhàlaigh.	The horse going to Vallay.

"And this is a finger rhyme (this has loads of variants):

Òrdag	Thumb
Sgealbag	Index finger [same word as
Gunna Fada	'splinter']
Mac an Aba	Long gun
Cailleach bheag an airgid.	MacNab
	the little lady with the money."

With all of the finger rhymes I'd come across, this was the only one I'd seen that started with the thumb instead of the pinky!

Which seemed typically, paradoxically, Scottish.

I wrote to Mairi again for more information, but didn't hear back. This was more than enough, though. Certainly much more than I'd hoped for!

Shortly after getting this email, I was reading about the author and translator Willa Muir, who was born the same year (1890) as my great-grandfather James Glen, and grew up in exactly the same small coastal town in Scotland (Montrose).

By incredible luck, Muir had made a study of the children's singing games she'd learned on the playgrounds of Montrose as a child, in a book called *Living With Ballads*. My great-grandfather was apparently a great reciter of aphorisms, short rhymes and old Scottish songs. It's entirely possible they knew each other (being the same age in a town with, in those days, one public school). There's no doubt they would have known the same childhood songs.

Of all the interesting examples Muir collected, this was my favourite:

Water, water wall-flower, growing up so high
We are all maidens and we must all die.
All except Lavinia [any girl's name]
She is young and she is pretty
She is the girl of the golden city.

Nowadays this may sound a little morbid, but in 1890 it wasn't uncommon for children to die of fevers, or of tuberculosis, and so "we must all die" would have had a more poignant meaning for children of that place and era.

CHAPTER TWENTY-ONE

WAR, CHILDREN, SANDCASTLES AND MY COAT

PREPARING OUR CHILDREN FOR THE NEXT ONE

In late April 1945 my father survived a sniper attack while crossing the Isar Canal near Landshut, Bavaria. As the soldier standing beside my father was shot through the head, a quick-thinking sergeant, seeing my father standing still in a state of shock, ran up from behind and knocked him out of harm's way.

My father told me about this when I was a child, and I thought about it a great deal, imagining this vivid scenario over and over again. I was not impressed with my father's role in the story: why had he become frozen to the spot, standing as an open target on a narrow bridge after the soldier beside him was killed?

I knew, of course, that I wouldn't have stood there frozen, waiting to be shot down. No one would have had to save *me* – I wouldn't have had any problem leaping out of the way all by myself. And I would have seen what was going to happen ahead of time – I would have seen the sniper.

After hearing this story, I always looked at the upper windows of buildings, and searched the foliage of tall trees. I knew there weren't snipers lurking in the Dundas, Ontario, of the 1970s, but I also knew that it was important to be vigilant, to be always on the lookout.

Later when I played capture the flag at camp, I had no trouble tricking people and capturing the flag – I did it many times, never using the same strategy twice. I wasn't an athletic boy, I wasn't great at expressing myself

– I was pretty unremarkable – but I knew that I had an edge when it came to watchfulness. If I had a high opinion of myself for any reason at all, it was for this. Even then, I knew it was related to my father's stories from the war. Because of them, I was able to create a state of mind where my life depended on the outcome of what I was doing, or not doing.

This particular story about the sniper attack had changed how I thought and behaved, and this had an influence, looking back, on where and how I focused my attention. My children heard about a sniper attack in the news recently, and JoJo was saying he would dodge any bullet that was fired at him. Ashey explained that a bullet wasn't like a ball – a bullet moves too quickly to be dodged. I watched JoJo take this in, but I could tell he was still thinking about ways to dodge bullets.

Just as lap, finger and bouncing games are a preparation for certain ways of being, veterans and civilian survivors of war also prepare their children, often unconsciously, to survive.

There are compelling studies showing that PTSD may be passed on genetically, somehow – that genes can be changed by trauma. This wouldn't surprise me at all. If so, therapeutic approaches to families where PTSD occurs should be changed, so that a multi-generational dynamic is taken into account.

But while there is the hope for peace, there is also a pervading sense that long-term peace is unlikely anywhere in the world. And when war comes, you'd want your child to be able to react quickly.

The author Jack Gantos and I had a whole exchange about this issue once, because he also felt that his father, who was a veteran of the Second World War, had prepared him for war experiences. This was something I felt strongly when reading his book *Dead End in Norvelt*, which is why I wrote to him about it. Jack, it turned out, was highly conscious of how this played out in the book, and its sequel.

I believe you can see the same phenomenon in *The Hunger Games* and its sequels – Suzanne Collins' father was a veteran of the Vietnam War, and was, apparently, traumatized by his experiences there.

The fact that so many classics of English-language children's literature were written by authors who experienced war first-hand – C.S. Lewis, J.R.R. Tolkien, Louisa May Alcott, A.A. Milne, Theodor Geisel, Roald Dahl, Robert Graves, Eric Carle, John Ciardi, Hans and Margret Rey, Judith Kerr, Tomi Ungerer, et cetera – is something that deserves more research and attention as well, I think.

In 1939, in England, the German refugee and journalist Sebastian Haffner wrote a book called *Defying Hitler,* analyzing the reasons why he believed Nazism had become such a powerful force in Germany. He believed that the impact of the First World War on the imaginations of German children, including himself, was crucial in creating the atmosphere that allowed the Nazis to take power. He describes what he believed happened here:

> What counted was the fascination of the game of war, in which, according to certain mysterious rules, the numbers of prisoners taken, miles advanced, fortifications seized and ships sunk, played almost the same role as goals in football and points in boxing. I never wearied of keeping internal score-cards. I was a zealous reader of the army bulletins, which I would proceed to recalculate in my own fashion, according to my own mysterious, irrational rules: thus, for instance, ten Russian prisoners were equal to one English or French prisoner, and fifty aeroplanes to one cruiser. If there had been statistics of those killed, I would certainly not have hesitated to 'recalculate' the dead. I would not have stopped to think what the objects of my arithmetic looked like in reality. It was a dark, mysterious game and its never-ending, wicked lure eclipsed everything else, making daily life seem trite. It was addictive, like roulette and opium. My friends and I played it all through the war: four long years, unpunished and undisturbed. It is this game, and not the harmless battle games we organized in streets and playgrounds nearby, that has left its dangerous mark on all of us.

Further, Haffner's description of the impact of war reporting on children is just as relevant today, and may help explain some of the strange political movements that have become powerful in many different parts of the world, very much including our own part of it:

A generation of young Germans had become accustomed to having the entire content of their lives delivered gratis, so to speak, by the public sphere, all the raw material for their deeper emotions, for love and hate, joy and sorrow, but also all their sensations and thrills – accompanied though they might be by poverty, hunger, death, chaos and peril. Now that these deliveries suddenly ceased, people were left helpless, impoverished, robbed and disappointed. They had never learned to live from within themselves, how to make an ordinary private life great, beautiful, and worthwhile, how to enjoy it and make it interesting. So they regarded the end of political tension and the return of private liberty not as a gift, but as a deprivation. They were bored, their minds strayed to silly thoughts, and they began to sulk. In the end they waited eagerly for the first disturbance, the first setback or incident, so that they could put this period of peace behind them and set out on some new collective adventure.

Play has many purposes, and certainly one purpose of play (not just for humans, but for many mammals) is to prepare for future fighting, for sometimes perilous struggles, both physical and verbal. But as an optimistc coda to these ruminations on perilousness and play, and the general precariousness of everything, you can read below an account of an active and creative form of engagement with hazardous conditions that my children made up one day by the seaside.

SANDCASTLES

If you're by the ocean, building a sandcastle in close proximity to the waves so that the castle is under constant threat can be very exciting.

When I first saw my children doing this I couldn't understand it.

To me the whole point of building a sandcastle was to make something amazing – something to stand back and gaze at with a sense of accomplishment. I tried to discourage them from building at the edge of the waves, to make them build further back – but they ignored me.

From their point of view, they were *doing* something amazing – not *making* something amazing, or the making was only part of the doing. To build with a sense of peril and then to try a dozen different methods of preventing the inevitable, that was the exciting thing.

How long could they salvage it for? What could they find to help them? Driftwood? Seaweed? They built up barriers, reinforced peninsulas – but the waves kept pushing them back – inside walls became outside walls. The struggle never stopped for a moment – the sandcastle changed form every few minutes.

Sophie called the ruler of the castle the prime minister, and Ashey decided the prime minister needed a co-prime minister, which he promptly transformed into KoKo Prime-Injet.

The people were all represented by seashells.

In the end there was no sandcastle, but it didn't matter – they carried away an experience that seemed to be far more gratifying.

MY WINTER COAT

And as a reminder that there are ways for adults to be more playful with each other, too, I offer this:

Rough, repetitive searching for mittens had torn the pockets of my winter coat. As soon as it was warm enough I dropped my coat off at the Baygins, a wife and husband who've been tailoring at their store on Eglinton West for decades.

A few weeks later I dropped in to see if it was ready.

Mr. Baygin smiled at me. He stood up, gently took my arm and led me outside. Gesturing to the sidewalks full of people in shorts and T-shirts, he said, "Are you sure you need your winter coat today?"

He might have gotten impatient – he might have looked panicked and apologized, and promised to fix the coat as soon as possible. Instead, employing humour – and he did this gently, without any sarcasm – he improvised a little scene for the two of us. He engaged in a little theatre.

It wasn't just a rhetorical question, or a humorous question that he was asking me; it was a philosophical question.

"Why, on a summer day, are you worrying about your winter coat?"

There were many sensible, reasonable answers I could have provided, but that wasn't the point. Mr. Baygin was redirecting my attention to the reality of the outside world at that moment. I laughed, he waved and I went on my way.

EPILOGUE

I started this book in 2006, not fully realizing that I was starting a book.

Some of what you'll read here I wrote that long ago, many parts I wrote while I was working on other books and much of it was also written, or rewritten, over the past year.

Once I realized I was writing a book about the games people play with children, cross-culturally, I did my very best to make the sources as globally representative as I could. I had to work hard to track some of these down – and sources for some countries or cultures proved impossible to find, for me, anyway. Finding people from places all over the world isn't difficult in Toronto, but finding people who had knowledge of what I was after was sometimes a different matter.

At other times, what I was hoping to find literally fell into my lap. A chance conversation with someone would lead to a rich vein of information – this happened many times, as well. I envisioned something almost encyclo-pedic at the zenith of my ambitions for this project, but in the end, it's really a very small sample – in some ways it's more of a father's memoir shaped around children's games and rhymes.

As a project, the research for this book has sprawled itself across ten years of my life, and no doubt the collecting itself will continue to sprawl beyond the publication of this book. It's become a habit. The same thing happened after I wrote a book called *A Voweller's Bestiary* – for a few years I kept track of vowel patterns and combinations in every word I heard or read. While I don't track vowels obsessively anymore, the habit has never entirely left me either. And I'm sure that for the rest of my life, whenever I hear a different accent, or encounter a last name I've never come across before, my first thought will still be "Should I ask them where they're from, and about the games they play with babies?"

ACKNOWLEDGEMENTS

First, and most of all, I want to thank my wife, Amy, who talked over most of these pieces with me, and suggested and introduced me to many of the contributors, as well. I've learned more from Amy and her incredible, natural sensitivity to children and her big loving heart than from anyone else in the world.

My children, Sophie, Ashey and JoJo, steered me into unexpected territory again and again as I worked on this book – many of their ideas are included in the pieces above.

Next, my huge thanks to all those I interviewed. I must have seemed terribly obtuse at times. No doubt I asked questions that seemed insensitive, intrusive or otherwise off the mark – if so, I was always, in every case, treated with great patience. My enormous thanks to everyone named in the book, and to many who aren't named, as well.

And of course my boundless gratitude to Noelle Allen, for believing in the value of the project, and for all of her expert and necessary editorial advice, which included an essential (and major) restructuring of the material – no small task. Ashley Hisson's editorial acumen and careful copy-editing helped me (and this book) enormously, too – I'm very grateful to her. My thanks, as well, to Sheila Barry who discussed the project with me in its early stages while I was trying to figure out the best way to present the material in book form.

Below is a favourite story to summarize my gratitude to those who bore with me:

An aged man, whom Abraham hospitably invited to his tent, refused to join him in prayer to the one God. Learning that he was a fire-worshipper, Abraham drove him from his door.

That night, God appeared to Abraham in a vision and said: "I have borne with that ignorant man for seventy years: could you not have patiently suffered him one night?"

– The Talmud (also in Saadi's *Bostan*)

283

Many of you suffered with me for more than just one night!

The Chalmers Arts Fellowship, administered by the Ontario Arts Council, which I received in the fall of 2007, came at a crucial moment. It allowed me to do the bulk of research I needed to do, though – and this was one of the beautiful things about it – I wasn't expected to produce a book! I was doing research to broaden the horizons of my discipline – to help me shift gears professionally, and that's exactly what this research allowed me to do.

Some sections above also appeared as papers given at conferences or as university talks: the 2005 MLA conference in Washington, DC, Modern Masters panel, chaired by Dr. Lissa Paul; the 2009 Simmons College Childrens Literature Summer Institute in Boston (Crimes and Misdemeanours conference), organized by Professor Susan Bloom and Dr. Cathie Mercier; the UBC Master of Arts in Children's Literature Program colloquium 2013, in Vancouver, organized by Professor Judi Saltman; and in a presentation at Acadia University in Wolfville, NS, organized by Dr. Andrea Schwenke Wyile.

Certain organizations have been very helpful to me, as well, by making me aware of books, articles, monographs and ideas I wouldn't (and couldn't) otherwise have come across:

The Institute for Cultural Research, and The Octagon Press, both of which have been superseded by The Idries Shah Foundation (http://www.idriesshahfoundation.org).

As well, the Institute for the Study of Human Knowledge (http://www.ishk.net).

The website Mama Lisa's World is an incredible resource for lullabies and games from around the world, and for cross-referencing different versions you might know, or collect – I highly recommend it to anyone doing similar research (http://www.mamalisa.com/?t=eh).

Thank you to Lore Segal for permission to use her translation (with W.D. Snodgrass) of the poem "Delayed Action" from Christian Morgenstern's *Gallows Songs*.

Thank you to Alison Gopnik for permission to quote from her book *The Gardener and the Carpenter*.

Thank you to Julian Marks for permission to quote the poem "Hey, Hey, Hemerl" from Ruth Rubin's book *Voices of a People: The Story of Yiddish Folksong*

Thank you to librarian Chantel Prashad of the Toronto Public Library's Osborne Collection of Early Children's Books and Eddie Robertson, Digital Collections Technician, for providing the image for "Horse Turned Driver" from Ann and Jane Taylor's *Signor Topsy-Turvy's Wonderful Magic Lantern: Or, The World Turned Upside Down*.

APPENDIX 1: SUNNY VIEW WORKSHOPS

DEVELOPING THE IDEAS

Sunny View is a school for special-needs students in Toronto, which opened in 1953 and is still open today (in 2017). Close to a hundred students bused in from around the city receive intensive support to address multiple physical, communication, intellectual and health care needs. I conducted the workshop described below with Gyongi "Gingi" Venczel and Dawna Duff in 2004.

After going to watch Gingi demonstrate techniques for getting students involved in creating their own artwork, and after reading Tim Lefens' book, I started to feel more confident that something interesting could be done. While Gingi and I were talking over some of our ideas after her art-class demonstration, a speech pathologist named Dawna Duff suddenly appeared through the door and said, "I'm sorry to interrupt, I was just eavesdropping and I'd be interested in helping out with the project you're developing." Dawna offered to advise us on adaptations needed to involve students in the workshops who might not be able to see, hear or move their limbs easily, or at all. And so began a lively three-way collaboration that lasted almost three months.

It was one of the most rewarding collaborations I have ever been involved in. Even now, over a decade later, I get a funny feeling when I think of my time at Sunny View. I still think of the many insurmountable problems the students there were facing. Some were facing the prospect of an early death. Most were confronting severe limitations imposed on them by their vulnerable physical selves. Nadezhda Mandelstam, a survivor of the Soviet era, once wrote:

In war, in the camps and during the periods of terror, people think much less about death (let alone suicide) than when they are living normal lives. Whenever at some point on earth mortal terror and the

286

pressure of utterly insoluble problems are present in a particularly intense form, general questions about the nature of being recede into the background. How could we stand in awe before the forces of nature and eternal laws of existence if terror of a mundane kind was felt so tangibly in everyday life? Perhaps it is better to talk in more concrete terms of the fullness or intensity of existence, and in this sense there may have been something more deeply satisfying in our desperate clinging to life than what people generally strive for.

In any case, we decided that I would send Gingi and Dawna lesson plan ideas I had for the workshops, and that they would give me feedback about how they saw them being adapted for students at Sunny View.

Dawna and Gingi responded with a wealth of ideas. When we met again a month or so (and many emails) later, everyone felt that it would be a good idea to come up with something completely new for the primary level. None of the ideas I'd sent them seemed workable.

Dawna suggested that I get away from the idea of doing something strictly "creative," and instead focus on rhythm and rhyme, and to offer some choices within the activity to engage the students. She showed me a number of different lessons she had done and provided me with the framework I'd need to make a new lesson plan. I came up with the idea of a dragon taking two children on its back to different "beautiful places." The children would choose the places where they landed, and they would choose which of the objects they wanted to look at after they arrived.

Gingi was positive about the primary lesson plan, but she thought that some of the places and things were too abstract. Instead of having objects that rhymed, she suggested saying the names of the objects together as a group in an emphatic and rhythmic way once they'd all been chosen. For instance:

In the *bathtub* they saw:
Bubbles!

A bath towel!
Soap!
A rubber duck!
A bathrobe!

After each word was said the student holding the object (being called out) would shake it in the air or have someone help them shake it, or they would look at it. At the same time I would be standing by the visual icons of the objects and pointing at them.

We had thought through the choreography of the workshop very carefully, but we still didn't know how it would work once we were up there, in front of the class. There was a lot to think through in terms of timing with the many visuals, tactile objects and audio devices we needed to use. Before we started the first workshop, Gingi said to me, "Don't worry, I won't let you drown." I relaxed a lot after that.

We planned as much as we could, but what we were doing was also an experiment and we knew we would have to figure some things out as we went along.

THE WORKSHOPS

Gingi modelled the enthusiasm I would need to show in front of the students. This was an invaluable lesson. To feel enthusiastic and to show enthusiasm are two different things, I was to learn.

She had me say things along with her in a dramatic way. Dawna took the same approach, modelling the behaviour and the pacing I needed to have if I hoped to reach the students.

"You were hanging back a bit at first," Gingi said after the first primary workshop. "The students will connect and understand better if you go in close."

What I had thought of as a respectful distance was, in other words, probably being experienced as alienating. I got down on a stool with wheels that allowed me to scoot back and forth and up close, as Gingi and Dawna were doing. Gingi had suggested that I do this in the first place, but I felt too self-conscious until I saw how much more effective it was.

This kind of scenario happened time after time over the five days we worked together; I would feel inhibited or doubtful about what I was doing until I saw and experienced the connections that were being made when I followed leads provided by Gingi and Dawna.

Sometimes they had to teach me directly – sometimes I learned just from watching them.

The following is a good example of how an idea was adapted as we went along. I had written a short rhyme that the students (and adults) repeated several times during the primary workshop.

Dragon, dragon, we can't fly
We've never been up in the sky.
Dragon, dragon, take us there
On your back up through the air.

At first the plan was that I would say it and ask the students to repeat it. Gingi then transformed my overly quick and quiet reading with a more dramatic rendition, which we added gestures to for the students to mimic.

The gestures were suggested by a teacher who saw one of the first versions of the workshop. This was another fascinating thing about Sunny View: collaboration was taken for granted – criticisms were always constructive, and suggestions were given constantly. Teachers and adult-helpers viewing the workshops made helpful suggestions as we went along, such as putting the objects in context when we read them out loud.

For example, saying "and in the *kitchen* I found . . . a cooking spoon, a rolling pin," et cetera. Initially I had just had them read the poem, and then the objects, without repeating where it was we'd found them. Another teacher suggested that the dragon puppet be made to "fly" about in front of the children as I said the poem.

This was definitely an improvement.

Dawna also suggested that the rhyme be put one line at a time on a device called a Step-by-Step so that students who couldn't speak could press the button and take part. We tried this during one session, but found that it slowed down the momentum too much, so in the next session we tried having a student press it after everyone else had said it.

This still seemed anticlimactic. Finally Gingi had the idea of a student pressing it first, and then everyone else repeating it after. This worked very well; the momentum was maintained. I also found a large and dramatic-looking dragon puppet and this gave the students an animated focal point to look at when repeating the rhyme.

APPENDIX 2: TANYA WINER

While this book was being copy-edited, Ilya and Michael Winer, the
grandchildren of Amy's zaeda's brother, found our family after decades of
fruitless searching. We had also searched for them in the past, without any
success. Amy's zaeda's brother had stayed in the Ukraine in 1924 when
her zaeda left, so the two branches of the family hadn't seen each other
for ninety-three years. It was an amazing reunion – there was almost a full
century of news to catch up on.

When Ilya and Michael came for dinner, as we looked at old family
photos and filled in many missing pieces, I couldn't help asking about the
"Tsip, Tsip" rhyme . . . had they been raised with it, too? Ilya and Michael
had no memory of it, but Judaism and the Yiddish language were completely suppressed by the Soviet government when they were growing up
in the Ukraine. They promised to ask their mother, Tanya Winer, who was
ninety years old and now living in Israel. A few weeks later, Ilya sent me an
email. He said, "When I next see you, I will show you a video of my mother singing 'Tsip, Tsip' with her great-grandchildren!" All these years later
she remembered it from her own father, and was able to teach it to her
great-grandchildren. It had been passed on in both branches of the family,
but because of religious and cultural persecution in the Soviet Union, and
the subsequent move to Israel (the everyday language of her family had
changed twice – from Russian to Hebrew to English), it had missed two
generations on Tanya's side.

She knew the four-line version, with the two extra lines Amy hadn't
remembered:

Tsip, tsip, hemerl
kum tsu mir in kemerl
ikh vel dir epes vayzn
shiselekh mit ayzn.

It absolutely delighted me that this research allowed for it to be passed on directly in another part of Amy's family after such a long break. Tanya's exuberance in the video, which Ilya later showed us, and the clear enjoyment of her great-grandchildren, was wonderful to see.

APPENDIX 3: RECOMMENDED BOOKS

The list below influenced this work in important (though often indirect) ways, and it would seem wrong to let them go unmentioned.

Ascherson, Neal. *Black Sea*.
Ascherson, Neal. *Stone Voices: The Search for Scotland*.

Barghouti, Mourid. *I Saw Ramallah*.
Bateson, Mary Catherine. *Peripheral Visions: Learning Along the Way*.
Bernhard, Thomas. *My Prizes: An Accounting*.
Bitov, Andrei. *A Captive of the Caucasus*.
Bolaño, Roberto. *The Savage Detectives*.
Bonhoeffer, Dietrich. *I Loved This People*.
Borges, Jorge Luis. *Professor Borges: A Course on English Literature* [or any of his books].
Bortoft, Henri. "Goethe's Scientifc Consciousness" in *The Wholeness of Nature: Goethe's Way Toward a Science of Conscious Participation in Nature*.
Burckhardt, Jacob, *The Greeks and Greek Civilization*.
Busk, Rachel Harriette. *The Valleys of Tirol: Their Traditions and Customs, and How to Visit Them*.
Byron, Kevin. *Inventions and Inventing: Finding Solutions to Practical Problems*.

Cashore, Kristin. *Graceling*.

Davis, Aubrey. *Bagels from Benny*. Illustrated by Dušan Petričić.
Deikman, Arthur J. *The Wrong Way Home: Uncovering the Patterns of Cult Behavior in American Society*.

Elliot, Jason. *An Unexpected Light: Travels in Afghanistan*.

Fermor, Patrick Leigh. *A Time of Gifts*

Fernyhough, Charles. *The Baby in the Mirror: A Child's World from Birth to Three*.

Findley, Timothy. *Inside Memory: Pages from a Writer's Workbook*.

Furedi, Frank. *Paranoid Parenting: Why Ignoring the Experts May Be Best for Your Child*.

Ginsberg, Allen. *Composed on the tongue*.

Gopnik, Alison. *The Philosophical Baby: What Children's Minds Tell Us About Truth, Love, and the Meaning of Life*.

Grossman, David. *Writing in the Dark: Essays on Literature and Politics*.

Graves, Robert. *The Common Asphodel: Collected Essays on Poetry, 1922–1949*.

Graves, Robert. "A Journal of Curiousities" in *But It Still Goes On: An Accumulation*.

Graves, Robert, and Alan Hodge. *The Long Week-End: A Social History of Great Britain, 1918–1939*.

Hachiya, Michihiko. *Hiroshima Diary: The Journal of a Japanese Physician, August 6–September 30, 1945*.

Haffner, Sebastian. *Defying Hitler: A Memoir*.

Hall, Edward T. *The Dance of Life: The Other Dimensions of Time* [or any of his books].

Hall, Tarquin. *Salaam Brick Lane: A Year in the New East End*.

Heaney, Seamus, and Ted Hughes, eds. *The Rattle Bag*.

Herbert, Zbigniew. *Barbarian in the Garden*.

Heyman, Michael. *The Tenth Rasa: An Anthology of Indian Nonsense*.

Holub, Miroslav. *The Dimension of the Present Moment*.

Hope, Sebastian. *Outcasts of the Islands: The Sea Gypsies of South East Asia*.

Horwitz, Anthony. *Into the Blue: Boldly Going Where Captain Cook Has Gone Before*.

Hughes, Ted. *Poetry in the Making*.

Jaimoukha, Amjad. *The Circassians: A Handbook*.

Joe, Rita. *Song of Rita Joe: Autobiography of a Mi'kmaq Poet.*
Joseph, Michael. The uncollected and mostly unpublished works.

King, Thomas. *The Inconvenient Indian: A Curious Account of Native People in North America.*
Knockwood, Isabelle. *Out of the Depths: The Experiences of Mi'kmaw Children at the Indian Residential School at Shubenacadie, Nova Scotia.*

Langbein, Hermann. *People in Auschwitz.*
Lee, Dennis. *Body Music.*
Lessing, Doris. *African Laughter: Four Visits to Zimbabwe.*
Lessing, Doris. *Time Bites: Views and Reviews.*
Levi, Primo. *The Search for Roots: A Personal Anthology.*
Lorde, Audre. *Zami: A New Spelling of My Name.*

Magris, Claudio. *Danube.*
Mandelstam, Nadezhda. *Hope Abandoned.*
Mandelstam, Nadezhda. *Hope Against Hope.*
Marcus, Leonard S., ed. *Dear Genius: The Letters of Ursula Nordstrom.*
Marshall, Elizabeth, and Özlem Sensoy, eds. *Rethinking Popular Culture and Media.*
McCloud, Scott. *Understanding Comics.*
Mommsen, Katharina. *Goethe's Art of Living.*
Morland, Polly. *The Society of Timid Souls: Or, How to Be Brave.*

Nel, Philip, and Lissa Paul, eds. *Keywords for Children's Literature.*
Nessel, Denise D., ed. *Awakening Young Minds: Perspectives on Education.*
Nichol, bp. *Organ Music.*

Obraztsov, Sergey. *My Profession.*
Ornstein, Robert. *The Evolution of Consciousness* [or any of his books].

Ornstein, Robert, and Paul Ehrlich. *New World New Mind: Moving Toward Conscious Evolution.*

Pendlebury, David. *Absorbing Persian: An Adventure Trail for Beginners in the Classical Language.*
Pendlebury, David. *Creative Translation.*
Pendlebury, David, trans. *The Walled Garden of Truth* by Hakim Sanai.
Pendlebury, David, trans. *Yusuf and Zulaikha* by Jami.

Queneau, Raymond. *Exercises in Style.*

Rich, Adrienne. *What is Found There: Notebooks on Poetry and Politics.*
Ringelblum, Emmanuel. *Notes from the Warsaw Ghetto.*
Roethke, Theodore. *On the Poet and His Craft: Selected Prose of Theodore Roethke.*
Rukeyser, Muriel. *The Life of Poetry.*

Sacks, Oliver. *On the Move: A Life.*
Schad, Wolfgang. *Man and Mammals.*
Seligman, Martin E. P. *Learned Optimism: How to Change Your Mind and Your Life.*
Shah, Amina. *The Tale of the Four Dervishes of Amir Khusru.*
Shah, Idries. *The World of Nasrudin* [or any of his books].
Shah, Safia, ed. *Afghan Caravan.*
Shah, Saira. *The Storyteller's Daughter: One Woman's Return to Her Lost Homeland.*
Shah, Tahir. *In Arabian Nights: A Caravan of Moroccan Dreams* [or any of his books].
Steinbeck, John. *The Log from the Sea of Cortez.*
Stern, Mario Rigoni. *The Sergeant in the Snow.*
Stringer, Chris. *Lone Survivors: How We Came to Be the Only Humans on Earth.*

Thomas, Elizabeth Marshall. *The Old Way: A Story of the First People*.

Thomas, Joseph T., Jr. *Poetry's Playground: The Culture of Contemporary American Children's Poetry*.

Thorpe, Nick. *Adrift in Caledonia: Boat-hitching for the Unenlightened*.

Thorpe, Nick. *Eight Men and a Duck: An Improbable Voyage by Reed Boat to Easter Island*.

Tsvetaeva, Marina. *Art in the Light of Conscience: Eight Essays on Poetry*.

Twigger, Robert. *The Extinction Club*.

Twigger, Robert. *Walk: A Self-help Book* [or any of his books]

Waddell, Helen. *The Wandering Scholars of the Middle Ages*.

Webster, Jason. *Duende: A Journey in Search of Flamenco*.

Winston, Mark L. *Bee Time: Lessons from the Hive*.

Wiseman, Richard. *The Luck Factor: Changing Your Luck, Changing Your Life*.

Wood, Ramsay. *Extraordinary Voyages of the Panchatantra: And How We Limit Our Understanding of the Word Story*.

Xenophon. *Anabasis*.

Zimmer, Heinrich. *The King and the Corpse*.

Zipes, Jack, Lissa Paul, Lynne Vallone, Peter Hunt and Gillian Avery. *The Norton Anthology of Children's Literature: The Traditions in English*.

Zoshchenko, Mikhail. *Before Sunrise*.

BIBLIOGRAPHY

Ager, Simon. "One Language is Never Enough." Omniglot: The Online Encyclopedia of Writing Systems & Languages. http://www.omniglot.com/language/phrases/onelanguage.htm.

Baldacchino, Christine. *Morris Micklewhite and the Tangerine Dress.* Illustrated by Isabelle Malenfant. Toronto: Groundwood Books, 2014.

Barghouti, Mourid. *I Was Born There, I Was Born Here.* Translated by Humphrey Davies. London: Bloomsbury, 2011.

Batanda, Jackee Budesta *The Blue Marble.* Accra, Ghana: Sub-Saharan Publishers, 2005.

Bateson, Mary Catherine. *Peripheral Visions: Learning Along the Way.* New York: HarperCollins, 1994.

Berry, James. *When I Dance.* London: Hamish Hamilton, 1988.

Bijvoet, Tom. "Tracks and Traces: The Extinction of Jersey Dutch." *DUTCH the Magazine,* January 2, 2014. http://www.mokeham.com/dutchthemag/tracks-and-traces-the-extinction-of-jersey-dutch/.

Boyd, Brian. *On the Origin of Stories: Evolution, Cognition, and Fiction.* Cambridge, MA: Harvard University Press, 2009.

Bracho, Coral. *Firefly Under the Tongue: Selected Poems of Coral Bracho.* Translated by Forrest Gander. New York: New Directions, 2008.

Braque, Georges. *Illustrated Notebooks: 1917–1955.* Translated by Stanley Appelbaum. New York: Dover Publications, 1971.

Brown, Donald E. *Human Universals.* Boston: McGraw-Hill, 1991.

Burckhardt, Jacob. *The Age of Constantine the Great.* Translated by Moses Hadas. New York: Pantheon Books, 1949.

———. *The Greeks and Greek Civilization.* Translated by Sheila Stern. New York: St. Martin's Press, 1998.

Challenger, Charlene. *The Voices in Between.* Toronto: Tightrope Books, 2014.

Chekhov, Anton. *The Island: A Journey to Sakhalin.* Translated by Luba and Michael Terpak. New York: Washington Square Press, 1967.

Chenciner, Robert. *Daghestan: Tradition and Survival.* Caucasus World, edited by Nicholas Awde. Abingdon, UK: RoutledgeCurzon, 1997.

Chesterton, G.K. *The Defendant.* Mineola, NY: Dover Publications, 2012. First published 1902 as the second edition of *The Defendant* by R. Brimley Johnson.

Cohen, David Steven. *The Dutch-American Farm.* The American Social Experience 24. New York: New York University Press, 1992.

Collins, Suzanne. *The Hunger Games.* New York: Scholastic, 2008.

Darwin, Charles. *A Biographical Sketch of an Infant.* Philadelphia: Lippincott, 1971. First published in "A Biographical Sketch of an Infant." *Mind: A Quarterly Review of Psychology and Philosophy* 2, no. 7 (July 1877): 285–294.

Davis, Russell, and Brent Ashabranner. *Ten Thousand Desert Swords: The Epic Story of a Great Bedouin Tribe.* Boston: Little, Brown, 1960.

Doi, Takeo. *The Anatomy of Self: The Individual Versus Society.* Translated by Mark A. Harbison. New York: Kodansha America, 1988. First published 1985 as *Omote to ura* by Kōbundō.

Doniger, Wendy. *The Woman Who Pretended to be Who She Was: Myths of Self-Imitation.* Oxford: Oxford University Press, 2004.

Fernyhough, Charles. *The Baby in the Mirror: A Child's World from Birth to Three.* London: Granta Books, 2008.

Fitch, Sheree. *Breathe, Stretch, Write: Learning to Write with Everything You've Got.* Markham, ON: Pembroke, 2011.

Gabler, Neal. *Walt Disney: The Triumph of the American Imagination.* New York: Alfred A. Knopf, 2006.

Gantos, Jack. *Dead End in Norvelt.* New York: Farrar, Straus and Giroux, 2011.

Ghosh, Pallab. "Infants' Brains Attuned to Baby Talk and Nursery Rhymes." *BBC News*, November 16, 2016. http://www.bbc.com/news/science-environment-38002105.

Goffman, Erving. *The Presentation of Self in Everyday Life.* New

York: Anchor Books, 1959. First published 1956 by University of Edinburgh Social Sciences Research Centre.

————. *Stigma: Notes on the Management of Spoiled Identity*. New York: Touchstone, 1986. First published 1963 by Simon & Schuster.

Goldman, William. *The Princess Bride: S. Morgenstern's Classic Tale of True Love and High Adventure*. San Diego: Harcourt Brace Jovanovich, 1973.

Gopnik, Alison. *The Gardener and the Carpenter: What the New Science of Child Development Tells Us About the Relationship Between Parents and Children*. New York: Farrar, Straus and Giroux, 2016.

Grahame, Kenneth. *The Wind in the Willows*. London: Sterling, 2005. First published 1908 by Charles Scribner's Sons.

Graves, Robert. *The Less Familiar Nursery Rhymes*. The Augustan Books of English Poetry 2, no. 14. London: E. Benn, 1927.

Haffner, Sebastian. *Defying Hitler: A Memoir*. Translated by Oliver Pretzel. London: Picador, 2002. First published 2000 as *Geschichte eines Deutschen: Die Erinnerungen 1914–1933* by Deutsche Verlags-Anstalt.

Hall, Edward T. *The Dance of Life: The Other Dimension of Time*. New York: Anchor, 1984.

Heighton, Steven. *Workbook: Memos & Dispatches on Writing*. Toronto: ECW Press, 2011.

Howe, Irving, Ruth R. Wisse and Khone Shmeruk. *The Penguin Book of Modern Yiddish Verse*. New York: Penguin, 1987.

Iskander, Fazil. *Sandro of Chegem*. Translated by Susan Brownsberger. New York: Vintage, 1983.

Jastrow, Joseph. *Fact and Fable in Psychology*. London: Macmillan, 1901.

Jones, Brian Jay. *George Lucas: A Life*. London: Little, Brown, 2016.

Jzin. "Chinese Children's Songs: Trishaw / Strange or not 三輪車." Castle of Costa Mesa. http://castleofcostamesa.com/song-list-trial-page/song-list/chinese-childrens-songs-trishaw-strange-or-now/.

Khan, Rukhsana. *Big Red Lollipop*. Illustrated by Sophie Blackall.

New York: Viking Books for Young Readers, 2010.

———. *Dahling, If You Luv Me, Would You Please, Please Smile.* Toronto: Stoddart Kids, 1999.

King, Thomas. *The Truth About Stories: A Native Narrative.* Toronto: House of Anansi, 2003.

Kumove, Shirley, ed. *Words like Arrows: A Collection of Yiddish Folk Sayings.* New York: Schocken, 1985.

Lawson, JonArno, ed. *Aloud in My Head.* Illustrated by Jonny Hannah. London: Walker Books, 2015.

———. *Sidewalk Flowers.* Illustrated by Sydney Smith. Toronto: Groundwood Books, 2015.

Le Clézio, J.M.G., and J. Le Clézio. *Sirandanes: Suivies d'un petit lexique de la langue créole et des oiseaux.* Paris: Seghers, 2005. First published 1990.

Lee, Dennis. "Commentary." In Lawson, *Aloud in My Head*, 40.

Lefens, Tim. *Flying Colors: The Story of a Remarkable Group of Artists.* Boston: Beacon Press, 2002.

Lessing, Doris. *Shikasta: Re, Colonised Planet 5.* London: Jonathan Cape, 1979.

———. *Walking in the Shade: Volume Two of My Autobiography, 1949–1962.* New York: HarperPerennial, 1997.

Levi, Primo. *Survival in Auschwitz.* Translated by Stuart Woolf. New York: Touchstone, 1996. First published 1959 by Orion Press.

Lewin, Olive. *Rock It Come Over: The Folk Music of Jamaica.* Kingston: University of the West Indies Press, 2009.

Lewis, C.S. *Prince Caspian.* London: Puffin, 1951.

Lobe, Mira. *Das Städtchen Drumherum.* Illustrated by Susi Weigel. Vienna: Verlag Jungbrunnen, 2015. First published 1970 by Herold Verlag Brück.

Lomax, Alan. *The Land Where the Blues Began.* New York: Dell, 1993.

Lomax, John A., and Alan Lomax. *American Ballads and Folk Songs.* New York: Dover, 1994. First published 1934 by Macmillan.

Majrouh, Sayd Bahodine. *Songs of Love and War: Afghan Women's Poetry*. Translated by Marjolijn de Jager. New York: Other Press, 2003. First published 1994 as *Le suicide et le chant: poésie populaire des femmes pachtounes* by Editions Gallimard.

Mandelstam, Nadezhda. *Hope Abandoned*. Translated by Max Hayward. London, Collins Harvill Press, 1974.

———. *Hope Against Hope*. Translated by Max Hayward. London, Collins Harvill Press, 1970.

Milne. A.A. *When We Were Very Young*. London: Methuen, 1924.

Moore, Marianne. *The Complete Poems of Marianne Moore*. New York: Viking, 1967.

Mordecai, Pamela. *de book of Mary*. Toronto: Mawenzi House, 2015.

Morgenstern, Christian. *Gallows Songs*. Translated by W.D. Snodgrass and Lore Segal. Ann Arbor: University of Michigan Press, 1967.

Muir, Willa. *Living with Ballads*. London: Hogarth Press, 1965.

Mukherjee, Siddhartha. *The Gene*. New York: Scribner, 2016.

Nel, Philip. *Crockett Johnson and Ruth Krauss: How an Unlikely Couple Found Love, Dodged the FBI, and Transformed Children's Literature*. Jackson: University Press of Mississippi, 2012.

Nessel, Denise D., ed. *Awakening Young Minds: Perspectives on Education*. Los Altos, CA: Malor Books, 1997.

Ornstein, Robert. *The Mind Field: A Personal Essay*. 3rd ed. Los Altos, CA: Malor Books, 1996.

Oxenbury, Helen. *It's My Birthday*. Somerville, MA: Candlewick Press, 2010.

Peerbaye, Soraya. *Poems for the Advisory Committee on Antarctic Names*. Fredericton, NB: Goose Lane Editions, 2009.

———. *Tell: Poems for a Girlhood*. St. John's, NL: Pedlar Press, 2015.

Potter, Beatrix. *The Tale of Ginger and Pickles*. London: Frederick Warne, 2002. First published 1909 by Frederick Warne.

Ramanujan, A.K, trans. *Speaking of Siva*. London: Penguin, 1973.

Rich, Adrienne. *What is Found There: Notebooks on Poetry and Politics*.

New York: W.W. Norton, 1993.

Roethke, Theodore. *The Collected Poems of Theodore Roethke*. New York: Anchor, 1975.

Rothenberg, Jerome, ed. *Technicians of the Sacred: A Range of Poetries from Africa, America, Asia, Europe and Oceania*. 2nd ed. Berkeley: University of California Press, 1985.

Rubin, Ruth. *Voices of a People: The Story of Yiddish Folksong*. New York: Thomas Yoseloff, 1963.

Sacks, Oliver. *Oliver Sacks: The Last Interview and Other Conversations*. Brooklyn: Melville House, 2016.

Shah, Idries. *The World of Nasrudin*. London: Octagon Press, 2003.

Shivkumar. *Stories from Panchatantra*. Illustrated by Anil Vyas. New Delhi: Children's Book Trust, 1970.

Singer, Isaac Bashevis. *Love and Exile: A Memoir*. New York: Doubleday, 1984.

Spiegelman, Art. *Maus: A Survivor's Tale*. Vol. 1, *My Father Bleeds History*. New York: Pantheon, 1986. First published 1980–85 by *RAW* magazine.

Strauss, Frederic, ed. *Almodóvar on Almodóvar*. London: Faber & Faber, 2006.

Sully, James. *Studies of Childhood*. New York: D. Appleton, 1895.

Taylor, Ann, and Jane Taylor. *Rhymes for the Nursery*. London: Harvey and Darton, 1824.

———. *Signor Topsy-Turvy's Wonderful Magic Lantern: Or, The World Turned Upside Down*. London: Tabart, 1810.

Taylor, Patrick, and Frederick I. Case, eds. *The Encyclopedia of Caribbean Religions*. Champaign: University of Illinois Press, 2013.

Thorndike, Lynn. *Michael Scot*. London: Nelson, 1965.

Tjia, Sherwin. *The World Is a Heartbreaker*. Toronto: Coach House Books, 2005.

——— [Sully, pseud.]. *The Hipless Boy*. Wolfville, NS: Conundrum Press, 2009.

Tolkien, J.R.R. *The Fellowship of the Ring.* New York: HarperCollins, 2007. First published 1954 by George Allen & Unwin.

Truth and Reconciliation Commission of Canada. *Final Report of the Truth and Reconciliation Commission of Canada.* Vol. 1, *Summary: Honouring the Truth, Reconciling for the Future.* Toronto: James Lorimer, 2015.

Ungerer, Tomi. *Moon Man.* New York: HarperCollins, 1967.

"What is the Zulu word for peek-a-boo?" WordHippo. http://www.wordhippo.com/what-is/the/zulu-word-for-c4185f84be1c73176e5d-4650f5bfd1a0271148fe.html.

Wilbur, Richard. *The Disappearing Alphabet.* New York: Harcourt, 1998.

Williams, William Carlos. *Kora in Hell: Improvisations.* San Francisco: City Lights, 1957.

Wood, Ramsay. *Extraordinary Voyages of the Panchatantra: And How We Limit Our Understanding of the Word Story.* London: Institute for Cultural Research, 2011.

———. *Kalila and Dimna.* Vol. 1, *Fables of Friendship and Betrayal.* London: Saqi Books, 2008. First published 1980 by Alfred A. Knopf.

———. *Kalila and Dimna.* Vol. 2, *Fables of Conflict and Intrigue.* London: Saqi Books, 2008.

Zeldin, Theodore. Oxford Muse: Conversation, Dining and Dancing. http://www.oxfordmuse.com/?q=conversation-dinners.

POEM, GAME AND SONG INDEX BY COUNTRY

Poems are listed by title, when available, or by first line

POEM, GAME AND SONG INDEX BY LANGUAGE

Poems are listed by title, when available, or by first line

311

JONARNO LAWSON

JonArno Lawson is the author of many books for both adults and
children, including the well-received wordless book, *Sidewalk Flowers*. He
lives with his family in Toronto.